AN ILLUSTRATED HISTORY OF
CATHOLICISM

AN ILLUSTRATED HISTORY OF
CATHOLICISM

An authoritative chronicle of the development of Catholic Christianity and its doctrine with more than 300 photographs and fine-art illustrations

A comprehensive and vivid account of the Church's early days in the Holy Land, through the middle ages, to its position today as a global religious power

MICHAEL KERRIGAN & MARY FRANCES BUDZIK
CONSULTANT: REVEREND RONALD CREIGHTON-JOBE

southwater

This edition is published by Southwater,
an imprint of Anness Publishing Ltd,
Blaby Road, Wigston,
Leicestershire LE18 4SE;
info@anness.com

www.southwaterbooks.com;
www.annesspublishing.com

Anness Publishing has a new picture agency outlet for images for publishing,
promotions or advertising. Please visit our website www.practicalpictures.com
for more information.

Publisher: Joanna Lorenz
Editorial Director: Helen Sudell
Project Editor: Elizabeth Young
Production Controller: Bessie Bai

Produced for Anness Publishing by Toucan Books:
Managing Director: Ellen Dupont
Editor: Theresa Bebbington
Project Manager: Hannah Bowen
Designer: Elizabeth Healey
Picture Researcher: Marian Pullen
Proofreader: Marion Dent
Indexer: Michael Dent
Cartography by Cosmographics, UK

Ethical Trading Policy
Because of our ongoing ecological investment programme, you, as our
customer, can have the pleasure and reassurance of knowing that a tree is
being cultivated on your behalf to naturally replace the materials used to
make the book you are holding. For further information about this scheme,
go to www.annesspublishing.com/trees

© Anness Publishing Ltd 2011

Previously published as part of a larger volume, *The Illustrated Encyclopedia
of Catholicism*

Publisher's Note
Although the information in this book are believed to be accurate and true at
the time of going to press, neither the authors nor the publisher can accept any
legal responsibility or liability for any errors or omissions that may have been
made nor for any inaccuracies nor for any loss, harm or injury that comes about
from following the advice in this book.

A CIP catalogue record for this book is available from the British Library.

CONTENTS

Above *Detail from* The
Presentation in the Temple
by Fra Angelico, 1442.

Above *A 5th-century carved
ivory relief illustrating the
Resurrection of Christ.*

Above *A 6th-century mosaic
of the prophet Isaiah, San
Vitale Basilica, Ravenna, Italy.*

Above *Pope John Paul II
celebrating Mass in Knock,
Ireland, in 1979.*

Above Christ refusing the banquet offered by Satan, by William Blake, c. 1816–18.

Above A Roman legionary killing a barbarian from a 3rd-century marble sarcophagus.

Above A 15th-century French depiction of the capture of Antioch in the First Crusade.

Above The interior of the 13th-century Notre-Dame Cathedral, Reims, France.

INTRODUCTION

With its spiritual, cultural and historical heritage, spanning more than 2000 years, the Catholic religion has a great influence across the globe and has a special place in the hearts and minds of millions.

Catholicism is the oldest and the largest of the Christian churches, and has become one of the world's largest religions. More than half of the world's Christians take their leadership from the pope in Rome. The number of Catholics in the world stands at around 1.16 billion people – 17.4 per cent (about one-sixth) of the planet's population. (Islam, if all its branches are taken together, just tops that total; none of the other creeds comes close.) One of the world's biggest and most formidably organized institutions, the Catholic Church can call on around 136,000 priests and 750,000 nuns, along with a multitude of loyal

Above Moses and Elijah look on as St Apollinare tends his flock. Ravenna's first bishop was buried in the 6th-century basilica that contains this painting.

lay supporters. It is too important a force to be ignored, and is capable of exerting an influence on public policy and international affairs. Its religious teachings have shaped many millions of lives.

HEAVEN AND EARTH

The Catholic Church would be nothing if it were only an earthly institution – "My kingship is not of this world," its founder Jesus stated (John 18: 36). Looking beyond this life to the hereafter, the Church views humankind's existence in an eternal perspective: the living and departed come together in the Communion of Saints. As this book sets out to demonstrate, Catholicism offers its followers an account of God's Creation, of life and death – along with the possibility of salvation for devout Catholics, with everlasting joy in heaven.

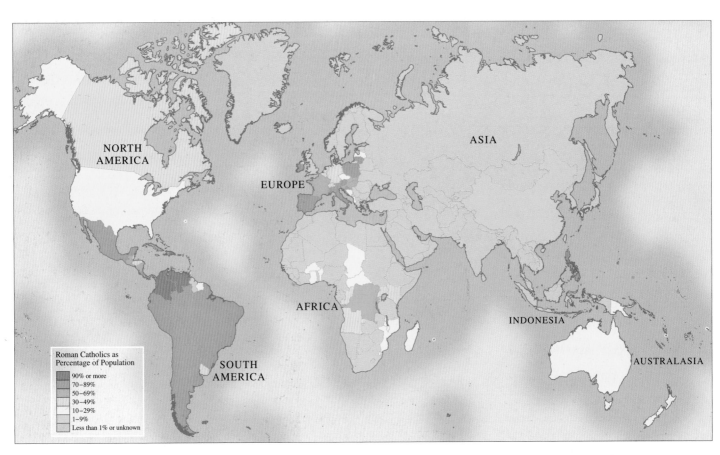

Roman Catholics as Percentage of Population

- 90% or more
- 70–89%
- 50–69%
- 30–49%
- 10–29%
- 1–9%
- Less than 1% or unknown

NORTH AMERICA

SOUTH AMERICA

EUROPE

AFRICA

ASIA

INDONESIA

AUSTRALASIA

AN EVENTFUL HISTORY

The history of the Catholic Church begins with the coming of Christ. In the early Church, Christ's followers suffered persecution, yet the Church gained power and managed to survive difficult times in the Middle Ages and the Restoration. From a small, informal community, the Catholic Church expanded to become one of the largest religions in the world in the 21st century.

At key turning points in its history, the Church was able to grow in strength even through suffering and struggle; however, at other moments, it persecuted those who stood against it. An inspiration to creativity, Catholicism has played a central role in the Western artistic tradition, if at times it has arguably been too involved in acquiring these splendours. The papacy has provided vital leadership, yet an absolute authority it was endowed with by Christ himself has not always been wielded as conscientiously as it should have been.

DIVINE DOCTRINES

As the early Catholic Church grew in numbers, it struggled to express its teachings to its followers, many of whom were poorly educated. In a confusing time when there were conflicting ideas about God, the Catholic Church had to present an official source for its followers, and leading Church members fromulated Catholic doctrine. This "deposit of faith" is at the core of the Church's teachings and provides Christians with an understanding of the mysteries of Catholicism, including the Trinity, original sin and salvation.

Left This demographic map illustrates the percentage of the Roman Catholic population around the world. It is increasing fastest in Africa and Asia, and although 25 per cent of Catholics live in Europe, it has the slowest growth rate.

ABOUT THIS BOOK

This book provides a fascinating and detailed insight into the history of Catholicism. It discusses the doctrine and unravels the myths, and looks at how places became holy sites, the significance of relics and the purpose of pilgrimage.

Divided into two sections, the first section of this book, Catholic History, shows how eventful and exciting the story of the Church has been – and sometimes how difficult, even contradictory. Catholicism's truths might be eternal, yet they took many centuries to articulate. Although Catholicism's inspirations might be divine, many of its practitioners have been all too human.

The second section of the book, Catholic Doctrine, looks at the various teachings that constitute the Catholic faith. It considers beliefs about the eternal truths of existence as well as those that goven the everyday dilemmas of social and personal morality. From the Trinity and transubstantiation to the status of the Scriptures and the significance of the saints, the complete range of the Church's teachings are examined here. Among the questions explored are: What is sin? What does Christ's redemption mean? How are we to understand the concepts of salvation and damnation?

Catholicism is a complex creed and the Church a vast and venerable institution, and the purpose of this volume is to offer an accessible and detailed account of the history and doctrine of Catholic Christianity. Illustrated throughout with more than 300 photographs, including images of magnificent churches, relics and fine-art paintings, this expert guide will inform all readers interested in discovering more about Catholicism and its teachings.

Below St Peter's Basilica, in the Vatican within Rome, Italy, is both the historic centre of an ancient Catholic Church and at the heart of the modern world. Catholicism continues to flourish amid changing times.

TIMELINE

THE CATHOLIC CHURCH HAS A LONG HISTORY. THE TIMELINE BELOW LISTS SOME OF THE MAJOR EVENTS THAT HAVE AFFECTED IT.

1ST CENTURY BC
- Romans conquer Judaea, 63 BC.
- Herod the Great begins renovations on the Temple of Jerusalem, *c.*19 BC.

1ST CENTURY AD
- *Anno Domini* – by tradition, the year of Christ's birth.
- Saul witnesses the martyrdom of St Stephen, *c.*AD 35.
- Council of Jerusalem convened by St Peter, the first pope, *c.*AD 50.
- Nero launches the first persecution of Rome's Christians in AD 64.

2ND CENTURY
- Monumental shrine erected around St Peter's tomb in Rome, *c.*150.

3RD CENTURY
- Persecution of Valerian, 253–60.

4TH CENTURY
- Diocletian's "Great Persecution", 303–11.
- Emperor Constantine converts to Christianity in 312.
- Constantine calls the Council of Nicaea in 325.
- Proclamation of the Nicene Creed, 381.
- St Jerome begins work on his Latin "Vulgate" Bible, 382.

5TH CENTURY
- St Augustine starts writing his great work, *The City of God*.
- Leo the Great centralizes power in the papacy, 440–61.

6TH CENTURY
- St Benedict of Nursia establishes his monastic rule.

Above Detail from a fresco showing Pope Gregory the Great (540–604), from Vezzolano, Italy.

- Reforming papacy of Gregory the Great begins in 590.

7TH CENTURY
- Muhammad begins receiving his revelations of Islam in 610.
- Arab armies occupy Jerusalem in 638.

8TH CENTURY
- The Church is given temporal authority over Rome and its environs under the "Donation of Pepin", 754.

9TH CENTURY
- The legendary "Pope Joan" supposedly succeeds to the papacy in 853.

10TH CENTURY
- The reformist abbey of Cluny is founded in eastern France, 910.

11TH CENTURY
- The Cistercian order tries to take monasticism back to its first Benedictine principles.
- The Eastern Orthodox Church formally parts company with Rome, 1054.
- Urban II calls the First Crusade in 1095. Jerusalem is taken four years later.

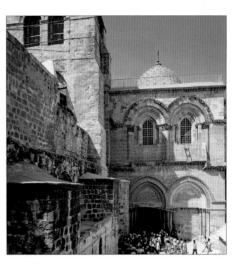

Above Worshippers gather outside the entrance to the Church of the Holy Sepulchre, Jerusalem, Israel.

12TH CENTURY
- The beginning of the Gothic movement in religious architecture.
- The Second Crusade of 1145 breaks down in chaos.
- The Third Lateran Council begins in 1179.
- Saladin recaptures Jerusalem for the Muslims in 1187. The Third Crusade that follows is a failure.
- Peter Waldo denounces the wealth of the Church from 1177.

13TH CENTURY
- The forces of the Fourth Crusade (1202–4) sack Christian Constantinople.
- Innocent III proclaims the Albigensian Crusade against the heretical Cathars in 1208.
- St Francis of Assisi begins his ministry in 1209.
- Thomas Aquinas writes the *Summa Theologica*, 1266–74.

14TH CENTURY
- Clement V transfers the papacy to Avignon in France, 1309.
- Gregory XI makes Rome the centre of papal power again in 1377 – but rival popes continue in opposition in Avignon after his death in 1378.

15TH CENTURY
- The Council of Pisa (1408) fails to resolve the Western Schism. A solution is found in 1417.
- Czech heretic Jan Hus is burnt at the stake in 1415.
- The Spanish Inquisition is at its height, encouraged by the "Catholic Monarchs", Ferdinand and Isabella.
- The Reconquista is complete, with the expulsion of the Moors from Granada in 1492. That same year Columbus starts opening up an empire for Spain in the Americas.

16TH CENTURY
- The reconstruction of St Peter's Basilica, Rome, begins in 1505.
- Martin Luther nails his "95 Theses" to the door of the cathedral in Wittenberg, Germany.
- Clement VII is taken prisoner by German forces during the Sack of Rome, 1527.
- The Ottoman Siege of Vienna is successfully repulsed in 1529.
- Henry VIII announces that he and his successors will henceforth be heads of the Church of England, 1534.
- Ignatius Loyola founds the Society of Jesus in 1534.

- Copernicus' theories are published after his death in 1543.
- St Francis Xavier undertakes his mission to the East, 1542–52.
- The Council of Trent gets under way in 1545. Church leaders resist the Reformation.
- Turkish naval power is defeated by the Christian fleet at the Battle of Lepanto, 1571.

17TH CENTURY
- Galileo is forced to recant his claims for Copernican astronomy.
- A Congregation for the Evangelization of Peoples is founded to co-ordinate missionary endeavours, 1622.
- The Thirty Years' War ends in 1648, with Europe divided along religious lines.

18TH CENTURY
- Denis Diderot and friends begin work on their secularizing *Encyclopédie* in 1750.
- Revolution convulses France from 1789.

19TH CENTURY
- Pius IX denounces modern liberalism in his *Syllabus of Errors*, 1864. Papal infallibility will be proclaimed six years later.

- The "White Fathers" are at work evangelizing in Africa, from 1868.
- Papal rule in the city of Rome is brought to an end in 1871.
- Leo XIII throws the Church's weight behind the cause of workers' rights in *Rerum Novarum*, written in 1891.

20TH CENTURY
- The Lateran Treaty of 1929 sees the Church enter into partnership with Mussolini's Fascist state.
- A Concordat is signed with Nazi Germany in 1933.
- Pius XI condemns anti-semitic violence in Germany, 1937.
- John XXIII calls the Second Vatican Council in 1962.
- Liberation theology takes root in Latin America from the 1960s. Its followers play a leading role in the Nicaraguan Revolution of the 1980s.
- Pope John Paul II is elected by an enclave in 1978.

21ST CENTURY
- Protestant Pentecostalism is on the rise in Latin America.
- Pope John Paul II makes the first papal visit to Israel, in 2000. That same year he becomes the first pope to pray in a Muslim mosque.

Above The striking Gothic façade of the 14th-century Duomo di Milano, or Milan Cathedral.

Above An 18th-century Peruvian painting of St Francis Xavier. He is the patron saint of all missions.

Above John Paul II (served 1978–2005), an influential pope, was the second longest-serving pope to rule in Rome.

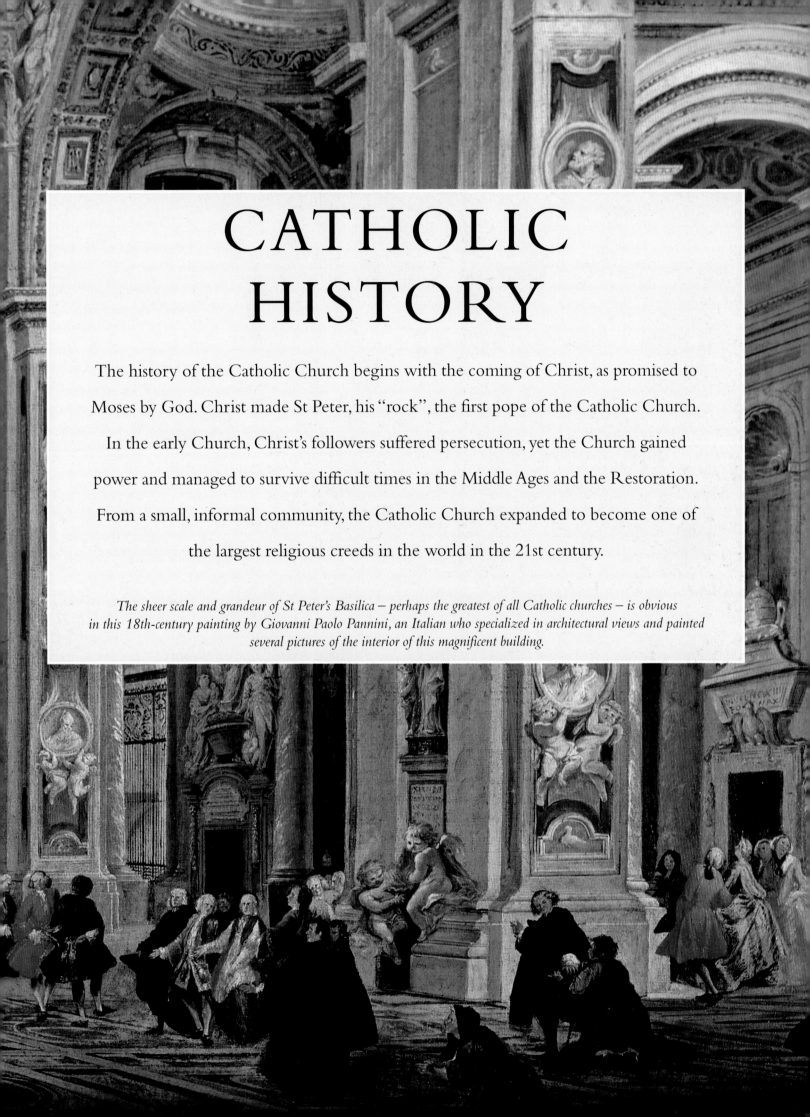

CATHOLIC HISTORY

The history of the Catholic Church begins with the coming of Christ, as promised to

Moses by God. Christ made St Peter, his "rock", the first pope of the Catholic Church.

In the early Church, Christ's followers suffered persecution, yet the Church gained

power and managed to survive difficult times in the Middle Ages and the Restoration.

From a small, informal community, the Catholic Church expanded to become one of

the largest religious creeds in the world in the 21st century.

*The sheer scale and grandeur of St Peter's Basilica – perhaps the greatest of all Catholic churches – is obvious
in this 18th-century painting by Giovanni Paolo Pannini, an Italian who specialized in architectural views and painted
several pictures of the interior of this magnificent building.*

THE EARLY CHURCH

The gospels tell an inspirational story. "The word became flesh," says John's Gospel, "he lived among us and we saw his glory." The coming of Christ was the fulfilment of a promise. His remarkable life and death, and above all his Resurrection, made good God's undertaking to both Moses and Abraham. It realized the predictions of the prophets and renewed humanity's hope.

However, inspiration was not enough: as Christ incarnated the word of God, so his message had to be embodied in the institutions and practices of a living, working Church. Catholicism's structures evolved slowly, sometimes painfully, over centuries. Tried in the fire of persecution and torn by dissension – and, ultimately, division – the Church faced many difficulties as it developed. Christian theology was still comparatively new and unexplored, and it had to be systematized by learned scholars.

There were also the difficulties that come with success. The bigger and more secure Catholicism became as a worldwide institution, the greater the political pressures. The emergence of the papacy as a seat of spiritual authority and political power was a temptation as well as a triumph for the Church. Even so, as the 1st millennium came to an end, the faith was the dominant spiritual and cultural force across much of Europe. Catholicism had come a long way in its first thousand years.

Above The Greek letters Iota (for Iesu, or "Jesus"), Chi (for Christos, or "Christ") and Theta (for Theou, or "Saviour") spell Ichthus, Greek for "fish". The fish, as seen in this 4th-century Italian mosaic, became a Christian emblem.

Left In this 1485 painting The Life of Mary by the Master of Aachen, the old priest Simeon blesses the baby Jesus on his presentation in the Temple.

IN THE DAYS OF KING HEROD

THE COUNTRY IN WHICH THE CHRISTIAN STORY STARTED WAS A TERRITORY OF THE ROMAN EMPIRE, ALTHOUGH THE ROMANS WERE JUST THE LATEST IN A LONG SUCCESSION OF INVADERS.

Above A Bedouin tends his flock in the rocky Judaean Desert, just as Jewish shepherds would have done 2,000 years ago.

Jesus' birthplace, Bethlelem, and the surrounding regions have an ancient history. Christ was born among the Jews, who saw themselves as the "Chosen People" of Jehovah. However the "Holy Land" that was so important to the Jews was one of the less signicant corners of the world at the beginning of the first millenium.

Judaea and Israel, its neighbour to the north, had been brought together under King David from *c.*1007 BC. The state he created, with its capital in Jerusalem, had come to prominence under his son, Solomon, in the 10th century BC. Though known for his legendary wisdom, Solomon had in reality all but ruined his kingdom; the construction of his celebrated Temple had bankrupted the state. Eventually, the country disintegrated and was conquered by the Assyrians in 841 BC.

UNDER OCCUPATION

The Jews never accepted their subject status, despite being subjugated for centuries, first under the rule of the Assyrians, then the Babylonians. In the 6th century BC, leading Jews were taken from their country to the imperial capital in what is known as the "Babylonian Captivity", but this failed to break their spirit of resistance.

Persian power proved more benign: after conquering Babylon in 539, Cyrus the Great of Persia let the exiles return to Israel. (He even ordered the reconstruction of the Temple, which had been sacked by Babylon's King Nebuchadnezzar after a Jewish uprising in 587 BC.) The Persians, however, were swept aside by the eastward march of Alexander the Great, who came with his Greek army in 332 BC. After Alexander's death, his vast empire was fought over by his surviving generals. Along with much of the Middle East, Israel fell to Seleucus, a boyhood friend and comrade-at-arms of Alexander. His descendants reigned after him, in what is known as the Seleucid line.

A TASTE OF FREEDOM

Attempts by the Seleucid ruler Antiochus IV to suppress the religious rituals of the Jews sparked a revolt in 167 BC. Simon

HEROD..."THE GREAT"?

Herod's honorific title, "the Great", strikes modern Christians as strange, given his client-king status – and the part he played in the Gospel account of Jesus' birth. The Magi, wise men who had journeyed from the east by following a star to where they had been told a new king of the Jews would be born, went to Herod and sought his assistance in finding the infant. He was horrified to hear of a rival's birth. However, he begged his visitors to tell him when they found the boy, so that he, too, could pay him homage. Warned by an angel not to tell Herod anything, the Magi instead returned home by another route, whereupon the enraged king had all the infant boys in Israel – the "Holy Innocents" – massacred. This is a cruel and ignominious role in the Christian Scriptures, but

Jewish tradition and mainstream history have judged Herod more kindly. He is called "Herod the Great" on account of his reconstruction of the Temple.

Below A 14th-century Italian mosaic shows King Herod enjoying a lavish banquet.

Above Herod lives in Jewish memory as the rebuilder of the Temple, shown here in a 19th-century painting by James Jacques Tissot (1836–1902).

Maccabaeus' Hasmonean Dynasty took power and Jewish sovereignty was restored. Jewish rule lasted until 63 BC, when the country was conquered once again – this time by the Roman general Pompey. He let the Hasmoneans stay in office, but as client-kings of what was now named Judaea. They reigned at the beck and call of the Roman emperors, but in return their subjects could still find some comfort in the fact that their country was a kingdom, rather than a mere province.

That the Jews were allowed this degree of autonomy indicates the strength of their identity – however, it also reflects the comparative irrelevance of a people living on the margins. The main centres of wealth and civilization in the ancient world were to the east in Mesopotamia (modern-day Iraq) and Persia, and to the west in the Mediterranean. Palestine was peripheral to both these spheres. Regardless, as insignificant as they were, the Jews had been allowed considerable freedom to live and worship God in the way they had for generations. This freedom was a dangerous thing: many Jews were in no way reconciled to their subjection and were eager to shake off the Roman yoke.

KING OF THE JEWS

For the moment, Rome was firmly in charge and King Herod was the Empire's servant. He had been appointed by the Romans as King of Judaea in 37 BC and was given the title "King of the Jews". In return for his loyalty, Herod won certain privileges for the Jews, and the Romans made no objections to his request when, in 19 BC, he renovated the Temple.

Above "No foreigners shall enter…" reads the tablet King Herod placed in the Temple. Christ, by contrast, was to reach out to all people.

15

AND IT CAME TO PASS…

THE JEWS HAD BEEN EXPECTING A MIGHTY KING AS A SAVIOUR, BUT INSTEAD CHRIST WAS BORN IN A LOWLY STABLE IN BETHLEHEM. COULD THIS REALLY BE THE MESSIAH THEY HAD BEEN WAITING FOR?

Jewish scriptural tradition had long foreseen the coming of a "Messiah" – whom the Book of Daniel (9:24) referred to as the "anointed one" or "prince". "The people who lived in darkness have seen a great light," prophesied Isaiah (9:2–9). As a king descended from the House of David, it was believed that the Messiah would introduce an eternal era of justice and peace.

Most Jews expected a king to come in glory, but there were Old Testament writers with another vision. Zachary's Messiah (9:9) was envisaged as "lowly, and riding on a donkey". In a chapter of Isaiah (53:3–6), there is a fore-shadowing of how the Christian

Below "Behold the handmaid of the lord…", begins the Latin inscription beneath this Annunciation by the Italian painter Filippo Lippi, c.1440.

servant-saviour was received: "despised, and rejected by men… he was wounded for our transgressions…and with his stripes we are healed."

A VISIT FROM AN ANGEL

"Behold, a virgin shall conceive," promises Isaiah (7:14), "and bear a son, and shall call his name Immanuel." That prophecy found fulfilment in the gospel account (Luke, Chapter 1) in which the archangel Gabriel announced to the astonished Virgin Mary the miraculous part she had been appointed to play as the Messiah's mother. The angel's words were later to form the first line of the prayer that is still repeated daily by many Catholics: "Hail Mary, full of grace, the Lord is with thee."

The angel also told Mary that her much older relative Elizabeth was pregnant, despite years of

Above The Messiah was expected to renew the reign of King David, writer of the Psalms, shown in this c.1500 painting by the Master of Riofrio.

childlessness, so the Blessed Virgin went to see her in the "Visitation". Elizabeth greeted Mary with the words that became the second line of the Hail Mary: "Blessed art thou amongst women, and blessed is the fruit of thy womb."

THE ANGELUS

Although the custom has fallen victim to the mounting pressures of modern life, for centuries, throughout the Catholic world, the rhythm of the day was set by the sound of the angelus bell. Three sets of three slow, solemn strokes rang out at 6 a.m., 12 noon and 6 p.m. as a signal to the faithful to stop whatever they were doing to meditate on the Annunciation and what it meant. The call-and-response devotion that followed re-enacted the abrupt arrival of the angel in the Virgin Mary's presence and Christ's conception by the power of the Holy Spirit.

Mary's reply ("Behold the handmaid of the Lord…Be it done to me according to thy word") is also recollected in the angelus, as are John's words (1:14) on the Incarnation of Our Lord ("And the word was made flesh, and dwelt amongst us").

THE NATIVITY

Mary, though a virgin, was betrothed to Joseph, whose occupation as a carpenter has made him the patron saint of working men. However, the Gospels of Matthew and Luke are at pains to make the point that he is also a descendant of the House of David: as his son, then, Christ is from Israel's royal line. Yet his is anything but a kingly birth.

At the time when Mary was due to deliver her child, she and her husband were in Bethlehem. The Romans were conducting a census in Judaea and all families had been ordered to go to the ancestral home of the father to be counted. There was no room for them at the inn, so Mary had to give birth in a stable and lay her baby in a manger.

The baby was attended, not by great Jewish dignitaries, but by shepherds from the surrounding hillsides. Although the Magi, "kings" or "wise men", had come to honour the newborn, they were outsiders, summoned from afar. The manner of Jesus' arrival in the world anticipates his later remark (Matthew 13:58) that "a prophet is not without honour except in his own country". By the same token, the coming of the Magi may be seen as a signal that Christ will ultimately find most of his followers abroad.

Above The most momentous of events, Christ's Nativity in the stable was painted by Hans Leonhard Schaufelein in the 16th century.

Below The Holy Family fled to Egypt when they learned that Herod had ordered the slaughter of all male babies, as shown here in this late 15th-century manuscript.

ANNO DOMINI

The "Year of the Lord" – from the Latin *anno domini* (which is commonly abbreviated to AD) – has been taken as a chronological starting point in western tradition. Supposedly, it was the year in which Christ was born. But was it really? Luke's account has the holy family travelling to Bethlehem to take part in a census ordered by the Romans. This could only refer to the survey conducted by Quirinius, Rome's governor in Syria, which is known to have taken place in AD 6–7. However, Matthew implies an earlier date, and some scholars believe that the Nativity might have taken place in 8 BC.

"YOU ARE MY SON, THE BELOVED..."

JESUS GREW UP QUIETLY IN NAZARETH, A LITTLE TOWN IN GALILEE. NO ONE GUESSED THAT THE BOY THEY SAW HELPING OUT IN HIS FATHER'S WORKSHOP WAS ACTUALLY THE MORTAL SON OF GOD.

Christ may have been born, but "Christianity" was as yet unheard of, and Jesus was raised by his parents in the traditions of Judaism. Like any other Jewish baby boy, he was circumcised at eight days old and, on the 40th day after his birth, Jesus' mother took him to the Jewish Temple for his presentation. Tradition demanded not only that the mother herself should be ritually "purified" after giving birth but that the baby should be formally presented. Jewish law decreed that the Temple had the right to claim any

Below Simeon, an elderly priest, sees the Messiah during his presentation in this 15th-century painting by Giovanni Bellini.

firstborn boy for the priesthood, unless he was redeemed with a token payment.

SEEING SALVATION

The Gospel of Luke (2:29–31) describes how Simeon, an old priest who had prayed to God to let him live long enough to see the Messiah, finally saw the infant saviour during his presentation and realized that God had answered his prayers. "Now master you are letting your servant go in peace," he said in gratitude, "for my eyes have seen the salvation which you have made ready in the sight of the nations." The child was destined to be the deliverance of his people, though he would also face great opposition from

Above The adolescent Jesus is shown astonishing the elders of the Temple with his knowledge in this early 19th-century Russian icon.

them and others. Simeon also warned Mary, "a sword will pierce your soul, too" (2:35).

A SPECIAL BAPTISM

At 12 years old, Jesus disappeared during a pilgrimage his family was making to Jerusalem. His frantic mother found him in the Temple talking to the elders. These experienced scholars were in raptures at his knowledge and insight.

Above Jesus is determined to be purified through baptism, like any sinner, in this early 14th-century painting entitled The Baptism of Christ *by Giotto.*

The boy – a little impatiently – dismissed his mother's reproaches: "Why were you looking for me?" he asked (Luke 2:49). "Did you not know that I must be in my father's house?" Though his parents did not understand what their son was saying, this is a clear indication that Jesus' own mind was already on his heavenly kingdom and his earthly mission.

The gospels agree that it was not until many years later, when Jesus was about 30 years of age, that he left home and made his way into the desert beside the River Jordan. There he found John – Elizabeth's son and his relative. Known as John the Baptist, he had already embarked on his own sacred ministry, living simply in the wilderness and preaching to the people, calling on them to change their lives. He baptized the repentant and prophesied the coming of a saviour.

When Jesus appeared, John pointed him out as the one who was to come. John was perplexed when the man he regarded as the Messiah asked to be baptized like any sinner, but Jesus was adamant, and John agreed. As Christ arose from the water, the heavens parted and the Holy Spirit descended in the form of a dove. A voice rang out, saying "You are my Son, the Beloved; my favour rests on you" (Mark 1:11).

THE TEMPTATION

After his baptism, Matthew tells us, Jesus went into the wilderness alone to fast and pray in preparation for the task that awaited him. He spent 40 days and 40 nights in the desert, with his solitude being interrupted only by the devil, who had come to test his resolve.

Satan appeared three times to tempt Jesus. First he offered Jesus all the kingdoms of the world if he would bow down and worship Satan. Then he challenged Jesus to turn stones into bread to satisfy his hunger. Finally, Satan took Jesus to the highest point on the Temple and dared him to jump off (the angels will make sure you are not hurt, he said). Christ refused to rise to these provocations. Dismayed, the devil left and angels arrived with bread to ease Jesus' hunger.

Right Christ is tempted by the devil in the desert, shown here in this c.1225 stained-glass scene in Troyes Cathedral, in France.

"BLESSED ARE THE POOR IN SPIRIT"

IT IS UNCLEAR WHETHER CHRIST'S MINISTRY LASTED FOR WEEKS OR YEARS. EITHER WAY, HE HAD TIME TO PERFORM MIRACLES AND PROCLAIM THE MOST REMARKABLE MESSAGE EVER HEARD.

Jesus first performed a miracle at his mother's urging during the Wedding Feast at Cana. Supplies were running low, so he turned jars of ordinary water into wine. Once his ministry got under way in earnest, Jesus cast out demons and healed the sick – and, in the case of Lazarus, he even gave life back to the dead.

From a modern perspective, the early miracles appear to have established Christ's credentials as the Messiah. Certainly, when the apostles saw him walking across the waters of the Sea of Galilee toward their boat, they were left in no doubt of his divinity (but Peter's own faith faltered as he attempted to walk out to meet his Lord).

A DIVINITY KEPT SECRET

Jesus himself did not necessarily want his divinity known to others. At a number of points, in the

Left Jesus is surrounded by his followers as he gives his Sermon on the Mount. He is standing in this painting by James Jacques Tissot, but traditionally Jesus is shown sitting – rabbis often sat while teaching.

Gospel of Mark especially, he urged his hearers to keep what is called the "Messianic Secret". Even when his apostles witnessed him standing on a high mountain in the episode known as the "Transfiguration", blazing forth in all his godly radiance, they were urged to not tell others what they had witnessed.

After one of his first miracles, the healing of a leper (Mark 1), Christ gave the man strict orders that he should tell no one of his cure. However, in his exhilaration, the man ignored this injunction and told everyone he met what Jesus had done for him. Crowds came from far and wide to see this marvellous miracle worker. Some came in hopes of being cured themselves; some to witness miracles or to hear what this new prophet had to say.

THE BEATITUDES

Christ's teachings have their single, most sustained exposition in the extraordinary episode known as the Sermon on the Mount – although on which particular mount the discourse was delivered is unclear. Wherever it occurred, it was during this sermon that Jesus formulated the Beatitudes (literally, Blessednesses), as is recorded in Matthew 5:3–12:

Above Christ cures a blind man in this warm and intimate scene by an 11th-century Italian artist.

- *How blessed are the poor in spirit; the kingdom of heaven is theirs.*
- *Blessed are the gentle; they shall have the earth as inheritance…*
- *Blessed are the merciful; they shall have mercy shown them…*
- *Blessed are the peacemakers; they shall be recognized as children of God…*

These blessings gave encouragement to his listeners. However, there were many other components to this thought-provoking sermon, including the Lord's Prayer and what are considered by many people to be the central tenets of Christianity. The convention is that Jesus' life and death created a "new covenant" between God and humankind. This was a merciful reaching out, a second chance for the fallen descendants of Adam and Eve.

This interpretation is true enough, but at the same time, for all the generosity and love it represented, the "deal" Jesus offered was extremely exacting. Those who followed his way, he warned, could expect to endure abuse and persecution. Harder than the insults and violent treatment they were to expect, would be the duty they would have to respond to their oppressors with friendship and forgiveness: rather than retaliate if anyone hit them, they must offer them the other cheek (Matthew 5:39). They should love their enemies, do good to those who wish them harm, and treat others as they would hope to be treated themselves.

NOT ONLY FOR THE JUST

Jesus found his first followers when, walking by the Sea of Galilee, he met the fishermen Simon (whom Jesus promptly renamed Peter) and his friend Andrew, along with two brothers, James and John. Other "apostles" followed: 12 in all, including Philip, Bartholomew and Thomas. None was rich or learned; they represented the working poor rather than the priestly elite. Matthew, a tax collector, was a member of a despised class. But Christ had come to call sinners, he said. His later friendship with Mary Magdalene, the repentant prostitute, underlined his concern that his redemption was for all, not just the traditionally pious.

Right Jesus dismisses the disapproving stares of his pious companions as Mary Magdalene prostrates herself at his feet in this 16th-century painting attributed to the French School.

TEACHING TALES

Arriving as he did to bring God's Word to the poor and uneducated, Christ made his message as vivid as he possibly could. Rather than setting out an abstract code of instructions, he expressed his teachings in strikingly human terms. He spoke of the Sower whose seed fell largely on stony ground; the Samaritan who remembered his charitable duty when his "betters" forgot theirs; and the Prodigal Son, welcomed home from his wanderings by his joyful father. Such parables demonstrated, more strongly than any commandments could, what it might mean to follow in the way of Christ.

Right Christ's parable of fishermen making an abundant catch but only keeping the best fish is recalled in this c.1530 illustration for medieval readers.

THE WAY OF THE CROSS

CHRIST MAY HAVE COME TO BRING HUMANITY EVERLASTING LIFE, BUT FIRST HE HAD TO SUFFER AND DIE. THE AGONIES OF HIS CRUCIFIXION WERE THE PRICE HE PAID FOR MAN'S REDEMPTION.

The climax of Christ's ministry occurred when he made his triumphal entrance into Jerusalem. He did not do so in a chariot or on a noble stallion but mounted on a donkey. This is kingship in the humble spirit of the Beatitudes. The huge crowd cheered the Messiah through the streets, scattering palm leaves before him as he went. The crowd cried out the words of Psalm 118, "Hosanna! Blessed is he who is coming in the name of the Lord!"

However, he received a decidedly cooler welcome from his country's religious establishment. The Christ who had come to call sinners had already alienated both the learned scribes and the self-consciously pious Pharisees. Their devotion, he said, was to the letter of the law, while his was to its spirit. In Jerusalem, it became clear just how radical a reformer he was prepared to be. He was even willing to violate the peace of the Temple, driving out the moneychangers from its sacred precincts. For Jesus, they had turned the house of God into a den of thieves.

Above Christ's entry into Jerusalem, with palm leaves spread before him, has been captured in this 15th-century fresco by an unknown artist.

THE LAST SUPPER

Jesus had journeyed to the capital to join the celebrations for the Passover feast. As a good Jew, he wanted to take the traditional supper of lamb and unleavened bread with his apostles, but he gave the occasion a new and very special slant. Breaking the bread, he gave it to his friends, telling them solemnly, "This is my body". He offered them wine, telling them to drink it and saying, "This is my blood". What was to be his "Last Supper" with his apostles thus became a foreshadowing of the sacrifice he was so soon to be making on Calvary, and, of course, the Catholic sacrament of the Eucharist.

When the meal was over, Jesus and his apostles withdrew to the Garden of Gethsemane to pray in seclusion. Jesus felt all-too-human fear and panicked at the thought of what he was about to face. Men sent by the Sanhedrin – the sacred judges of the Jews – arrived to arrest him, away from the public eye. He was pointed out by his own apostle Judas, who betrayed him for 30 pieces of silver.

ON TRIAL

Jesus' captors accused him of blasphemy, although the evidence against him proved exasperatingly slight, until he told them that he was Christ, the son of God. His guilt established to their own satisfaction, the judges handed

Below Jesus feared death, as any mortal would. In the Agony in the Garden, *painted by Giovanni Bellini c.1465, he prays for help.*

Above The Crucifixion, and the sign of the Cross, became emblematic of Catholicism. This 13th-century Italian painted cross was an object of devotion.

him over to the Roman governor Pontius Pilate, claiming that he had been scheming against the state. Pilate was unconvinced, but the clamour of the Sanhedrin and their supporters was so great that in the end he called for water and literally "washed his hands" of the problem. Christ's accusers could have their way, he said.

THE EXECUTION

Jesus was scourged at a pillar before being made to carry a heavy timber cross to his place of execution. He was mocked and spat upon as he made his slow, painful way through the streets of Jerusalem. Outside the city, on Mount Calvary, he was placed on the Cross, attached to it by nails through his hands and feet, and set up on the hilltop between two condemned thieves. "Father forgive them; they do not know what they are doing," he said of those who tormented him. Only after hours of agony did he die. On that day, a Friday, darkness fell upon the earth, which was convulsed by tremors; the curtain that screened the holiest part of the Temple ripped down the middle.

Below Jesus staggering under the weight of his heavy Cross is depicted in this sumptuously carved, c.1460 wooden altarpiece from Antwerp.

Above Judas betrayed Jesus with the sign of love, a kiss, as captured in this 14th-century Spanish painting by the Master of Rubio.

PASCHAL PAST

The feast of Passover dates back to the deliverance of the Jews from Egyptian enslavement, as told in the Old Testament's Book of Exodus. God had sent nine plagues to afflict the Egyptians, but they still refused to let Moses and his people go. At last God sent an angel down to kill the firstborn of every family. So no Jews should be punished, Moses was instructed that each Israelite household should kill a lamb and mark their doorpost with its blood.

Christ was going to his own death, sacrificing himself to atone for all of humanity's sins. Where the Jehovah of the Old Testament had meted out punishment to the Egyptians for their wickedness, now the "lamb of God" was going to take on the sins of all the world. His death and Resurrection marked the beginning of a "new covenant" in which justice would be tempered with mercy and in which sins might be forgiven.

HE HAS RISEN

CHRIST'S DEATH WAS THE ULTIMATE EXPRESSION OF LOVE, BUT IT WAS HIS RESURRECTION THAT GAVE IT MEANING. STRIVING HUMANITY HAD A WAY BACK TO GOD, A CHANCE AT LIFE IN HEAVEN.

Numbed by shock and stunned by disbelief, Jesus' friends took him down from the Cross, and his mother cradled him in her arms for the last time. One of his followers, Joseph of Arimathea, had a burial chamber already prepared for himself in a cave nearby. He got Pontius Pilate's permission to lay Christ to rest inside.

With that done, fear for their own physical safety being the least of their problems, Jesus' followers turned to despair. What were they to do? Where were they to go? They had been left emotionally and spiritually bereft by the death of their saviour, the one who had promised them eternal life. The darkness that still enveloped the earth matched their complete disorientation and their utter gloom.

AN EMPTY TOMB
But life had to go on, and part of life is the ritual responsibility of the living to the dead. So on Sunday morning, Mary Magdalene and "the other Mary", mother of the apostle James the Less, made their way to the tomb. (The gospels

Above Christ cuts an awe-inspiring figure as he floats triumphantly above his open tomb in The Resurrection of Christ, *painted c. 1502 by Raphael.*

differ, but Mark's Gospel mentions a third woman, another friend and follower, Salome.) There, they found that the stone protecting the entrance had been rolled aside. In the doorway, an angel greeted them, informing them that they had made a wasted journey: "He is not here, for he has risen, as he said he would."

In Matthew's account, as the astonished women ran to tell their friends the news, they met Jesus himself nearby. He asked them to tell the disciples to meet him in Galilee. Just hours later, two disciples walking along the road to Emmaus joined a stranger and went to an inn to eat with him. Only when this "stranger" blessed the bread before handing it to them did they realize who he was.

THE ASCENSION
The risen Christ then revealed himself to a number of disciples at various points, although these tended to be fleeting encounters. The apostles themselves were frightened and demoralized, and

Below Christ appears to two travellers on the road to Emmaus in this 15th-century fresco from the Church of the Trinity, Piedmont, Italy.

Above The apostles gaze up as Jesus is borne aloft on a cloud by angels in this 12th-century Spanish stone relief.

Thomas was at first reluctant to believe that the sightings had even taken place. Finally, 40 days after the Resurrection, Jesus appeared before them in a room where they were all gathered. He urged them to carry his message to all the nations of the world. He told them not to fear: the Holy Spirit would protect them. He also said they would be able to pick up serpents and not be harmed, and they would have the power to cast out demons and heal the sick.

What happened next is unclear because the gospels differ on the details. However, there is agreement among the gospel writers that Jesus ascended to heaven: "a cloud took him from their sight", says the Acts of the Apostles (1:9).

PENTECOST

Left behind again, the apostles withdrew with Mary, the mother of Jesus, and other supporters to an "upper room" – the same one in which the Last Supper was celebrated. For the next few days they prayed together until, on the Jewish feast of Pentecost, the house was suddenly filled with a roaring noise, "as of a violent wind". Tongues of fire came to rest above their heads as the Holy Spirit descended upon them. With this inspiration, they ventured out into the streets to start spreading the word. Miraculously, those who listened, no matter what country they came from, could hear them speaking in their own native language.

THE GOSPELS AND THE GRAIL

Joseph of Arimathea is referred to in the gospels for the part he played in the burial of Christ, where he had a limited role in the event. However, he was given a more important role in a later legend. The tradition, most recently popularized by Dan Brown's novel *The Da Vinci Code,* has him carrying Christianity to Britain, along with the Holy Grail. This sacred vessel (widely assumed to be a chalice, although some sources see it as a serving dish) is said to have been used by Christ at the Last Supper. It is a colourful story, but no more than that. The earliest accounts of Christianity in Britain make no mention of Joseph of Arimathea, and it is not until the 9th century that we hear of his involvement. As for the Holy Grail narrative, that is even later in its origins, first appearing in French romances of the 12th century.

Below Mary takes pride of place among the apostles in this representation of Pentecost, painted in Florence by Jacopo Orcagna (active 1368–98).

THE DISCIPLES

"COME AFTER ME," CHRIST HAD TOLD THE FISHERMEN BESIDE THE SEA OF GALILEE, "AND I WILL MAKE YOU IN TO FISHERS OF MEN." HIS WORDS CAME TO PASS IN THE EARLY DAYS OF THE CHURCH.

Pentecost is a day of inspiration, marking the day of the descent of the Holy Spirit on the apostles. The disciples' joy was all but intoxicating – although cynics claim that they had, indeed, been drinking. Yet their euphoria, born of the Holy Spirit, is only heightened when they find ordinary people in the streets receptive to the message of Christ. As predicted by Jesus, these disciples became the "fishers of men". On that first day alone, the Acts of the Apostles assures us (2:41) some 3,000 converts were made, and more were recruited daily in the weeks that

Below Jesus sends his followers to "make disciples of all nations" in a 20th-century stained-glass window by Gabriel Loire.

followed. Christianity, it seems, was gathering momentum. This was a mass movement, no longer a community – but a Church.

A NEW WAY OF LIFE

At the time, the disciples' religion was more fervent than thoughtful; Christian doctrine and ritual were works in progress. However, one thing is clear: at this stage the Christians were still emphatically Jewish. At the heart of their ritual, we are told (Acts 2:46), were their daily visits to the Temple together; afterwards, they adjourned to the homes of the community members for the "breaking of bread". This appeared to be both a eucharistic ritual and an act of sharing. The same verse tells us that they "shared their food gladly

Above The apostles were soon finding many ordinary people willing to convert to Christianity, as shown in this late 15th-century illumination by Jean Poyet.

and generously". We are told, too, that they sold their possessions and divided up the proceeds so that everybody had what they needed. It is said that they were "looked up to by everyone", and were joined by a steady stream of new recruits.

Like Jesus before them, the apostles worked miracles, but they were careful that the glory went to God, not themselves. They fell foul of the Sanhedrin (the sacred judges of the Jews, who did not believe in resurrection), but they had no grounds on which to condemn them – nor could they explain how the Christians cured the sick and lame.

A FAITH FOR ALL

These Christians were indeed still scrupulous in their Jewish observance, worshipping regularly and

maintaining all the dietary laws. However, that was soon to change. St Peter had a dream in which God instructed him that from now on no animal or bird should be deemed "unclean" (Acts 10:10–15). Additionally, there was news that an angel had appeared to a Roman centurion, Cornelius, and this persuaded Peter that God wanted Christianity to be open to all, regardless of nationality.

For hundreds of years, the Jews had prided themselves on being God's "chosen people", so what Peter was saying was a complete departure. As he was addressing Cornelius and his Roman friends

Above St Peter continued the ministry of his departed Lord. In this Italian fresco, by Masolino da Panicale, he raises Tabitha from the dead.

and relatives, the Holy Spirit descended upon them – just as it had earlier on the disciples at Pentecost. Peter's Jewish companions were shocked, but their leader, unruffled, explained that this was a sign that "God has no favourites" (Acts 10:34).

The historical record shows that this principle was ratified at the Council of Jerusalem, held around AD 50 under Peter's guidance. The Council also agreed

that gentiles (non-Jews) could be baptized without circumcision. This was the start of the divergence of Christianity and Judaism. So, too, was St Peter's transfer of his ministry from Jerusalem to Antioch in Syria (modern-day Turkey), and later to Rome, where he was to take his message to the centre of the ancient world.

A CHRISTIAN CAPITAL

Antioch, or Antakya, now in modern-day Turkey, is not an attractive place to visit. It is a noisy, congested city. However, behind this façade hides a historic and spiritual centre of extraordinary importance. The beautiful buildings may have been swept away, but the legacy of this past has endured in the people, in its small but active Christian community. Today, Antakya's Christians are in an often uncomfortable position: they are caught between the aggressive secularism of the Turkish state and the Islamic devotion of the majority of the population. Yet, they feel strengthened by their sense of 2,000 years of continuous Christian worship here. Under its old name, Antioch, this was a major metropolis. More than that, for a crucial period in the 1st and 2nd centuries, it was the capital of Christianity. St Peter himself is said to have made it his headquarters, and by the 3rd century, according to St John Chrysostom, there were 100,000 Christians in the city.

Left St Peter preaches in a street that has the distinct look of 15th-century Florence. The painting is from the Linaiuoli Triptych *by Fra Angelico (c. 1387–1455).*

ST PAUL THE CONVERT

SAUL STARTED OUT AS AN IMPLACABLE PERSECUTOR OF THE NEW
RELIGION, BUT REBORN AS PAUL HE BECAME A TIRELESS EVANGELIST.
HE PLAYED AN IMPORTANT ROLE IN BUILDING THE EARLY CHURCH.

Saul was born in Tarsus, in what is now the south of Turkey. In the 2nd century BC, this country had been conquered by the Romans. Tarsus had been given an unusual amount of say over its own affairs, and Saul's well-born Jewish family had been granted citizenship. This set Saul apart from the Jews of his time and made him doubly suspicious of Christ's followers, who were a potential threat to Judaism and the Roman Empire.

According to the Acts of the Apostles (Chapters 7–8), Saul first came into contact with Christianity as a witness to the martyrdom of St Stephen, who was stoned in Jerusalem around AD 35. Saul appeared as a mere bystander: those about to kill the young man placed their cloaks at his feet for safe keeping. The man from Tarsus did not remain detached for long. Oddly enough, it does not seem to have been either Stephen's proclamations of Christian faith or his criticisms of the Jews that upset Saul. What got his attention was the serenity with which the first martyr met his death and the magnanimity with which he asked God to forgive his killers.

Saul, in anything but magnanimous mood, hurled himself into the task of hunting down and destroying the rest of Stephen's fellow Christians. It was with the aim of rounding up the Christian community in the Syrian city that Saul was on the road to Damascus.

THE LIGHT OF GOD

As he travelled, a dazzling light appeared. Felled by its force, Saul pitched forward, falling on the

Above Saul was stopped on the road to Damascus, as seen in this 19th-century stained-glass window from Lincoln Cathedral, England. His conversion greatly influenced the course of Christianity.

stony road. "Saul, Saul, why are you persecuting me?" thundered God from the sky. Saul, in his shock, lay cowering and helpless. "Who are you, Lord?" he said. "I am Jesus, whom you are persecuting," came the reply. This was a revelation for Saul, and his conversion on the road to Damascus was to be a defining moment for Christianity. Saul had never set eyes on the living Christ, yet, as Paul, he did much to shape the development of Christ's Church.

SIGHT RESTORED

Having been blinded by the light, Saul was taken on to Damascus by his companions. A disciple named Ananias was told in a dream to go to the house where Saul was staying and restore his sight. Having heard what type of man Saul was, Ananias questioned this instruction. To his amazement, the Lord told him that Saul had to be cured because he was central for his plans for his Christian Church.

The restoration of Saul's sight was of course a symbolic as well as a physical cure: he had been morally blind before but was now enlightened. He became as eager a proselytizer as he had been a persecutor, dedicating his life to the spreading of the gospels.

Below Paul preaches Christ's message in Luca di Tommè's 14th-century representation. The disciple believed the gospels should be spread to all people.

THE LETTERS OF THE LAW

Paul covered thousands of miles in the course of his ministry. He took his duty to the gentiles very seriously. Never satisfied with simply making converts, he kept in touch with the communities he had come to know in a series of letters. Part personal greetings, part sermons, part theological arguments with himself, the Epistles were to be incorporated into the Christian Scriptures. Paul's opinions, as set down in his Epistles, had an incalculable influence not only on his various congregations around the ancient world but on the way Christianity was to develop in modern times.

Right A page of Paul's Epistles can be seen in this detail from a 1473 polyptych (a many-panelled altarpiece) in Ascoli Piceno's Sant' Emidio Cathedral, Italy.

APOSTLE TO THE GENTILES

The Holy Spirit, we are told (Acts:13), specifically chose Saul for the task of taking the divine word to the gentiles, or non-Jews. It is no surprise, then, that he changed his name to the Roman "Paul" during his first mission to Cyprus, Greece and Asia Minor – or that he took sides with Peter in discussions at the Council of Jerusalem, which were to open the new religion to non-Jews. In subsequent missions, Paul criss-crossed the eastern Mediterranean and Middle East regions, making new converts and revisiting existing Christian communities.

Arrested in Jerusalem, allegedly for bringing gentiles into the Temple in defiance of Jewish law, Paul was accused of blasphemy – just like Christ had been before him. However, because of his background, Paul could appeal to his rights as a Roman citizen, which meant that he was eventually transported to Rome for trial there. His arrival coincided with the first major persecution of the Christians in AD 64. He died a martyr, though the exact date and circumstances are unknown.

Right Masaccio's 15th-century painting of St Paul shows the disciple armed with the sword of the fighter (and the martyr) and the Bible.

A FAITH IN FEAR

"BLESSED ARE YOU WHEN PEOPLE ABUSE YOU AND PERSECUTE YOU," CHRIST SAID. HIS FOLLOWERS WERE TO FIND OUT WHAT THAT FELT LIKE AS THEY BRAVED TORTURE FOR THE SAKE OF THEIR BELIEFS.

Toward the end of AD 64, Nero, Emperor of Rome, launched the first "Great Persecution". In these early days of Christianity, its disciples could pose no conceivable threat. By this time, the numbers in their community in the capital could have been only in the low hundreds at the most.

However, Nero had an agenda. He was widely blamed for the Great Fire of Rome, which had swept through the city that year.

There were reports that the emperor's own household slaves had been seen intentionally setting the fire so that Nero could advance his redevelopment plans for parts of the city centre. As things turned out, the conflagration gutted 10 of the capital's 14 districts. Under the circumstances, Nero was only too eager to have someone else to blame, and the Christian community made the perfect scapegoat.

Above A man is attacked by wild beasts in the arena in this 2nd-century mosaic from North Africa.

CRUEL DEATHS

On his orders, Christians were taken prisoner by the score. Some were tossed on to fires – alive – thrown to savage dogs to be torn apart or, notoriously, cast into the arena to be killed by wild animals as a public spectacle. Others were crucified, a common form of execution at the time, but also a sneer at the way the Christians' Messiah had been killed. Peter, who had arrived in Rome at the start of Nero's Great Persecution, was one of those crucified in Rome during this period. One tradition has it that he was hung upside down, at his own request, presumably because it would be presumptuous to be executed in the same manner as his saviour.

PROLONGED REPRESSION

In many places and for long periods, Christians were tolerated. Yet, sometimes, persecution came not

Left St Peter is often depicted being crucified upside down, such as in this 16th-century French manuscript.

from the state but from the general public. Christians were harassed – even physically attacked – by their pagan neighbours. Sometimes there were also more serious and sustained outbreaks of mob violence against Christians, with or without the connivance of the authorities.

As is generally the way with such things, hostility increased at times of political uncertainty or economic crisis. There were significant crackdowns during the reigns of Domitian, Trajan, Septimius Severus and Decius. Many priests and bishops were martyred in the reign of Valerian (253–60), including St Laurence, reputedly burnt on an iron grill.

In fairness, part of the problem was the Romans' incomprehension of what was motivating the Christians to resist. As far as they were concerned, they had given the Christians every chance to

Left St Sebastian, who was martyred in 287, is shown gazing stoically heavenward as arrows pierce his body in this 1480 painting by Mantegna.

Many others were killed during the eight years of the Great Persecution, but some modern scholars are sceptical about claims by contemporary sources that 10,000 martyrs were crucified on the first day of Diocletian's crackdown. Yet even the conservative estimates are in agreement that thousands were martyred and many thousands more had suffered harassment and torture. Again, the persecution appears to have been prompted by an economic crisis brought on by Diocletian's financial mismanagement. The emperor was also a religious conservative, concerned at what he saw as the abandonment of the traditional Roman gods in favour of new faiths, such as Christianity.

THE EMPEROR AND THE ANTICHRIST

After being driven underground by Nero's persecution, the Christians communicated using a code based on what was known as "gematria". This was a type of numerological theory that attributed mystical properties to different numbers and saw significance in their relations to the letters of the Hebrew alphabet. Some scholars have studied all the infinite subtleties of gematria for many years, but at its crudest level it can be used to make a straightforward cipher. For Nero, the figures came to 666: the "Number of the Beast" in the Book of Revelation. Many early Christians did, indeed, see this Roman ruler as the model for the "Antichrist".

save themselves by abjuring their religion. They simply could not understand that this new creed could be worth dying for.

ANOTHER PERSECUTION

In 303, Emperor Diocletian issued his "Edict Against the Christians", ordering that churches should be demolished and Christians enslaved. This would have been bad enough even if it had not been the signal for the start of another Great Persecution. Again, Christians were given a chance to save themselves by offering sacrifices to the pagan gods. Some were intimidated into compliance. Some sources say (though others deny this) that even the pope of the day, Marcellinus, had been persuaded to burn incense before Roman idols. However the pope repented his weakness, reasserted his Christian faith and died a martyr some time in 304.

Above The grisly manner of St Catherine's execution in Alexandria around 305 has clearly caught the imagination of this late medieval painter, whose work appeared in the 1280 History of Four Saints.

New Life among the Dead: The Catacombs

BENEATH ROME, MEN, WOMEN AND CHILDREN CAME TOGETHER IN SECRET WORSHIP. THEY FOUND A SANCTUARY IN THE DOMAIN OF THE DEAD, WHERE THEY HAD BURIED THEIR LOVED ONES.

In the face of persecution in the world above for their adherence to the creed of Christ, early Roman Christians ventured deep into the earth to the homes of the dead to give their thanks and praise to the living God.

A PRACTICAL SOLUTION

The catacombs were first and foremost a place to bury the dead, but for the Christians, and perhaps others, they became a place of refuge in times of persecution. As many as 40 of these underground burial complexes existed around the periphery of Rome; construction had begun in pre-Christian times. The pagan Romans, while

Below Ancient skulls seem to survey the scene in a chamber at the heart of Rome's San Callisto catacombs.

revering the dead and making offerings at their graves, had also viewed them with fear and banished them beyond the city limits. Burial grounds had sprung up along the main routes out of town. Many people were cremated and their ashes stored in special columbaria ("dovecots"), so-called because the regular niches in which the urns were placed in their hundreds resembled the pigeonholes in which the birds nested in the dovecots of the day.

With pressure growing on space around the city, these facilities were tucked discreetly away underground. More subterranean complexes were built in Christian times, and these had to be more spacious. Burial had replaced cremation for the Christian faithful, who looked forward to

Above The catacombs were primarily a way of warehousing the dead: floor-to-ceiling niches line this passage.

the resurrection of the body. Fortunately, the soft and porous "tuff" (volcanic ash) on which much of Rome is founded made excavation easy, and these underground cemeteries quickly grew.

SAN CALLISTO

Rome's biggest catacombs, the San Callisto, are named after an early pope, St Callistus (although

Above Inside the Roman church of San Callisto, the "Crypt of the Popes" houses the relics of Church leaders from the 3rd and 4th centuries.

he was actually one of the few 3rd-century pontiffs not to have been buried in its rectangular "Crypt of the Popes"). They were rediscovered in 1849 by the Italian Giovanni Battista de Rossi, and while more than 20km (12½ miles) of tunnels and chambers have been mapped, there are large areas of labyrinthine passages that have yet to be explored. Tunnels were often created one on top of another, in up to four separate layers.

SACRED AND SECRET

For decades at a time the Christians had been left alone, and during these settled periods the catacombs appear to have been nothing more than burial places. It was only natural, though, that during periods of official crackdowns, when worshipping in public basilicas or homes was too hazardous, families that had grown used to visiting these underground passages to honour and pray for their dead thought of seeking a sanctuary here. The tombs of martyrs put to death in the persecutions became sacred sites in themselves, and their fellow Christians would visit them later to gather for worship and prayers.

Even in times of toleration, then, the catacombs were a powerful focus for Christian faith. And then, of course, there was the symbolic resonance: the sense of life and affirmation flourishing in the midst of death. It is inconceivable that this could have been lost on the men and women of the early Church.

MODERN INSPIRATION

Today we can marvel at the courage of these early Christians and see their story as exemplifying hope. The vanquishing of death, the triumph of new life – even in the grave itself – Christianity can hold out no greater promise to the believer. Hence, perhaps, the continuing hold the catacombs exercise over the imagination of the faithful.

UNDERGROUND ART

Areas in the catacombs were crudely customized as churches, and frescoes were painted showing what appear to be eucharistic scenes. The fish often crops up as a symbol – not just because Christ and his apostles had been fishermen but because the letters of the Greek word *Ichthus* ("fish") spelled out the secret slogan *Iesu Christos Theou* (or "Jesus Christ Saviour"). Old Testament scenes are represented as well, such as Moses striking the rock and sending water gushing forth and Jonah being swallowed by the whale.

San Callisto's "Gallery of the Sacraments" has some fascinating paintings. There are more in the San Domitilla catacombs, where key saints of the 4th century were laid to rest in an underground basilica. One side room has a ceiling adorned with a 3rd-century fresco of the Good Shepherd; in nearby niches and passages are paintings of Jesus, his apostles and the Magi.

Above Abraham prepares to sacrifice Isaac, his son, in this fresco. The catacombs hold some of the earliest Christian art.

THE CHURCH OF ROME

INCREASINGLY, CHRISTIANITY WAS EASING AWAY FROM ITS JEWISH ROOTS. ROME, THE CENTRE OF THE 1ST-CENTURY WORLD, WAS THE NATURAL HEADQUARTERS FOR THIS NEW RELIGION.

Why, despite its Middle Eastern origins, did this new religion become known as the "Roman" Catholic Church? To some extent, the development might seem accidental. The scene of so many martyrdoms had acquired strong emotional and spiritual associations for the early Christians. As early as the 2nd century – long before the age of persecutions had run its course – men and women were making pilgrimages to the tombs of St Peter and St Paul.

WORLD CAPITAL

There were other reasons that were also important. Rome was the capital of a vast empire: to all intents and purposes the centre of the world. Important decisions were all made there, and Rome ruled in many subject nations. The city was the centre of a web of well-made roads and busy shipping lanes.

Below Tertullian was a pagan who converted to Christianity c.AD 197. His writings covered many issues in the theological field, providing a picture of religious life and beliefs in his time.

These advantages would not always have been of interest to the Church, of course. To begin with, Christianity had been influenced by Judaism. In fact, debate had raged over whether gentiles should be baptized at all, and many had been resistant to this change. However, Peter and Paul had prevailed with their literal interpretation of Christ's words, "Go…and make disciples of all nations" (Matthew 28:19).

LATIN TAKES OVER

Significant, too, was the decision of Tertullian, the Church's leading thinker, to write his works in Latin, the Roman language. Until now, there had been two languages of Christianity: Hebrew, the tongue of the Jews, and Greek, the language of the Seleucid kingdom and the Middle East. The word "Christ" came from the Greek *Christos* ("the Anointed"). Tertullian's decision in *c.*AD 200 made clear the ambition of the Church to reach out beyond its territories of origin to the rest of the known world.

CONSTANTINE'S CROSS

In 312, the Church found an unexpected supporter in Emperor Constantine I. At noon, in the hours before an important battle with a rival for imperial power, Constantine the Great had been praying to the sun – as Sol Invictus, the supreme deity of his religion. Suddenly, he and his army were astonished to see the blazing face of the sun overlain by the figure of the cross. The unmistakable symbolism was spelled out by an

Above Rome is revealed to St Augustine as the "City of God", as shown here in a 15th-century French manuscript.

inscription written across the face of the heavens: *in hoc signo vinces* ("in this sign prevail").

Constantine's conversion at the Battle of Milvian Bridge and his patronage gave the Church a welcome boost. With the threat of persecution lifted, its members could meet and worship openly; its clergy could conduct its affairs in public. What had been – necessarily – a low-profile faith, with its adherents meeting quietly, was able to establish a presence in the world. Constantine advanced this process, endowing the Church with resources and working hard to build up its institutions. It was he who called the Council of Nicaea in 325, where important doctrinal questions were debated and resolved. While some felt that Constantine's patronage made Catholicism too "official", it allowed access to the structures of the imperial establishment that helped the Church to grow.

Constantine's Christianity was what the Church had needed at a tricky time. Even if the emperor himself was at times less than wholehearted in his commitment to his new faith, his mother St Helena ensured that he stayed loyal to its cause. Having converted following her son's example, she became his religious guide.

THE NEW CAPITAL

At the same time, Constantine took steps that were to lead to one of the saddest developments in the Church's history: he transferred the empire's capital to Byzantium, or Constantinople as he called it. In the centuries that followed, the city on the Bosporus became the real centre of the "Roman" world, while Rome itself sank into stagnation and decline. In time it was to recover, but by then the Eastern Church had broken away and Christ's followers were divided.

Above Constantine I is depicted in this 16th-century fresco with his mother, St Helena, the traditional finder of the relics of the "True Cross". She ensured her son never wavered in his beliefs.

Below In this 13th-century fresco, Pope Sylvester I baptizes Constantine – a breakthrough for the Church. In fact, the emperor postponed this sacrament until his deathbed.

A DOUBTFUL DONATION

Constantine gave Christianity his generous backing, building (among numerous other things) the original Basilica of St Peter's in Rome. However, the one thing the Roman does not appear to have given the Church is the rumoured "Donation of Constantine", in which he supposedly gave Pope Sylvester I and his successors temporal authority over Rome and many of its possessions in Europe and North Africa. Most of these realms fell to a variety of invaders and other rulers, but the popes held on to power in parts of central Italy into modern times. Even today, the Vatican remains a sovereign nation, its status sanctioned by custom, if not by legal title. In fact, the "Donation of Constantine" was revealed as a forgery in the 15th century. It is believed to have been created in the 8th century.

Below A colossal head of Emperor Constantine from the Roman Forum. It was once the topmost part of a 4th-century full-length statue.

THE FIRST POPES

THE INSTITUTION OF THE PAPACY BEGAN WITH CHRIST'S COMMISSION TO PETER, "I WILL GIVE YOU THE KEYS OF THE KINGDOM OF HEAVEN: WHATEVER YOU BIND ON EARTH WILL BE BOUND IN HEAVEN…"

The papacy started to take shape as an institution over time, but the first pope was Peter. His name had been Simon, but Christ gave him a new name to go with his new and crucial role. "You are Peter," he says (Matthew 16:18), punning on the Greek word *petros*, or "stone", "and on this rock I will build my community." The Church over which he presided would be proof against the powers of Satan, Jesus promised, and its leader would have complete spiritual authority on Earth.

CHRIST'S SUCCESSORS

The "apostolic succession" is key to Catholicism's claims to be the one true Church of God. According to this theory, authority has been transmitted via an unbroken line of pontiffs from Christ and Peter down to the present day.

Below Christ hands the keys of heaven to Peter, who becomes the first pope, as depicted by Pietro Perugino in this 15th-century fresco.

That authority is embodied in the office of the pope, who has as his emblem the crossed keys that recall the "keys of heaven" that Christ promised to Peter.

In its early days, of course, the Church was small and less structured, so to be its bishop would not have been a great honour in worldly terms. Christianity was often – due to Roman persecution – a furtive faith, forced to operate underground or on the run. There was no point in its bishops attracting attention to themselves, and they did not need to. Peter had no palace, no Vatican. Even so, his pre-eminence as "Prince of the Apostles" was acknowledged by Christ's followers. He was the Saviour's anointed successor here on earth, and no Christian would have dreamt of questioning his command.

A CHANGING CHURCH

In the Edict of Milan (313), the Roman state recognized the legitimacy of the Church. Larger and

Above The keys of heaven have been incorporated in Pope Leo X's coat-of-arms, which were carved in this Roman stone relief of 1513–20.

no longer persecuted, the Church had become a very different kind of institution. Leadership in what was now a big and international organization became not just a spiritual challenge but also an administrative one. Maintaining doctrinal discipline was proving to be more difficult as well. Individual teachers started striking out in their own directions and, by the end of the 4th century, theological anarchy was threatening the integrity of the Church.

This, moreover, occurred at a time when Rome was in steep decline, beset by both barbarian invasions and by instability that came from within. The centre of political power had shifted to the East, where Constantinople was booming as the capital of a more Asian-orientated "Roman" state. Rome had become a backwater in its own empire. All the indications were that, as the Western Empire declined, the Church was going to go down with it. It seemed that its brief history was going to end in oblivion.

A POWERFUL PAPACY

Pope Leo I, the Great, was influential in the development of the Church. His approach was far from subtle. He was unashamedly tough in his response to opposition. Democracy was a luxury he felt the Church could not afford. He was confronted with an organization that was in disarray, so he exercised dictatorial powers and centralized all power and doctrinal authority in himself. He formulated the view that the pope was heir to the powers of Peter, as stated in Matthew 16:18. Earlier generations of Christians had looked up to their popes, had valued the apostolic succession and had read and been inspired by Jesus' words to Peter, but they had not necessarily thought of the popes as heirs to Peter. Through these actions Leo the Great helped to strengthen the Church.

Below When Pope Fabian was elected in 236, the Church was a large organization. In this depiction of his coronation by an artist of the 15th-century Spanish School, a dove (symbolic of the Holy Spirit) is perched on his head.

A PERSUASIVE POPE

Leo the Great may have been a masterful pontiff, however he was not a tyrant. He could compel people by his kindness, and won people over with his warmth. That he had a gift for getting his own way could hardly be denied: however, this was, after all, the man who managed to talk Attila the Hun out of attacking Rome. Their meeting, in 452, came after the Asiatic warlord and his army had invaded Italy and were poised to sweep down and sack the capital. Despairing of defending their city against such a ferocious enemy, the military and civic leaders of Rome approached the Pope to ask for his help. Taking two officials with him, Leo went to meet Attila and ask for peace. The latter "was so impressed with the presence of the high priest," wrote one chronicler of the day, "that he ordered his army to give up warfare and, after he had promised peace, he disappeared beyond the Danube".

Below Leo the Great saved Rome from attack by Attila's forces when he met the Hunnish leader in 452. This c.1860 woodcut was inspired by a fresco in Munich.

THE CHURCH FATHERS

MANY SCHOLARS HAVE HELPED IN DEVELOPING THE DOCTRINAL
DETAILS OF CATHOLICISM — BUT FOUR IN PARTICULAR STAND OUT
AS THE "DOCTORS" OF THE EARLY CHURCH.

The Church owes an immeasurable debt to the great "doctors", or teachers, of the early Middle Ages, who helped shape not just its rituals but its faith. Clear though they were in essence, Christ's teachings had implications that had to be explored and examined, principles to be drawn out and systematized. The Church existed in the real world: Christians looked to it not just for inspiration

Below Gregory, Ambrose, Jerome and Augustine: the four Church Fathers attend the Virgin and Child in this 15th-century altarpiece.

but also for explanations, for moral guidance and for help in dealing with their doubts and fears. At first, it was ill equipped for this task. Its theology was undeveloped, and its institutional structures were limited.

AN UNBAPTIZED BISHOP

Just how disorganized it was is clear from the fact that, when the Bishop of Milan died in 374, his successor, Ambrose, had not been baptized or ordained as a priest, and he had not received any serious schooling in theology. Yet Ambrose understood the need for

Above St Jerome had reputedly taken the thorn from a lame lion's paw, hence the cat with which he is traditionally shown, as here in this 15-century painting by an unknown Swiss artist.

THE CONFESSOR

Today, St Augustine is best known for his autobiography, *The Confessions* (397) and for his youthful cry, "Lord make me chaste, but not yet!" However, in his eagerness to underline the fact that humanity was, from the beginning of existence, in a "fallen" state, he belaboured himself about offences that far predated this. As a boy, he lamented he had stolen fruit that he did not need; even as a baby, he believed that he had cried deliberately to unsettle the adults around him. This is a strange book in some ways, yet Augustine's self-examination is today admired far beyond the Church for its striking insights into what we would call psychology.

Right The Devil holding up the Book of Vices to St Augustine *is the title of this work by Michael Pacher (c.1435–98). St Augustine saw evil and its temptations as a constant threat.*

theological rigour. His first move on his appointment was to give his possessions to the poor; his second was to embark on a programme of self-education. It was a spiritual and intellectual journey in which – thanks to the books he wrote – his fellow Christians were able to accompany him. Ambrose's courage was exemplary (his refusal to be bullied by Emperor Theodosius set the standard for subsequent pontiffs); so too was his piety. He was influential in his emphasis on the role of Mary, the Blessed Virgin.

LATIN WORDSMITHS

Ambrose benefited from his ease with the Greek sources in which much theological writing until that time had been set down. Writing in Latin, Ambrose can be seen as part of that same process of westernization that Tertullian had begun two centuries before. Jerome continued the process with his translation of the Bible into Latin, which he began in 382. Jerome was a Dalmatian-born

Right At "St Gregory's Mass", the Saviour appeared with his wounds bleeding and poured his blood into the chalice of the pope, as depicted in this c.1490 illumination.

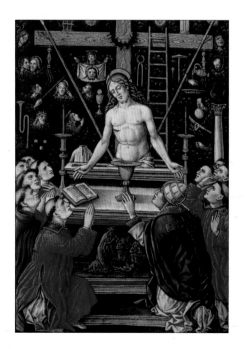

scholar who worked from Greek editions because it was recognized that the finest scholarship was to be found in that language. At the same time, the Church was starting to define itself as Western. Greek, since Alexander's day, had been the language not just of Greece itself but of Asia, the home – in the Church's eyes – of heresy.

FIGHTER FOR ORTHODOXY

St Augustine of Hippo refuted two powerful heresies. As a young man, he held Manichaean views. These views were a product of Persian tradition that pitted the powers of light and virtue against darkness and sin. Manichaeism had exerted a strong influence over Christianity in the East. Augustine rejected this phase of his development, just as he did the dissolute lifestyle of his youth, and became a staunch defender of Western orthodoxy.

Augustine also defended the Roman Christians against the comforting creed of the Pelagians. Pelagius, a 4th-century monk, had argued that humanity had not irrevocably fallen in the Garden of Eden, so had no need of Christ's redemption. Individuals could choose to be good themselves, unaided. It was Augustine who helped to formulate the doctrine of original sin.

A GREAT REFORMER

Gregory I, the Great, was elected pontiff in 590. His reforms were tireless and far-reaching. From the celibacy of the clergy to the idea of the remission of time in Purgatory for acts of public and private penance, they touched just about every area of religious life. The clamour for his canonization had begun in his own lifetime, though critics claimed he had practically bankrupted the Church with his charitable giving.

A CHURCH DIVIDED

"ROME HAS SPOKEN, THE CASE IS CLOSED" ARE STRONG WORDS ATTRIBUTED TO ST AUGUSTINE. THE CHURCH'S INSISTENCE ON ORTHODOXY CAME ABOUT AFTER A LACK OF DOCTRINAL DISCIPLINE.

Rome was the centre of the world in the 1st century AD, but the power and control of this empire didn't last. The Dark Ages, from c.500 to the 11th century, were not as black as some popular histories claim, but it was an era in which the Church struggled. The Roman Empire was under relentless attack from invaders, and Rome itself was imploding politically, so the survival not just of the state but also of a civilization was at stake – as was the Church. Yet, at a time when Christian unity was all-important, rivalry threatened to tear the faith apart.

A CITY UNDER SIEGE

Augustine saw the danger. Rome had just been sacked by the Visigoths when, in the latter part of 410, he started writing *The City of God*. Many Romans believed the fall of their capital had been a judgement of the gods on its

Above The Church, a fortress, is defended against heresy and sin in this illumination from a 15th-century French manuscript.

toleration of the Christian religion. However, Augustine's vision was of the city of Rome and the Church as parallel states, beset by barbarism and paganism respectively. Hence the impassioned urgency with which he strove to secure the spiritual integrity of his Church.

DIFFERENCES OF OPINION

Augustine thought the heretics were the enemies within. There was no shortage of them at this time, and they were often powerful. The adherents of Arianism followed the teaching of Arius, an Egyptian monk who had claimed that Christ, though saintly, was not divine. St Ambrose had led the fight against this heresy as Bishop of Milan in the 4th century, but it flourished and was believed in by many within Europe's ruling class. This heresy was halted when Emperor Theodosius I spoke out against it at the Constantinople Conference of 381. That year's

Left A series of Nicaean Councils in the 1st millennium allowed important doctrinal issues to be thrashed out. It is represented in this Russian calendar dating from the mid-18th century.

revised Nicene Creed (*see below*) clearly rejected Arianism's claims. Yet its influence persisted in outlying regions of the West.

The 5th century brought the Nestorian Schism. An Archbishop of Constantinople, Nestorius asserted that Christ as God and Christ as man were not two different aspects of the same being but two distinct persons. This heresy was taken up in the East, leading to the breaking away of what became known as the Assyrian Church. Monophysitism, by contrast, held that Christ had only one aspect, the divine. Its supporters were fiercely at odds with the Nestorians in the East.

OUT OF IRELAND

Augustine's fears for the Church under barbarian attack were by no means exaggerated. Within a century of the Sack of Rome, Christianity had been almost wiped out throughout western Europe. Only in the remotest reaches of Ireland's Atlantic coast were Christianity and its culture holding out. However, in the 6th and 7th centuries, missionaries from these far-flung monasteries fanned out across western and central Europe (even Italy), reintroducing the Church of Christ.

THE EAST–WEST SCHISM

With its own bustling capital at Constantinople, the centre of a thriving empire, the Church in the East was flourishing, and it was increasingly going its own way. Cultural and linguistic differences caused the two halves of the old Roman Empire to diverge: the West was European and Latin; the East Asiatic and Greek. The West was in apparently terminal crisis, while the fortunes of the East were buoyant, so the eastern patriarchs saw no reason to bow before the popes. They owed allegiance to

Left Heretical books are consigned to the fire in this illustration from a manuscript of the 9th century.

the Byzantine emperors, who had the right of appointing them. Their loyalty to the pontiff took second place. The authority of Rome was recognized formally, but deference was offered more grudgingly as time went on.

In 1054, Rome placed a papal bull denouncing the patriarch, Michael Kerullarios, upon the altar of Constantinople's great basilica, Hagia Sophia. Kerullarios responded in kind. Pope and patriarch had excommunicated one another – expelled each other from their Church community. The East–West Schism was under way, and the "Orthodox" Church of the East often existed separately from the Catholic Church.

THE NICENE CREED

We believe in one God,
the Father, the Almighty,
maker of heaven and earth,
of all that is, seen and unseen.

We believe in one Lord,
  Jesus Christ,
the only Son of God,
eternally begotten of the Father,
God from God, Light from Light,
true God from true God,
begotten, not made,
of one Being with the Father.
Through him all things were
  made.
For us men and for our salvation,
he came down from heaven:
by the power of the Holy Spirit
he became incarnate of the Virgin
  Mary,
and became man.
For our sake he was crucified
  under Pontius Pilate;
he suffered death and was buried.
On the third day he rose again

in accordance with the Scriptures;
he ascended into heaven
and is seated at the right hand of
  the Father.
He will come again in glory
to judge the living and the dead,
and his kingdom will have no end.

We believe in the Holy Spirit,
the Lord, the giver of life,
who proceeds from the Father and
  the Son.
With the Father and the Son he
  is worshipped and glorified.
He has spoken through the
  Prophets.
We believe in one holy Catholic
  and apostolic Church.
We acknowledge one baptism for
the forgiveness of sins.
We look for the resurrection of
  the dead,
and the life of the world to come.

Amen.

AVDI·TE CŌDITIO
MAGNI·ET NIS·ET
PARVI·CV GRADVS
IVS·CVNQ ESTIS·

ORDO·ISTI
FVIT·A·DEO
REVELATVS
SCE·BRIGI
DE·AD
HONOREM
VIRGI
NIS
MARI
E·PRICI
PIV·HVI
VS·RELIGIO
NIS·ET·SALV
TIS·E·VERA
VMILITAS·ET
PVRA·CAS
TITASATO
OLVTARIA
POVPERTES

·ORATE·
·PROPICTORE·
·1522·

THE MIDDLE AGES

The Church's second millennium could hardly have begun with a less auspicious start, split by the East–West Schism. What was really striking, though, was the easy assurance with which Catholicism shook off what should have been a catastrophic blow.

So-called in retrospect because it came between the classical period (Greece and Rome) and the Renaissance, the *medium aevum*, or Middle Ages, marked a breakthrough for the Church. Quite simply, in the West at least, there was no higher human institution: its teachings shaped the way men and women thought. The Church led the reconstruction of the West in the chaotic centuries that followed the fall of the Roman Empire in the 5th century, forming its institutions and culture and influencing architecture, music, literature and every area of learning. Catholicism had left its mark on all of these. The people saw the Church as the source of all their spiritual and moral laws, and rulers looked to it for their legitimacy.

Even so, there would be challenges. As early as the 7th century, Islam had emerged from Arabia. By the 11th century, the rapid expansion of its empire was seen as so great a threat to the West that a series of Crusades were mounted against the Muslims. Yet the existence of such a threat also gave Christendom an enemy against which it could define itself, and the Church continued to go from strength to strength.

Above Christ looks down from heaven as a choir of monks sings a hymn in this illumination from a c. 1300 manuscript of an English psalter.

Left St Bridget of Sweden issues the rule for the Brigettine Order (Giovannantonio di Francesco Sogliani, 1522). Monasticism flourished in Europe during the Middle Ages.

MEDIEVAL CATHOLICISM

THE MIDDLE AGES IN EUROPE WAS A HIGH POINT FOR THE CHURCH: EVERY ASPECT OF LIFE — FROM HOW PEOPLE FELT TO HOW THEY WERE GOVERNED — WAS SHAPED BY CATHOLICISM.

As the main religion throughout Europe, the sect that had hidden itself away in the catacombs was no more. No monarchy could match its pervasive power. Kings consulted closely with its prelates and its pope, and ordinary men and women looked to their priests with all the deference due to God's representatives on Earth. Its teaching set the tone – morally, intellectually and culturally. Its monasteries were repositories of learning, driving forces in literature and science, and its cathedrals displayed the latest and the best in art and architecture.

FEUDALISM AND FAITH

The Church's power and authority were not just awesome, they were integral to the way in which medieval Europe viewed the world. In the Middle Ages, along with the idea of "faith" went that of "fealty" (from the Latin *fidelitas*, or "faithfulness"). It defined the bond of obedience and loyalty the man had to his overlord. Just as the serf owed fealty to his lord, who in turn acknowledged the overlordship of his king, so the Christian obeyed his or her priest, who was directed by the religious hierarchy.

Medieval Europeans implicitly believed that God had created an orderly cosmos and everything in the universe had its place. It was the responsibility of those entrusted with power, both spiritual and temporal, to ensure that order prevailed here on Earth. The power of the Church and State were thus regarded as two sides of the same coin. Despite their differences – there were disputes between popes and kings – it would

Above This 12th-century golden orb, emblematic of the world, surmounted by a jewelled cross, was part of the crown jewels of imperial Germany.

never have occurred to a king to question the divine authority of the pope or his hierarchy any more than it would have occurred to the Church to undermine the power of the king. It was in neither's interest to jeopardize that principle of order on which the entire worldview of the Middle Ages rested.

POWER AND WEALTH

In truth, the Church wielded a great deal of power over secular affairs as well, and few temporal rulers dared defy its will. None would have dreamt of taxing its wealthy monasteries. Whether in a spirit of piety or in fear for their fate in the afterlife, wealthy magnates bequeathed lavish gifts in land and treasures to their local religious foundations.

Left Serfs who worked the land used the crop to pay their tithe to the aristocracy and the Church, as seen in this late 15th-century French illustration from The Playfair Book of Hours.

Meanwhile, year in and year out, poor peasants and craftsmen had to pay a "tithe" (one-tenth) of their income to the Church. Although priests at village level lived pretty much as modestly as their parishioners, things were different further up the hierarchy. In time, the ethics of this would come to be questioned, but, in the meantime, senior churchmen often lived like lords.

THE ARTS AND LEARNING

At the same time that these senior church members wined and dined stupendously, they also bestowed their patronage freely. As a result of their conspicuous consumption, art lovers today can appreciate what are considered the greatest masterpieces of Western art. Giotto, Cimabué and countless anonymous artists worked under the auspices of the Church. Church buildings were often also filled with the exquisite work of master woodcarvers and sculptors, whose works brought the stories of the Bible to the illiterate.

Education and learning were to all intents and purposes the monopoly of the Church – and this, too, would eventually become a source of friction. For the moment, though, intellectual discussion and debate all took place within the terms of reference established by the great Catholic teachers of the day. Pre-eminent among these was Thomas Aquinas, born in Sicily *c*.1225. His *Summa Theologica* (1266–74) was literally a "theological summary", setting out in a single vast and coherent plan all the Church's teachings about God, the universe and the place of man within it. Aquinas' work is valued in its own right by philosophers today, but it was also an important conduit for earlier thought: the ideas of Aristotle, of Arabic thinkers such as Ibn Rushd (Averroës) and Ibn Sina (Avicenna), and of Jewish doctors such as Maimonides all found their way into Western tradition through his work.

Above With Plato and Aristotle on either side, St Thomas Aquinas is shown with the Arab philosopher Averroës in the foreground in this 15th-century painting by Benozzo di Lese Gozzoli.

DANTE

Born in Florence *c*.1265, Dante Alighieri has been revered in modern times as the poet who envisioned hell. His *Inferno* is indeed awe-inspiring, striking in its dreadful beauty but also in the sympathy it shows for the sufferings of the damned. Yet Dante would have been surprised to see it abstracted from his *Commedia* ("Comedy") as a whole.

Hell's torments could make no sense for him except as aspects of a universal order. His *Inferno*, like his *Purgatorio* and his *Paradiso*, is founded in the love of God. He can weep for the sinner while still giving thanks for the overall scheme.

Below Dante enlightens the citizens of Florence with his vision of the universe in this 1465 painting.

THE CRUSADES

SOON AFTER ISLAM AROSE IN THE EAST, VICTORIOUS ARAB ARMIES
SPREAD THEIR FAITH TO THE VERY DOORS OF ROME. FOR NEARLY
500 YEARS, CHRISTIANS FOUGHT BACK IN A SERIES OF CRUSADES.

Roughly at about the same time that Catholicism had established itself as the dominant religion in Europe, Islam was on the rise in the East. This new expansionist religion posed a threat to Catholic authority, and the Church felt urgent pressure to try to stop its growth.

THE RISE OF ISLAM

The prophet Muhammad's mission to spread his Islamic religion began about 610. Arab armies carried his message to both the East and the West. By 638, less than three decades later, these armies were occupying Jerusalem.

Spilling across North Africa, the forces of Islam crossed the Straits of Gibraltar into Spain in the early 8th century. By 720 they were pushing into France, though they had been turned back at Tours in 732. Christian rulers in northern Spain had embarked on a long-term Reconquista, or "reconquest", but the south of the peninsula seemed securely established as al-Andalus, a Muslim kingdom. With the borders of the Islamic world expanding at an incredible speed, Christendom was in fear for its survival.

A CALL TO ARMS

In November 1095, Pope Urban II gave an electrifying speech at the Council of Clermont. The armies of Islam stood on the very doorstep of Christian Europe, he warned. His words were recorded by the chronicler Fulcher of Chartres, and he finished his speech with a desperate appeal:

Above Pope Urban II proclaims the First Crusade during the Council of Clermont in 1095 in this illustration from Jean Fouquet's Les Grandes Chroniques de France, *c. 1460.*

For this reason I beg and urge you – no, not I, but God Himself begs and implores you, as the messengers of Christ, the poor and the wealthy, to rush and drive away this mob from your brothers' territories, and to bring swift assistance to those who also worship Christ.

Below The crusaders travelled to the Middle East by both land and sea.

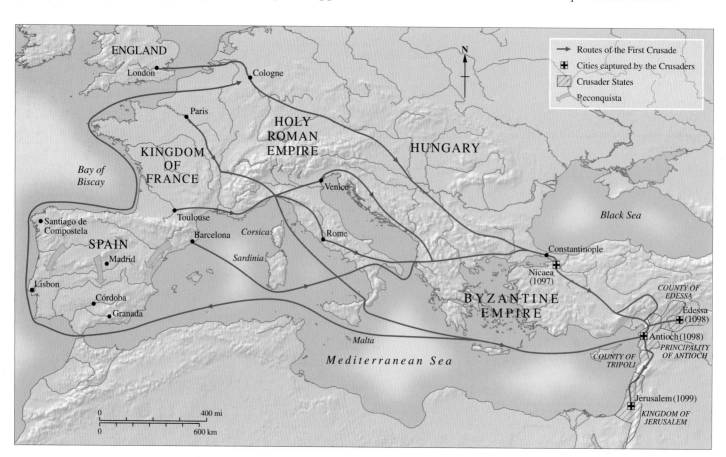

*Right Crusaders storm Constantinople –
a Christian city – in this 16th-century
painting of the Fourth Crusade by the
Italian painter Jacopo Tintoretto.*

In response to Pope Urban II's plea, a mass mobilization took place across Europe, involving not just knights and soldiers but also ordinary men and women – and children. Thousands were inspired by what they saw as their sacred duty. Others were drawn for secular reasons: the prospect of plunder or the promise of adventure.

TO JERUSALEM!

The Crusade had a difficult start. The army that arrived in Constantinople – ready to march through Anatolia (modern-day Turkey) and on to the Holy Land – was big, but it was poorly equipped. Of the 100,000 crusaders, only 40,000 survived the journey over the mountains to Antioch. It then took a seven-month siege to take the Syrian city. Afterward, the crusaders pushed on to Jerusalem. Amid ferocious fighting, the city fell on 13 July 1099, and thousands of its inhabitants were massacred.

CONTINUED CRUSADES

Jerusalem was soon under threat again from the resurgent "Saracens", as the Christians called the Arab forces. A Second Crusade occurred in 1147 but ended in an undignified rout. In 1187, the Kurdish leader Salah al-Din al-Ayyubi, or "Saladin", recaptured Jerusalem. The English king, Richard I, the Lionheart, and other Christian kings mounted a Third Crusade in 1189, but they fought in vain.

The Fourth Crusade (1202–4) was short of funds, so the crusaders sacked Constantinople, massacring thousands. This was followed by another tragedy: in 1212, thousands of young French and Germans enlisted in the Children's Crusade, but before they reached the Holy Land they starved or were sold into slavery in North Africa.

The Fifth Crusade (1217–21) approached Jerusalem from the south but proved no more successful than its predecessors. In 1228, Holy Roman Emperor Frederick II negotiated Jerusalem's return diplomatically, but it fell into Muslim hands again. Two further crusades were mounted in 1248 and 1270: both were catastrophic failures.

Retaking Jerusalem was out of the question after the Ottoman Turks took Byzantium in 1453, but the struggle against Islam went on. In Spain, the Reconquista was coming to a conclusion, which came with the capture of Granada in 1492. In 1529, the Ottomans besieged Vienna, but were finally repulsed. The West's decisive victory came at sea, at the Battle of Lepanto (1571). Christendom had been locked in conflict with Islam for five centuries. The struggle had been very costly in terms of lives and money, but it had done much to shape the Church.

*Left Even now an intimidating sight,
the 12th-century fortress of Krak des
Chevaliers in Syria was built by crusaders.*

MONASTICISM

THE MONASTERIES WERE IMPORTANT CULTURAL AND ECONOMIC CENTRES THAT HELPED SET THE TONE OF MEDIEVAL LIFE. THEY BROUGHT MEN TOGETHER IN COMMUNITIES OF WORK AND PRAYER.

From the beginning, Christians had met in informal communities, with sharing and co-operation being fundamental to their faith. For a beleaguered, sometimes persecuted, minority, the community provided comfort. However, as time went on, organized communities of Christians were established, often living far away from the distractions and temptations of society at large. St Benedict of Nursia (c.480–543) founded at least 12 such communities in the early 6th century.

THE RULE OF ST BENEDICT

One community in particular – the Benedictines, established about 430 at Monte Cassino, south of Rome – was to have enduring importance. This was where St Benedict first formulated his "Benedictine Rule", a regime prescribing set times for collective worship, private prayer and study. It also allowed time for daily stints of manual work, which Benedict saw as an important way of suppressing personal pride and of giving praise to God. The Rule also

Above The great pioneer of the monastic movement St Benedict of Nursia delivers the Rules of the Order to St Maurus in this 1129 illumination, produced at the Monastery of St Gilles, Nîmes.

put clear structures in place. One monk was to be elected "abbot" by his companions; he was to be in charge, though he had to consult with his community on key decisions and was not exempted from the general routines of work and prayer. With 73 points in all, the Rule gave detailed instructions about everything from forms of worship to food and clothing – it stipulated a lifestyle that was simple, but not punitively harsh.

MONASTIC LIFE

The Rule of St Benedict soon became the basis for an extensive network of monasteries across medieval Europe. Young men flocked to join these communities. They flung themselves into the monastic life in all its aspects, not just prayer and contemplation but also study and work. As beacons of learning, these monasteries soon commanded the respect of the wider communities in which they were based.

Run as they were by a well-motivated and educated workforce, their farms and market gardens thrived. So did their other economic ventures: some monks brewed beer

Left Monks work in the fields, as depicted by Breu the Elder (c.1475–1537) on this panel from an Austrian altarpiece.

St Benedict's, young men flocked to join the community. They were drawn by the possibility of a purer, more wholly dedicated religious life. Cluny subsequently became a major monastic centre.

Monasteries elsewhere begged the new community to send out teachers to instruct them in the new rule. The Cluniac Reform quickly spread throughout western Europe. Even where the Cluniac Rule was not explicitly adopted, its influence was felt. Its effects filtered beyond the monasteries and into the wider Church. Catholicism's conscience had been awakened, and individual believers, clergy and institutions all set about reforming themselves and the way they lived.

However, Cluny was a victim of its own success. It became so powerful and influential that some began to feel that it had become too worldly in its turn. In 1098, St Robert of Molesme and St Stephen Harding founded the Cistercian Order – so-called because it was established at the Abbey of Cîteaux. It too set out to restore the Benedictine Rule as originally ordained, and it did so with considerable success. From 1113, under the leadership of St Bernard of Clairvaux, it became an important force for monastic reform.

or other drinks while others prepared medicines from herbs they had grown themselves. The monasteries rapidly became important centres of industry and trade – and their abbots used their influence on local rulers.

MONASTICISM REINVENTED

But soon some people were asking whether this success had not come at too high a price. Were the monasteries losing their way, becoming too "worldly" in their concerns? In 910, William the Pious, the Duke of

Above The Cistercian Abbey of Sénanque, located in southern France, was founded in the mid-12th century.

Aquitaine, founded a new community at Cluny, in eastern France. His idea was that its members would return to the founding principles of monasticism, as originally set down in the Benedictine Rule. William had read the mood of the times and his call for a new kind of monasticism had struck a chord. Though, if anything, the code at Cluny was even stricter than

MONASTIC MYSTICISM

If the idea of community is as old as Christianity itself, so too is that of solitary contemplation. Christ's sojourn in the desert was emulated by a long tradition of hermits. Others wandered inward, deeper and deeper into their own minds, to find a peaceful place in which they could commune with God.

Some mystics, such as Julian of Norwich and Mechtilde of Magdebourg, can be seen as a kind of counterbalance to the monastic movement, pursuing the same aims as these religious communities but using contrary methods. The less these mystics attended to the world, they felt, the closer they could draw to God. In blindness to the world and its concerns, they could glimpse the truth that really mattered. Enlightenment, wrote one mystic, was to be found in a "Cloud of Unknowing".

Right Mother Julian of Norwich was one of the great mystics of the Middle Ages. She is depicted in this 20th-century statue in Norwich Cathedral, England.

SHRINES AND RELICS

TANGIBLE TESTAMENTS TO HEROIC LOVE AND SACRIFICE, HOLY SHRINES AND SACRED RELICS HAVE REMINDED BELIEVERS THROUGHOUT HISTORY WHAT THEIR FAITH IS ALL ABOUT.

A shrine is considered a sacred place, usually one that has been specially blessed by the presence of a holy person, who carried out an important act, or who lived, died or was buried there. A relic is an item once associated with a saintly personage, anything from a fragment of bone to a scrap of shroud, or a possession of some sort. Catholics believe that shrines and relics have been sanctified by their associations to these holy people, so shrines have often become places of pilgrimage, while holy relics have become objects of veneration.

Even Catholics today find it hard to imagine the transporting spiritual excitement their medieval forebears

Below The cloth said to have been worn by Our Lady at the birth of Christ has been kept at Chartres Cathedral, France, since AD 876. The cathedral is a popular site of pilgrimage.

experienced in the presence of holy shrines and sacred relics. Though the Catholic Church continues to encourage the veneration of genuine relics, this is often misunderstood outside the Church. There is discomfort with it among modern believers, and Catholics are still sensitive to any suggestion of superstition.

OPEN TO ABUSE

During the Middle Ages, there was undoubtedly an element of the grotesque in the cult of certain relics, and, indisputably, there was at times an air of opportunistic showmanship about their presentation. Much of their fascination for the faithful may well have been as much about vulgar curiosity as about faith.

At the time, businesses linked to the pilgrimages were thriving, and the possession of holy relics did not merely

Above St Veronica wiped Christ's face as he carried his cross to Calvary. Miraculously, an imprint of Jesus' face was left on the cloth, as shown in this 15th-century painting by Hans Memling.

confer prestige, it could also bring (sometimes spectacular) earning potential. Pride of place in Venice's St Mark's Basilica was the tomb of the apostle – the Venetians had actually stolen St Mark's remains from their original resting place in Alexandria. In England, Canterbury was quick to cash in on the martyrdom of St Thomas, with entrepreneurially minded priests selling what was purported to be vials of his blood and scraps of his clothing.

A VALID TRADITION

So many churches had parts of the True Cross or the bones of various saints that not all of them could have been genuine. Yet even if not all relics were what they claimed to be, over the centuries millions of Catholics have derived great comfort and inspiration from them. Relics were of value not least as a subject for meditation. A visitor to St Thomas à Becket's tomb in Canterbury could wonder at the courage of one who

Above Reputed to be the last resting place of the apostle St James the Great, Santiago de Compostela is an important place of pilgrimage.

had stood up to his own king for what he knew was right. German visitors to the shrine of St Sebaldus in Nuremberg could reflect on what his early mission to Rome and preaching in Nuremburg had meant for their country. Several successive German emperors visited the shrine to pay him homage.

CONTACT WITH THE SAINTS

There is no doubt that the sense of being able to touch the saintly was part of the reason behind making a pilgrimage. Accordingly, a certain amount of tension arose between the instinct to present sacred relics in what would be appropriate magnificence and the pilgrims' desire for up-close contact. As monuments for these relics grew in size and splendour, they were built with open cavities, or "squeezing places", left in the tomb surround so the faithful could feel they were getting as close as possible to the source of grace.

DISTRUST FROM OTHERS

This need for contact would eventually be viewed by non-Catholics as somewhat grotesque. Protestant reformers, like many other modern intellectuals, distrusted Catholicism's instinct for the concrete – what can be seen and touched – an instinct revealed in everything from crucifixes and rosaries to statues and stained-glass windows. To them, the desire to touch a fragment of the "True Cross" or a visit to a saint's tomb could be compared to the time when Jesus told St Thomas to put his fingers in his wounds (John 20:25–9) before the doubting man would finally believe in his Resurrection.

In the 18th century, the philosophers of pre-revolutionary France had denounced Catholicism as a conspiracy to prop up corrupt institutions. Voltaire was one of these philosophers, and among his anti-religious comments was a sneer about the veneration of Christ's foreskin and the Virgin's milk, designed to humiliate Catholics.

For believers, though, the desire for contact with Christ and his saints was not rooted in weakness of faith. Contact was made for love, like that of the woman who touched the hem of Jesus' garment (Luke 8:40–8).

Below Sacred shrines, such as the one in this 15th-century painting by the Master of San Sebastian, have sometimes been linked to miraculous healings, making them popular pilgrimage sites for the lame and the sick in search of succour.

MIRRORS REFLECTING THE RELICS

In Aachen, Germany, in 1440, so many pilgrims flocked to see an exhibition of sacred relics that there was little prospect of anybody actually touching the reliquaries. The most the pilgrim could hope for was glimpses of these sacred treasures through the crush of the crowd. This situation led to the selling of metal-framed "pilgrim mirrors". These mirrors were designed to be clipped to the cap. They supposedly allowed the radiance emitted by the sacred relics to be captured, which the pilgrims could even take home to share with their family and friends.

PILGRIMAGE

EVERY YEAR, ALONG EUROPE'S HIGHWAYS, TRAVELLERS MADE THEIR WAY, SINGLY OR IN GROUPS, CRISS-CROSSING THE CONTINENT TO SEEK OUT THE MOST SACRED SHRINES OF THE CATHOLIC FAITH.

The idea of the medieval pilgrimage is still well known today to students of literature, thanks to Geoffrey Chaucer's *The Canterbury Tales*. This 14th-century poem tells the story of a group of pilgrims from different walks of life, who travel from London to Canterbury in England. There they intend to offer their devotions at the tomb of St Thomas à Becket, who lies buried in the cathedral where he met his martyr's death. Like many Christians in the Middle Ages, Chaucer's pilgrims hoped to acquire grace in the eyes of God by the commitment they were showing in making a sacred journey.

AN OLD TRADITION
By this time, the tradition of pilgrimage, or spiritual journey, was already an old one. Since the 2nd century, believers had been travelling to Jerusalem to visit the scenes of their Saviour's ministry and sufferings and to think about what they meant in their own lives. The pilgrimage is by no means a uniquely Christian custom. By the 5th century BC, Buddhists had been trekking to the birthplace of their teacher, the Buddha, at Kapilavastu, Nepal.

Pilgrimage became embedded in the traditions of Catholicism. It was a gesture, a declaration of spiritual intent. Forsaking family, friends and everyday routines, the Catholic set out on what he or she hoped would be a new direction. The pilgrimage itself was just the start, but it could be a profoundly significant start. Removed from the rhythms of daily work and home life, the pilgrim could reflect on that life and how it might be led better. Arriving at the holy place itself, the pilgrim might meditate on the religious drama that had taken place there, or on the life of the saint whose mortal remains had sanctified the spot.

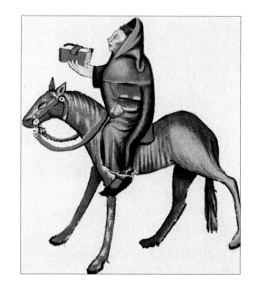

Above The Clerk of Oxenford, one of Chaucer's fictional pilgrims, is shown in The Canterbury Tales *(1400–10).*

Some made their pilgrimages in hopes of saving a sick relative, or to help secure their salvation in the life beyond. Others were motivated by piety, a desire to perfect themselves; still others went as penitential pilgrims. They might have made their own decision to make a pilgrimage in expiation of some great wrong they had done. Or they might have been ordered by a court to make the journey, or else face a far harsher

HOUSES OF HOSPITALITY
With thousands of pilgrims on the move, often travelling long distances, a considerable infrastructure was needed to feed, accommodate and protect them. It had to cope with such normal activities as treating their ailments, shoeing their horses and even mending their clothes. Every bit as important in its own time as the tourist industry is to travellers today, the pilgrimage acted as a powerful economic engine. Rather than the desire for leisure, however, it was harnessing Christian piety and spreading prosperity far and wide.

In Jerusalem, and on the great pilgrimage routes such as the road to Santiago de Compostela, monasteries and other religious houses created special hospices, where the pilgrims could stay overnight in safety. These hospices were not like today's hospices, used as places for the sick. The original hospices took their name from the Latin word *hospes*, or "host", which is the root of our modern word "hospitality".

Right A hospice (hostel) for pilgrims, one of many established across medieval Europe, is shown in this 15th-century illustration from Antoine de la Sale's Les Cent Nouvelles Nouvelles.

punishment. There were also those who were actuated by less pious motives: a yen for travel or adventure or simply a desire for change.

SACRED PLACES

The Holy Land, though the ultimate place of pilgrimage, was beyond most people's reach, geographically, financially, and often politically, given that Jerusalem was so long in Muslim hands. Even when it was not, Muslim pirates from Turkey and from North Africa's Barbary Coast preyed on Christian shipping, leaving no alternative to a long, costly and hazardous overland journey through the Balkans. Rome, as both the centre of the Church and with its shrine of St Peter, was another

Below A 17th-century French map shows the main pilgrimage routes to Santiago de Compostela in Spain.

popular place of pilgrimage. However, pilgrims from northern Europe had to find their way over the Alps on foot to get there, and many could not make their way across this treacherous mountain range.

There were less hazardous destinations, such as St Andrews in Scotland, reputedly the apostle's final resting place. In Galicia, Spain, the cathedral at Santiago de Compostela was supposed to house the remains of the apostle St James the Great. Another popular site in Spain was Zaragoza, where Our Lady had appeared atop a pillar before St James. Walsingham in Norfolk, England, had been the site of a different Marian apparition (appearance of Mary) in 1061, and it became an important place of pilgrimage.

Left A pilgrim badge was worn to show that a person had made a particular pilgrimage. This pewter badge of St Thomas à Becket was worn by a person who had travelled to Canterbury Cathedral.

SAFETY IN NUMBERS

Even short journeys could be hazardous, and pilgrims often felt obliged to travel in groups in order to avoid attack by brigands. According to an often-practised procedure, pilgrims gathered in their local town centre to receive a blessing from their priest before setting out on their journey together. On longer trips, these groups might join others, forming great congregations hundreds, sometimes thousands, strong.

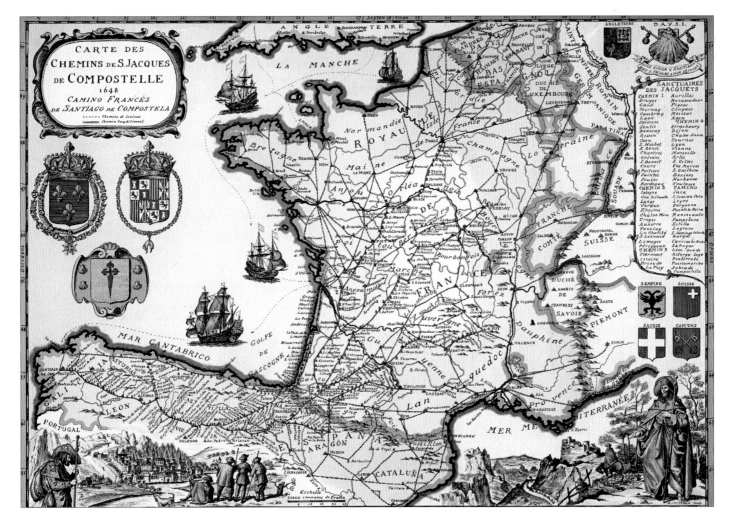

GOTHIC GLORY

BUILT TO CELEBRATE THE GLORY OF GOD AND AS HOUSES OF WORSHIP, EUROPE'S IMPRESSIVE GOTHIC CATHEDRALS ARE SPECTACULAR MONUMENTS TO AN AGE OF FAITH.

Imagine how a medieval peasant might have felt on seeing a great cathedral such as Chartres for the first time. Dumbstruck with amazement as far across the fields on the horizon, shimmering slightly in the haze of the August heat, the gigantic structure appeared to be rising out of the ground. They had heard of Chartres' new cathedral, of course – how its spire seemed to soar to heaven, how the clear lines of its solid stone structure dissolved into a riot of statuary figures as you approached. As for its vast interior, its wood carvings and statues bathed in the otherworldly light of a hundred stained-glass windows: that was a promise of paradise on earth. Even so, nothing had prepared them for their first actual experience of one of the great Gothic architectural monuments of the medieval age.

THE GOTHIC STYLE

Similar to most artistic movements, Renaissance architecture sought to better its predecessors. The term "gothic" was employed pejoratively by the Italian architects of the Renaissance to describe the architecture of the Middle Ages, which they had mistakenly attributed to the Germanic tribes known as the Goths. These tribes had sacked Rome in the 5th century AD, and thus had earned a reputation for barbarism. They were seen as the destroyers of classical civilization, which the Renaissance had set out to reinstate. But although the term "Gothic Style" is still in use, it no longer has a negative connotation, and the medieval period is now generally seen as a golden age of European architecture. In fact, the Gothic style enjoyed a major revival in the 19th century.

REACHING FOR THE SKY

One striking feature of the Gothic style was its thrilling emphasis on verticality. However, for all its aesthetic and symbolic resonances, the style was reliant on advances in engineering. The old Romanesque churches had been held up by the massive masonry of their walls, their rounded arches suitable for only small windows. Now pointed arches distributed the weight, replacing a great deal of outward thrust with downward thrust. This allowed constructions to be taller, and walls and columns to be more slender. The liberal use of pointed pinnacles and spires underlined the accent on the vertical, which made even the grandest Romanesque monuments look squat and stubby.

Since the walls no longer had to bear such a load, they could afford to be less solid and could be fitted with huge, decorative windows filled with stained glass. Chartres Cathedral has more than a hundred of these. All kinds of biblical scenes were presented, creating a stunning pictorial scripture

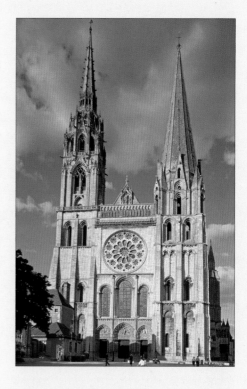

Above Built mainly in the 13th century, Chartres Cathedral in France is one of the great masterpieces of Gothic architecture (its second spire, on the left, was added on top of a previous tower in the 1500s).

for the illiterate. No longer dark and gloomy, the inside of the Gothic church could be turned over to the best artists and craftsmen to express themselves in paint and metalwork, carved wood and stone: they created saints' statues and fonts, elaborately ornate wooden pulpits, pews and choir screens.

To go to church in such a setting was to be bombarded with sensory impressions. In many ways it was an experience of wonder and delight. Given the enthusiasm with which medieval artists represented devils and hell's torments, it might also be an experience of fear – but it would always be an experience to be remembered. Demons bedecked the outside, too, with waterspouts turned into hideously decorative gargoyles. Chartres' exterior offers a crash course in medieval culture. Along with religious scenes, the door surrounds are lined with figures of famous kings and queens, prophets and even philosophers.

Above Stained glass, such as this one from a window in Chartres Cathedral showing Noah and his ark, gave the illiterate vivid access to the Bible stories.

COLLECTIVE EFFORTS

The creators of these stunning works were content to remain anonymous, though at the same time it is clear that they were given an astonishingly free hand in determining the design of their works. Where in a modern building the sense of unified, overall design is all-important, Gothic churches seem somehow to have grown organically.

All things considered, this should not be surprising. Such vast and ambitious edifices were beyond the capacity of any one man to construct or even oversee. These churches took years, decades, to build – longer than an artisan's working life – so it was not realistic to expect any continuity of craftsmanship, and generations of workers were involved in their construction. Skilled builders, masons, joiners, woodcarvers and glaziers accordingly went from place to place through the cities of Europe. On any given project, within rough parameters, they would have free rein in producing their work.

It was haphazard, but it worked. The great Gothic churches were essentially communal projects. Apart from that of praising God, and impressing and educating the public, their main purpose was to announce the wealth and prestige of the communities that built them. In that, they were triumphantly successful.

Right Satan stokes the fire, while demons plunge the souls of the damned into a cauldron in this 12th-century relief from England's York Minster Cathedral.

Below The Last Supper is represented in beaten gold in this stunning 11th-century relief from Aachen, Germany.

RENAISSANCE AND REFORMATION

The Renaissance was the age of undisputed Catholic supremacy in Europe, but it ended in dissension and strife. Outside the Church, the conventional view of modern historians has been of a papacy growing in corruption as it grew in power, with its hierarchy becoming increasingly remote from the people – even from parish priests. Although there is truth in this narrative, it tells no more than half the story of a great institution struggling to negotiate a time of extraordinary upheaval. Social, political, economic and intellectual life – all these were being transformed during this period. Great epidemics had ravaged the communities of Europe; the printing press was democratizing learning; Columbus' voyage had opened the door to the New World.

Martin Luther's stand at Wittenberg in 1517 was one reaction and the creed of Calvin another. In England, King Henry VIII's refusal to obey the pope marked a severing of the old accord between Church and State. However, there were changes within the Church, too. These had been gathering momentum for centuries, but they gained new impetus in the growing ferment.

The Reformation was a period of trauma for the Church, and in several countries it found itself driven back underground. All of Europe suffered from the wars the crisis brought, with martyrs on both sides. At the same time, in forcing a far-reaching process of reappraisal and renewal upon the Church, the Reformation also became a moment of rebirth.

Above The prophet Daniel as depicted on the Sistine Chapel ceiling, painted by the Italian artist Michelangelo, 1508–12.

Left Religion was the inspiration for much of the greatest Renaissance art, as in this early 15th-century painting, The Resurrection of Christ, *by Mariotto di Cristofano.*

RIVAL POPES

DURING PART OF THE EARLY RENAISSANCE, THE ROMAN CATHOLIC CHURCH WAS BASED IN FRANCE. THERE WAS A SHORT-TERM PAPACY IN AVIGNON AND MUCH CONFLICT WITHIN THE CHURCH.

The Church was not only a religious institution but was also an extremely powerful and prominent social organization. Inevitably, it was involved in political affairs. As the Middle Ages concluded and the Renaissance began, the Church was finding its independence increasingly difficult to maintain, with secular rulers seeking to harness its influence to their own ends.

POPES AND POLITICS

The 13th century had already seen the supposedly transcendent authority of the papacy called into question by the growing interference of kings and aristocratic clans. Pope Nicholas IV had created added difficulties for the papacy when he

Above Pope Boniface VIII is illustrated drafting canonical law in this 14th-century manuscript from the Decrees of Boniface VIII.

Below Built by Benedict XII and enlarged by Clement VI, the Palais des Papes in Avignon, France, was the home of a papacy in exile.

bought the support of the Colonnas – an important Roman family – by granting them favours, and when he agreed to crown the French Prince Charles of Anjou, making him King of Naples and Sicily in 1289. The family was in no mood to surrender its special status under Nicholas' successor, Celestine V. In deference to King Charles, he had established his papal court at Naples. However, Celestine was ignominiously out of his depth and abdicated just five months after his election in 1294, making way for the more formidable Boniface VIII, who moved the papacy back to Rome.

Boniface could not be frightened into submission by Charles – or by the French ascendancy he represented – but his confrontational manner served only to precipitate a crisis. From the first, Boniface had both the King of Naples and Sicily and the Colonna family against him.

Years of harassment culminated in an assassination attempt in 1303. Although Boniface survived the attempt, he died of natural causes only a few weeks later.

THE AVIGNON PAPACY

Boniface's successor, Benedict XI, was pulled one way and then the other by Charles and the Colonnas. The French won after Benedict's death with the election of Clement V, who as Bertrand de Got had been the Archbishop of Bordeaux.

Clement had never visited Rome, and four years into his reign, in 1309, he transferred the seat of papal power to Avignon, in southern France. This was just one of the most obvious of Clement's concessions to King Philip IV. A host of new French cardinals were created in an intiative urged by Philip, and Clement outlawed the Order of the Knights Templar in 1307 throughout Europe. Their immense wealth in France was confiscated by the king.

POPE AND "ANTIPOPE"

It almost seemed the move to Avignon had done the papacy good: it was growing in institutional splendour and in wealth. However, behind the scenes, the French crown was wielding unprecedented power. After Clement's death in 1314, six successive popes reigned from Avignon. The arrangement worked – but at a considerable cost to the Church's autonomy.

The transfer to France had left the Church in Italy in a rebellious mood; Rome was bereft, its purpose of so many centuries gone. There was unease in the wider Catholic Church as well. Queen Bridget of Sweden joined St Catherine of Siena in lobbying for a return. In 1376, Pope Gregory XI removed his court from Avignon to Rome. But the rejoicing was cut short by his death just a few months later.

The French had not finished with the papacy – their possession, as they now saw it. When an Italian, Urban VI, was named as pope in Rome in 1378, the French created their own "pope", Clement VII. In the decades that followed, four "antipopes" were elected as French counters to the popes of Rome. Called to arbitrate in the dispute, the Council of Pisa (1408) made matters worse: for a time the Church boasted not two popes but three, because the French

cardinals could not agree among themselves. Finally, in 1417 Pope Martin V (a member of the Colonna family) received the recognition of the entire Catholic Church, with the papacy back in Rome.

Above In Roma La Veuve, *an Italian manuscript produced in the Renaissance, the allegorical "Widow of Rome" is illustrated mourning her bereavement after the departure of the papacy, shown outside the city walls.*

THE WESTERN SCHISM

So-called to differentiate it from the earlier separation, which had seen the Orthodox Church established in 1054, the Western Schism had consequences far beyond the papal courts. Secular rulers had to decide which side to acknowledge: the Roman pontiff or the French-backed Avignon pope. Because both papal courts appointed their own bishops, the lower clergy and the people were left confused – and spiritually adrift. Each side had excommunicated the other's supporters, so ordinary people had no way of knowing whether the sacraments their priests were administering were valid; whether their marriages, or their loved ones' funerals, were acceptable to God.

Right Clement VII, the first "antipope" of the Western Schism, was enthroned at Avignon in 1378, shown here in the Chroniques de France ou de St Denis.

INDULGENCES

THE PAPACY HAD INITIALLY INTRODUCED INDULGENCES TO MEET A SPIRITUAL NEED. THESE REMISSIONS GAVE MILLIONS OF CATHOLICS THE HOPE TO STRIVE FOR THEIR SALVATION.

The Catholic Church is generally seen as being dogmatic in its teachings. It is easy to forget, then, that for much of the first millennium, its teachings in several areas were to some extent a work-in-progress in the development of doctrine. One issue that had from early on caused concern among Christians and their clergy was that they felt perilously poised between salvation and damnation. Surely, theologians reasoned, there must be a middle ground for those whose lives had been virtuous, though flawed?

PURIFYING THE SOUL

By the 5th century AD teachers were talking of a place of temporary chastisement, in which the soul would be purged or purified by the fire, but from which it would eventually be released into heaven, for eternity. The idea had been taken up and developed by Pope Gregory the Great in the 6th century. He had proposed that prayerful observance or good works in this life might lead to "indulgence".

An indulgence gives a period of remission to the sufferings of the soul in Purgatory after death, granted in return for some act of commitment – a pilgrimage, a programme of prayer, for example. It was a radical step, but it re-energized Christianity, giving ordinary men and women new grounds for hope. Few could hope to be saints in the hereafter, but anyone free of mortal sin could strive to do better in their daily lives, to throw themselves into their regimes of prayer and charitable works. The other great thing about the system was that, since people could earn "indulgence" not just for themselves but for their departed loved ones, it fostered a sense of solidarity between the living and the dead.

THE PLENARY INDULGENCE

As time went on, what had been an inspirational idea became a fully articulated system, with periods of indulgence established for certain observances or acts. In particularly special circumstances, a "plenary indulgence" might be granted, with a complete remission of temporal punishment for sin. If the receiver died in that moment, his or her soul could avoid going to Purgatory.

So far, this was nothing exceptional: the system may have seemed mechanistic, but it gave people a

Left The good are lofted heavenward by flights of angels, while the wicked are carried down into hell in a burning river in Jean Colombe's 14th-century painting.

Above Michael the archangel weighs souls, separating out the saved from the damned in this c. 1450 Last Judgement, painted by Rogier van der Weyden.

spiritual incentive to which they could respond. However, at the same time, it was open to abuse: the temptation was always there for the Church to harness it to meet its worldly ends. When Pope Boniface VIII proclaimed a jubilee year for 1300, for example, he promised a plenary indulgence to those who made the pilgrimage to Jerusalem that year. Two million people heeded his call. The suspicion that he was putting on a show of strength for his political enemies in Rome must be set against the wider benefit his jubilee did in reinvigorating the whole Church.

A FINANCIAL TRANSACTION

More problematic was the financial note, which may have been innocent to start with but became corrupt over time. It began with the payment of fees for masses offered for the souls of the dead, another way of gaining them remission. The token sums paid were a welcome supplement to the incomes of poor parish priests. However, the practice spread as the Church first relied on the contributions it gained in this way and then exploited its people's piety. The poor were bullied into paying for prayers, the wealthy bribed with offers of an easy afterlife. Soon high prelates and great religious houses were growing rich on the proceeds.

The perception spread that indulgences existed not for the sake of fallen humanity but for the Church's monetary enrichment. However, this was not always the case. When Jesus gave Peter his papal power, he gave him the keys of heaven; he also promised him that the "powers of death" would not prevail against his Church. Purgatory wasn't mentioned, but by giving his pope authority to "bind" and "loose" the laws of earth and heaven, he gave him, and the popes who followed him, the right to ordain these things as he decided through God's grace.

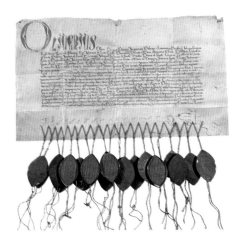

Above A bull of Julius II, issued in 1505, announces the indulgences that had been conferred on a group of wealthy benefactors.

SALVATION FOR SALE

In 1245, when England's King Henry III set out to rebuild Westminster Abbey, the venture won Pope Innocent IV's approval. More than this, it won his promise that any individual who made a contribution of money to this reconstruction would receive 20 days' indulgence from the sufferings of Purgatory. This was a clear cash transaction, even if it was for a good cause. By the 14th century, indulgences were being openly bought and sold. In Chaucer's *The Canterbury Tales*, the Pardoner carried a sheaf of printed "pardons" in his saddlebag. In 1344, Clement VIII issued 200 plenary indulgences in England alone, which were "earned" entirely by financial endowments to the papacy.

Below England's King Henry III is shown with Westminster Abbey, which he rebuilt, in this c.1253 illustration from History of the English.

THE FRANCISCAN REVOLUTION

ST FRANCIS IS AMONG THE MOST BELOVED OF SAINTS. TO HIS SPIRITUAL ARDOUR AND LOVE OF NATURE, HE ALLIED A TACTFUL RADICALISM THAT WAS TO HAVE A FAR-REACHING IMPACT ON THE CHURCH.

Francesco di Pietro di Bernardone (*c*.1181–1226) was one of Assisi's most fashionable young men, known for his love of all things French. He was devoted to music, poetry, fashion and flirtation. However, he also had a more serious side. In the 1200s, when he was a young man in his twenties, a series of spiritual crises caused him to question his worldly preoccupations. He left behind his old pursuits and his old friends to care for lepers. The romantic enthusiasm of old was evident in the way he hurled himself into this new life, though now the mistress of his heart, he said, was "Lady Poverty".

BEGGARS IN CHRIST

This was a huge transformation, but the change in Francis was by no means done. In 1209, he was in a church in Assisi when a priest gave a sermon on Matthew's Gospel, Chapter 10.

Take no gold, nor silver, nor copper in your belts, no bag for your journey, nor two tunics, nor sandals, nor staff; for the labourer deserves his food… Do not be anxious how you are to speak or what you are to say; for what you are to say will be given to you in that hour; for it is not you who speak, but the Spirit of your Father through you.

Above *Christ officiates as St Francis takes Lady Poverty as his bride, depicted in this 13th–14th century allegorical scene by Giotto.*

Francis would need no further encouragement to live the words of the gospels. He took to the roads as a beggar – with no money, no bag, no spare clothing, no sandals and no staff. However, he did soon have a companion: Bernard of Quintavalle, another wealthy young man from Assisi, and the first recruit to Francis' order of Friars Minor. Unlike the monks who lived in monasteries – and so, however hard they tried to avoid it, had worldly ties – the friars would have only the air they breathed and the food and water strangers gave them.

A NEW ORDER

This "mendicant" lifestyle could clearly be seen as an implicit criticism of the religious establishment at a time when its institutions had grown enormously in power and wealth. Already, there had been signs of restlessness, with certain heretics

Left *St Francis maintained good relations with the papacy. In this 13th–14th century painting by Giotto, he preaches before Innocent's successor, Honorius III.*

attacking the Church for its close relations with wealthy, worldly interests. The hierarchy could be forgiven for feeling defensive in the face of Francis' apparent challenge.

For his own part, however, Francis showed no interest in taking the hierarchy to task. On the contrary, he defended the institutions of the Church against all detractors and sued humbly to Pope Innocent III for his support. The Pope appears to have found Francis a perplexing character. One story claims that the Pope initially ordered the ragged, dirty vagabond before him to be sent away to tend swine; however, he then relented when Francis agreed without demur.

Above The Dominicans, shown in this 16th-century painting by the Spanish School, were writers and teachers.

Whatever reservations he might have had, Innocent came to the conclusion that Francis should be encouraged: that decision itself showed a certain vision on the pontiff's part. A movement that might have been profoundly destabilizing was accommodated by a Church already making conscious efforts to reform itself.

THE DOMINICANS
St Dominic was a teacher trying to hold back the rising tide of heresy in southern France. He founded his own order in 1214, which also took up mendicant proverty. Dominic saw that the poor were increasingly out of reach of the Church, not just in the scattered hamlets of the countryside but in the fast-growing cities. He wanted an order of young men to carry the Word to these lost sheep. Since Dominic had been placed in charge of a convent as early as 1206, these Dominican nuns actually predated the Dominican friars.

CHURCH MUSIC

FROM THE AUSTERE GRACE OF GREGORIAN CHANT TO THE GLORIOUS POLYPHONIES OF THE BAROQUE AND BEYOND, MUSIC HAS PLAYED ITS PART IN THE LITURGIES OF THE CHURCH.

Both solemn and spare, the sound of plainsong (also called "plainchant") as it echoes through the aisles and cloisters is for many people the quintessential sound associated with the Catholic Church. For others, however, it will be the thunderous chorus of the Lourdes pilgrims' "Ave Maria!", or the graceful harmonies of Haydn's *The Creation* or James MacMillan's *Mass*.

AN ORDERLY COSMOS

It seems likely that music formed part of the Christian liturgy from early on in its establishment, though in the absence of written notation from that time we have no real way of knowing for certain. Music had an almost theological significance for the people of the ancient and medieval worlds. The way in which

Left Whether a little pipe-and-bellows affair or an elaborate one such as this from the Chapel at Versailles, the organ is the standard instrument for church music.

the different notes could resonate harmoniously was seen as analogous to the relations between the earth and the planets and stars – all set in their own rotating spheres within the overall order of God's universe. Hence the phrase, "the music of the spheres", and therefore the importance attached to music – which went far beyond the aesthetic pleasure it provided.

SONG OF ST GREGORY

It was natural, then, that music would have its place in the monastic order, at the services offered by monks each day to mark the passage of the hours. The emphasis was on austerity: plainsong was indeed plain, involving no accompanying instruments and just a single sustained melodic line. Even so, its eerie beauty must have been an inspiration to the monks, reminding them each day of the mysterious majesty of God.

Pope Gregory the Great had encouraged the practice of singing plainsong, which, its inestimable beauties apart, helped foster the monastic virtues of co-operation and discipline. His support lent impetus to a musical genre that grew rapidly in scale and sophistication, and a rudimentary form of notation was developed during the 9th century.

Gradually, over the centuries that followed, moves were made toward simple two- and eventually more complex three- and four-part compositions – toward polyphony ("many voices"), in other words.

Above Much early music was performed by voice alone, as shown in this 15th-century illumination from the Bible of Borso d'Este.

The organ added yet another voice: it is thought to have been in use since the time of Pope Vitalian in the 7th century. The organ's pure tones were the perfect complement to the human voice, and it has been the mainstay of church music ever since. As the Middle Ages gave way to the Renaissance, other instrumental sounds were introduced to church music.

INFLUENCES ON MUSIC

Secular music was nourished by the church tradition. Though Claudio Monteverdi is famous for having composed the first operas in the 17th century, he was also a priest, and in this role brought baroque complexity to sacred music.

In his footsteps came fellow Italians, such as Antonio Vivaldi (1678–1741), a priest who wrote many of his great works for the orchestra of the Ospedale della Pietà, a church-run orphanage for girls. The kapellmeisters (or "chapel masters"), who wrote liturgical music for services at Austria's and

Germany's courts, also found time to write secular concerti, keyboard music and orchestral suites.

By this time, of course, the Reformation had swept Europe, and several of the great Baroque composers were Protestants. However, music was an ecumenical art: Catholic creativity was stimulated by the works of Bach and Handel, while the great Protestant geniuses themselves drew on the traditions of the Catholic past.

CLASSICAL TRADITION

Religion remained an important influence into music's classical heyday of the 18th and 19th centuries. Joseph Haydn was a committed Catholic. While he wrote many explicitly sacred works – such as his wonderful oratorio, *The Creation* (1798) – he saw the whole process of composition as an act of prayer, writing "Praise be to God" at the end of every completed piece.

His younger contemporary, Wolfgang Amadeus Mozart, may have been famously flawed as an individual, but his profound faith came through in the great *Requiem* he was working on when his own life was cut short in 1791. Franz Liszt, the great piano virtuoso and romantic composer of the 19th century, was notorious for his scandalous private life. Yet this intensely emotional man was also passionate in his attachment to Catholicism. He even took minor orders in the Church in 1865.

SONGS OF PRAISE

What might be called the elite culture of sacred music has endured in 20th-century works by several noted composers, from France's Olivier Messiaen to Scotland's James

Right Many of Vivaldi's works were premiered by the girls of the orphanage he served, seen here in this 18th-century painting entitled The Orphans' Cantata, *by Gabriele Bella.*

MacMillan. For most modern Catholics, though, Church music has taken the less sophisticated form of hymn singing. This has been more about participation than polished performance, but regardless it has been profoundly important to its participants. Communal singing can be crucial in bringing a congregation closer together, instilling in its members a sense of common purpose and common faith.

Right With such inspiring works as the Requiem, *Mozart created some of the most sublimely spiritual harmonies ever heard, enjoyed by Catholics and non-Catholics alike.*

HERETICS

SINCERE BELIEVERS WERE QUESTIONING THE AUTHORITY OF THE CHURCH. THE HIERARCHY HAD TO DECIDE WHICH CRITICISMS TO ACCEPT, WHICH TO IGNORE AND WHICH TO BRAND AS "HERESY".

An institution as far-reaching as the Church – and one with so many deeply thoughtful, idealistic individuals – was inevitably bound to have differences of opinion, even disputes, among its followers. To some extent these disputes could be contained and passionate debates took place with the Church's tacit acceptance – even its encouragement. However, some ideas were so wildly at variance with normal Catholic teaching that they could not be accommodated without the integrity of the Church being threatened. These contentious views became known as "heresies".

St Augustine had led the fight against heresy as early as the end of the 4th century, condemning the Pelagian view that humankind could earn salvation by its own efforts, without God's intervention. His view that humankind was dragged down so drastically by original sin that salvation came only and exclusively from the intervention of God

Above Although members of a Christian faith, Waldensian followers were linked to witchcraft in this 15th-century illustration from the Book of Occult Sciences.

was to be taken to heretical extremes in the 16th century, when it was known as Jansenism. However, the late Middle Ages turned out to be a period of particular ferment, and in hindsight we can see this as the beginnings of the Reformation.

THE WALDENSIANS

In 1177, Peter Waldo, a prosperous merchant from Lyon, France, had undergone a spiritual crisis. Like St Francis, he had given away all his possessions and become a mendicant preacher. However, unlike the Franciscans, the "Waldensians" confronted the Church, denouncing it as representing only the richest and most powerful in society. Ultimately, they rejected the authority of its priests when Pope Lucius III banned Waldo from preaching in 1184. He and his followers set up their own Church, which survived prosecution

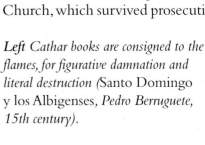

*Left Cathar books are consigned to the flames, for figurative damnation and literal destruction (*Santo Domingo y los Albigenses, *Pedro Berruguete, 15th century).*

during the following years. In 1848 the Catholic Church granted the Waldensians religious freedom.

THE CATHARS

Southern France had by this time become the centre of another great heresy: that of Catharism. This had its roots in the Manichaeism of earlier centuries, which preached a form of duelism that combined elements from several religions. A version of the heresy had been brought West through the Balkans by Pop Bogomil and his adherents, probably dispersed along the Mediterranean trade routes. Catharism carried to extremes the Manichaean opposition between good and evil, light and darkness, the spiritual and material. For its followers, the entire earthly Creation – the material world, the body and its desires – were evil. The aim of the godly was to transcend these things.

If the Word had been "made flesh" in Christ, that could only go to show that it, too, was evil – a fact the Cathars felt was confirmed by the wealth and power of the Church. Thousands flocked to the Cathar cause, despite the arguments of the Dominicans – newly formed to defend the faith. The violence of the official crackdown that followed (*see The Albigensian Crusade, below right*) has been condemned, but it is hard to imagine a more potent threat to the medieval order.

THE LOLLARDS

The teachings of John Wycliffe, an English priest and scholar of the 14th century, struck a chord with many of his country's less educated people. Like Waldo, Wycliffe thought the Church had no business being rich or involving itself with the concerns of temporal government. Even in religious affairs, he argued, the Church had made too much of its own role. He wanted a scaled-down hierarchy and translations of the Bible from Latin so that people could read the Word of God themselves. He denied the doctrine of "transubstantiation". The bread and wine, he said, remained bread and wine even as they took on the nature of Christ's body and blood.

Below An extravagant depiction of the persecution of the Lollards was illustrated in the fiercely Protestant John Foxe's Acts and Monuments, *16th century.*

Wycliffe's followers, known as "Lollards", were seen as a threat to both secular and religious authority. Their ideas were spread into Europe by Jan Hus (or John Huss), the Czech reformer who campaigned against the sale of indulgences in the 15th century. The Lollards were a short-lived group, but their ideas were taken up by the Protestants.

THE ALBIGENSIAN CRUSADE

Named after Albi, a town in the Languedoc, a region in southern France, where Catharism was officially denounced in 1178, the "Albigensian Crusade" was proclaimed by Pope Innocent III in 1208. By calling it a crusade, he equated the challenge of heresy within the Church with the threat of Islam in the Middle East and Spain. In the years that followed, the forces of the French Crown and powerful northern nobles attacked the southern peasantry and the local lords who supported them. As many as a million people may have been killed.

*Above Many atrocities were committed in the Albigensian Crusade. Here, Cathars are expelled from the city of Carcassonne (*Chronicle of France, *15th century).*

THE INQUISITION

FEW INSTITUTIONS OF CATHOLICISM HAVE BEEN MORE FEARED THAN THE "INQUISITION", OR SO WIDELY MISUNDERSTOOD. YET THE EXCESSES OF THE "HOLY OFFICE", AS IT WAS KNOWN, CANNOT BE DENIED.

Above Jan Hus is burnt at the stake for his heretical beliefs in this illustration from Ulrich von Reichenthal's Council Chronicle, *15th century.*

Throughout its history, the Catholic Church has fought against heresy, but it was not until the Renaissance that it formed an official institution against such preaching. The Albigensian Crusade, set up in France in 1208 in the hope of stemming the rising tide of Catharism, could be seen as a precursor to the official Inquisitions that followed. First ordered by Pope Gregory IX in 1232, an Inquisition was a tribunal ordered by the Catholic Church to suppress and punish heresy. The first inquisitors were chosen from the Dominicans and Franciscans, who were living mendicant lifestyles and therefore not influenced by worldly gains, and who were well educated in theology.

At about the same time an anti-Waldensian Inquisition followed in Italy, but then the Inquisition waned,

Below The Inquisition was especially active in the Netherlands and Ghent, where it was an arm of the Spanish occupation, as shown in this 16th-century engraving of the Flemish School.

to be revived in Spain and Portugal (and their overseas colonies) from the late 15th century. More of these ecclesiastical courts for suppressing heresy were constituted in France and Italy during the Reformation. The Congregation of the Holy Office, which is often shortened to the Holy Office, was formed to oversee the Inquisitions in 1542.

Although administered by the Church, the Inquisition worked with the temporal authorities. Generally, the state took the lead. Monarchs always had an interest in enforcing conformity and were happy enough to claim divine sanction for doing so. After the Reformation, religion took on a political aspect. A Protestant was no longer just a heretic but a dangerous subversive – potentially, an agent from another state in Europe.

SPANISH ACTS OF FAITH

It was in this febrile political context that the *Leyenda Negra* (or "Black Legend") was born. Spain, the Catholic superpower at the time, was

demonized by the propagandists of northern Europe's Protestant powers. Books and pamphlets were printed, describing in lurid detail the supposed excesses of the Spanish, from their American colonies to the torture chambers of the Inquisition. However, modern scholarship has shown that many of these accounts were mere fabrications, created by over-excited pamphleteers.

However, some of the accounts, though sensationalized, cannot be dismissed. Recent research has shown the scrupulous thoroughness with which the Holy Office sought to document its cases, avoiding prosecutions based on malicious denunciations. At the same time it

Above Spain's Grand Inquisitor, Tomás de Torquemada, was widely feared (Spanish School, 19th century).

THE SPANISH INQUISITION

The Inquisition in Spain had first been established in Aragon in the 13th century, but it came into its own in the 15th century under Ferdinand and Isabella, the "Catholic Monarchs". They bore that title, not because they staunchly defended Catholicism (though they did), but because by their marriage they had brought together the realms of Navarra, Aragon and Castile to form a single Spain. (The word "Catholic" originally meant "universal", "all-embracing" – hence its use for the Church of Rome.)

Ferdinand and Isabella saw the Holy Office as a way of using ecclesiastical structures as the basis for what we would now call a police state. Since the Reconquista was only recently completed, and many of the kingdom's Jews and Muslims had been converted by force, there was considerable fear that these alien groups were secretly upholding their old beliefs and practices in private meetings. Hence the drawing up of laws of *limpieza* ("cleanliness", "purity"), which anticipated the race laws of Nazi Germany. They were

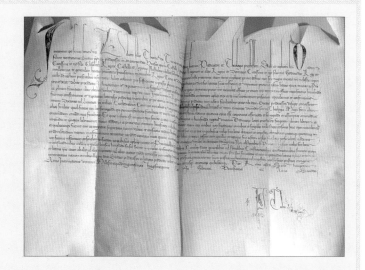

Above Torquemada received a bull of 1487 from Pope Innocent VIII, appointing him Inquisitor General of Spain.

imposed with terrifying thoroughness by the infamous Grand Inquisitor, Tomás de Torquemada, who was appointed to the position by the pope.

confirms the integral role of torture in the proceedings (after its explicit authorization by Pope Innocent IV in 1252). Although their frequency has been exaggerated, *autos-da-fé* ("acts of faith") assuredly took place. These rituals, in which there was a public penance for the guilty, were symbolic representations of the Last Judgement acted out before large crowds. An *auto-da-fé* ended with the accused being burnt at the stake.

OUTRAGEOUS ACTIONS

The readiness of the Church to consign its critics to the flames is easily exaggerated: the wilder claims of Reformation propaganda have proved obdurately persistent. The armies of the Albigensian Crusade did embark on a spree of slaughter, but the extent of the Church's blessing is unclear. Outraged though

Right St Dominic was committed to teaching – but when all else failed, the fear of death was used to persuade the people. Here, St Dominic presides over an auto-da-fé (Pedro Berruguete, c.1495).

it was by Wycliffe's teachings, the Church spent so long debating them that he had died of natural causes before he was denounced as a heretic.

However, Jan Hus, the Czech preacher who campaigned against the sale of indulgences, was burnt at the stake in 1415 (an act for which Pope John Paul II apologized in 1999). Nor was he alone in suffering this fate at the hands of the Church, which, with criticism mounting, was increasingly on the defensive – and all too ready to attack.

THE CHURCH IN TRANSITION

THE HISTORICAL HEADLINES MAY HAVE BEEN ABOUT THE STIFLING OF DISSENT, BUT QUIETER DEVELOPMENTS WERE TAKING PLACE BEHIND THE SCENES AS CATHOLICISM REFORMED ITSELF.

Above Convened in 1215, the Fourth Lateran Council, shown in this 19th-century engraving, introduced far-reaching reforms in the running of the Church.

The Church in the Middle Ages had been very much the establishment. Secure in its position, it had no real interest in changing. However, this does not mean that the spiritual status quo had gone unquestioned. The heresies of the time had only been the most extreme manifestation of a ferment of debate. This concerned not just the finer points of Christian doctrine but also the place that Catholicism occupied within society, and the developing relationship between Church and State.

COUNCILS FOR CHANGE

These issues were explored by the Church hierarchy at such gatherings as the Third Lateran Council of 1179 and the Fourth, which followed

Below Figures representing the Seven Liberal Arts – Arithmetic, Music, Geometry, Astronomy, Logic, Rhetoric and Grammar – are shown in a 1503 publication on humanism from Gregor Reisch, Margarita Philosophica Nova.

in 1215. These conclaves were held in the vast council chamber of the Lateran Palace, which was the pope's official residence in Rome. Leading clerics came together to discuss the changes the Church would have to make to adapt to a changing world while at the same time staying true to its original principles.

The great emphasis of the communiqués agreed by the Third Lateran Council was on the maintenance of orthodoxy, while the Fourth is today known chiefly for its decree that Jews and Muslims should have to wear distinctive garb to set themselves apart from Christians.

Yet the small print tells a slightly different story. Most of the Council's energies had gone into the attempt to get the Church's house in order. New measures were introduced to make the clergy more accountable for its actions and to control the activities of religious foundations.

THE RISE OF HUMANISM

At the end of the 15th century, the Italian scholar Giovanni Pico Della Mirandola advanced the views that became known as "humanism". God's greatest gift to us as humans, he argued, was the capacity to reason for ourselves. It was not just our right but our duty to use that gift. Traditional Catholic scholarship, he suggested, had seen its role as essentially a passive one of interpreting and implementing the will of God. Scholars had seen that will represented in the doctrinal judgements handed down over generations within the Church, which had come to have the force of legal precedent in Catholic thought.

Instead, Pico Della Mirandola claimed, people should be thinking for themselves and bypassing tradition to consult the ancient sources. In this view, he was reflecting the contemporary attitudes of the artists and writers of the wider Renaissance (rebirth), which was taking place in Italy at the time.

Inspired by the artwork of classical Greece and Rome, men such as Leonardo da Vinci saw the human form as the highest achievement of God's Creation. Scientists, too, were finding inspiration in the writings of the Greeks and Romans, gaining the confidence to set aside the perceived assumptions of centuries and to try out new theories and experiment with new ideas.

COUNCIL OF TRENT

Humanism, as then understood, did not dispute the greatness of God – still less his existence – but it did raise radical questions as to how he should be served. Church leaders were unsettled – not surprisingly, since humanist thinking did tempt some scholars toward the new Protestant theologies then emerging. However, in the works of writers such as St Thomas More and Erasmus, humanism offered a reinvigoration of a Catholic tradition, which had, to some extent, become fossilized over the passing years.

That the Church was capable of flexibility was to be demonstrated at the Council of Trent. Opening in 1545, when Europe was at the height of the Reformation, its sessions continued for several years until 1563. Its main conclusions were uncompromising, with the Church rejecting the theological heresies proposed by the Protestant rebels. At the same time, it tacitly acknowledged the justice of many of the criticisms of its own institution. It was these criticisms that caused the Church to institute root-and-branch reform. Measures were introduced to combat corruption, including regulation of the issuing of indulgences to prevent their sale. Diocesan seminaries were created to provide better training for priests, and disciplinary structures were formed to handle wrongdoers.

A CHRISTIAN JOKER

Desiderius Erasmus ("Erasmus of Rotterdam") was one of the most serious thinkers of the Renaissance, but it was with a joke that he caught the mood of an amazing time. His treatise, *Praise of Folly* (1511), was a masterly exercise in irony; among the absurdities it satirized were those of the Church. Its scholars' slavish reverence for tradition, its superstitions and its corruption: all these are ridiculed in its pages. However, this only makes the more moving the book's final reaffirmation of a Catholic faith whose truth transcends the earthly limitations of the Church.

Above Erasmus of Rotterdam, *painted in 1523 by Hans Holbein the Younger, was a brilliant scholar and thinker. He published many works and led the humanist movement within the Church.*

Left The Island of Utopia, *as imagined by the great English humanist St Thomas More, was illustrated by Ambrosius Holbein and published in 1518 in the book of the same title.*

POWERFUL POPES

THE RENAISSANCE SAW THE PAPACY AT ITS HEIGHT AS A POLITICAL FORCE – AND ITS MORAL REPUTATION AT ITS LOWEST EBB, RESPONSIBLE FOR SOME DISREPUTABLE CHAPTERS IN THE CHURCH'S HISTORY.

Today the idea of a "Renaissance Pope" suggests magnificence and political power. However, it also implies corruption on a huge scale. This is a stereotype, of course, but one that many pontiffs of the 15th and 16th centuries appear to have lived up to. To expect otherwise would perhaps have been unrealistic. The Church was the greatest institution of the day, and its leader commanded untold wealth and incalculable influence. At the same time it was very much a human institution. The meek and innocent might be blessed in heaven, but here on earth they were pushed aside by the ambitious, the unscrupulous and the ruthless.

A FAMILY BUSINESS

Among the Church's hierarchy, favours were exchanged, inducements were offered and friends and

Below Building the new St Peter's took many years. Antoine Lafréry's engraving (1575) shows a papal blessing being given beneath its uncompleted dome.

relations were taken care of. It was no surprise when the nephew of Pope Eugene IV followed him on to St Peter's throne as Pope Paul II in 1464.

Pope Sixtus IV followed in 1471. He made no fewer than six of his nephews cardinals during his papacy, on top of which he gave them benefices that brought in colossal wealth. (The Church had a vast income from a range of sources, including rents, donations, bequests and burial fees, all of which were a temptation to the corrupt.) Sixtus IV also married his nieces into Italy's leading aristocratic houses, building up a powerful network of familial connections, which he was ruthless in defending. He is believed to have been complicit in a plot carried out in 1478 in which two Medici brothers were attacked with daggers while attending Mass in the cathedral in Florence. One of them, Giuliano de' Medici, died of his wounds.

A strong sense of "family" was creeping in – of dynastic continuity and of bitter feuding – alien as this

Above Pope Sixtus IV appoints a new prefect to preside over his library, another monument to the majesty of his reign, in Melozzo da Forli's painting (1477).

should have been to a Church with a celibate clergy. Some popes were far from chaste. Pope Alexander VI (1492–1503) fathered nine children by an unknown number of different women. His most notorious son, Cesare Borgia, was a murderous wheeler-dealer; he became a cardinal before leaving the clergy to make an advantageous marriage.

PAPACY AND PATRONAGE

However far they may have fallen short of the principles they were supposed to serve, the Renaissance popes undoubtedly left us in their debt as the patrons of some of the most impressive Western art. It may have been extravagance, driven too much by human vanity, but their patronage had an impact on the whole history of Western culture.

Pope Sixtus IV spent a fortune beautifying the centre of Rome, which involved widening streets and constructing new churches and other buildings. His bridge, the Ponte Sisto, still spans the River Tiber.

Pope Julius II was also a great patron of the arts. It was this pope who asked Donato Bramante to design a replacement for the old

POPE IMPRISONED

In modern times, we have tended to think of the papacy as "above" politics, to some extent protected by their holy status. However, given the political power they wielded, the popes of the Renaissance could hardly claim to be simply men of God. Clement VII paid the price for this: though a member of the Medici family, ironically, he was innocent and unworldly by the standards of the times. His attempts to steer a safe diplomatic course between the great powers ruling Europe led to a dispute between him and Charles V, King of Spain and Emperor of Germany. In 1527, Charles' forces invaded Italy and sacked Rome. Pope Clement was held prisoner at Castel Sant' Angelo, from which he escaped.

Above The massive walls surrounding Rome offered the city some protection, but it lacked defensive troops, as shown in The Sack of Rome, *a 1527 painting by Johannes Lingelbach.*

St Peter's Basilica, and work on the greatest church built for Christendom began only two years into his papacy, in 1505. (That the astronomical costs were to be met by the greatest granting of indulgences yet seen was a fact that would not be lost on the Church's critics.) Julius was also responsible for commissioning Michelangelo to paint the ceiling of the Sistine Chapel.

The Medici family were already famous for their artistic patronage when the son of Lorenzo (the Magnificent) de' Medici became Pope Leo X in 1513. "God has given us the papacy," Leo X is said to have commented to a friend. "Now let us enjoy it." Fortunately for posterity, his greatest indulgence was art, including history-making works by the Italian artists Michelangelo and Raphael. He encouraged music, too, and writers such as Erasmus.

Right Raphael's *c.1517 portrait of his patron, Pope Leo X, captures the power and authority of the man.*

THE POPE AND THE PAINTER

THE CEILING OF THE SISTINE CHAPEL IS UNIVERSALLY ACCLAIMED AS A MASTERPIECE. IT HAS ALSO BECOME THE ARCHETYPE FOR THE DIFFICULT RELATIONSHIP BETWEEN THE ARTIST AND HIS PATRON.

If its ceiling had never been painted by Michelangelo, art lovers would still flock to see the Sistine Chapel for its frescoes by other great artists, which include Raphael, Botticelli, Perugino and Ghirlandaio. (The chapel is in the Apostolic Palace in the Vatican City, the official residence of the pope.) Some splendid tapestries, designed by Raphael, formed part of the plunder during Charles V's sack of Rome in 1527, but they were later restored and replaced. Although named after Pope Sixtus IV, who had built the structure, the chapel really found its role under Pope Julius II, who made it a magnificent showcase for the creativity of Renaissance art.

MICHELANGELO'S TASK

Today too many tourists look past the myriad wonders that line the walls, with eyes only for the ceiling, 20m (65ft) above. Admittedly, it is an astonishing sight: the whole sweep of human existence, from Creation to Last Judgement, in crowded scenes that seem to boil over in their energy. Yet if the artist had his own way, this masterpiece would not have existed.

Above The Deluge and the Drunkenness of Noah *illustrates transgression and punishment, important themes for the ceiling as a whole.*

Born outside Arezzo in Tuscany in 1475, Michelangelo had never doubted his artistic genius, but he saw himself as a sculptor first and foremost. When, in 1505, Julius II asked him to design his tomb, it seemed to Michelangelo to be the dream commission. He dedicated himself to the creation of his life's masterpiece. However, he was not to be left to his work for long. To his growing annoyance, Julius enlisted his help for various odd artistic jobs – and began to talk to him about a commission for painting frescoes on the ceiling of the Sistine Chapel.

A CONTEMPORARY REPORT

Giorgio Vasari, gossipy chronicler of the ins and outs of the Italian Renaissance art scene, says that this idea was not Julius' own. Raphael and Bramante talked him into it

Left Michelangelo and Julius II had a fractious – but finally fruitful – working relationship. The artist and patron are shown together in this 16th-century painting by Anastasio Fontebuoni.

mischievously, he maintained. The former was the leading painter of the time, the latter, the star architect – and both were feeling threatened by Michelangelo's prodigious talents. The pope's preference for sculpture was well known to his contemporaries, and Michelangelo's supremacy in that arena was undisputed. By getting the artist weighed down in what appeared an impossibly ambitious task for such a comparatively inexperienced and reluctant painter, his rivals saw an opportunity to level the playing field. There was even the chance that Michelangelo would blunder the job so severely that his artistic credibility would become fatally compromised.

In truth, this version of events is unlikely, but Vasari was possibly briefed by Michelangelo himself, and his account may well reflect the workings of the artist's extravagantly suspicious mind.

A GRUDGING LABOUR

Suffice it to say that Michelangelo tried every means to avoid taking on the project. In the end, when it became clear that he was not going to be able to do so, he decided to get it over and done with as quickly as he could. It took him four years in all, which is an astonishingly short time considering the enormous scale of the work – and the fact that Michelangelo seems to have worked largely alone, apart from an assistant who mixed his colours. Even so, the pope apparently asked him constantly about his progress. *The Agony and the Ecstasy* was the name given to the famous film about this episode in the artist's life – *The Irritability and the Impatience* might have been a more accurate title.

However, if these frescoes were not a labour of love, this hardly shows in a spectacular work that takes the continuity of Christian faith and worship as its theme. Seen in the artist's all-encompassing view, the

Above An uncompromising Christ makes his appearance as Judge of the World: *the climactic, culminating scene of the Sistine Chapel ceiling.*

Old Testament is the prefiguring of Christ's New Covenant; Christ and his Church the fulfilment of what the prophets promised. However, Michelangelo is undoubtedly a man of the Renaissance in the way he places humanity at the centre of God's Creation and in his depiction of the beauty of the human form as the ultimate expression of God's greatness. These values are summed up in the outstretched hands in *The Creation of Adam*, where we see the moment in which God transmits life to man.

A RICH LEGACY

Michelangelo never did get the opportunity to finish Julius' tomb – a mausoleum was built when the pope died in 1513, but it was placed in the Church of San Pietro in Vincoli, rather than St Peter's Basilica. Little of it is Michelangelo's work – although the one piece that is, an awe-inspiring Moses, confirms that this would indeed have been a special work. It is hard, though, to feel that humanity has been the loser, as the Sistine Chapel ceiling is one of the most famous and most visited artworks in the world.

Below The ceiling's most celebrated scene is The Creation of Adam, *where God reaches out to Adam, giving him life.*

NEW HORIZONS

WITH OVERSEAS EXPLORATIONS AND SCIENTIFIC DISCOVERIES BEING MADE IN SUCH QUICK SUCCESSION, RENAISSANCE EUROPE WAS AN EXCITING – BUT ALSO CONFUSING – PLACE TO BE.

Above Despite hurricanes and mutiny, the Portuguese navigator Vasco da Gama was the first European to reach Asia by going around Africa's Cape of Good Hope in 1497/8.

As the ideological certainties of the preceeding centuries were dissolving, the Church was facing an uphill struggle to maintain its old intellectual authority. The medieval period was the "Age of Faith", when men and women never questioned their duty of subservience in God's order; but then neither did they doubt their centrality in his cosmos. Paradoxically, even as Renaissance humanism proclaimed the pre-eminence of humanity, that centrality was coming under threat.

As the voyages of the great navigators pushed back the boundaries of the world known to the Europeans, astronomers explored an expanding universe – which might not actually be revolving around the earth as had been thought.

THE AGE OF DISCOVERY

Europeans were aware that their continent did not encompass the entirety of the world: Africa lay just beyond the Mediterranean, after all. Spices and other luxuries were brought along the Silk Route from the East: moreover, Marco Polo had brought back tidings from China in the late 13th century. However, few Europeans had followed him. The Crusades had left the Middle East a hostile environment, and the trade that continued in this region was conducted mostly by middlemen.

The soaring costs of luxuries imported overland helped motivate the search for a sea route, which receieved a boost when Prince Henry the Navigator of Portugal established a naval academy *c.*1450. Portuguese navigators made great progress with Bartolomeu Diaz finding his way down the coast of Africa to the Cape of Good Hope in 1487, while Vasco da Gama pushed on to India a decade later.

Christopher Columbus, sailing for Spain's "Catholic Monarchs", had reached the Americas, making landfall on 12 October 1492. However, he remained convinced until he died that he had found the westerly route to East Asia. The Europeans came to realize that he had instead stumbled on a "New World" – and the Old World would never be the same.

"Who is my neighbour?" Jesus had been asked by the lawyer in Luke 10:29. That question was looking harder to answer now. Difficult as it had always been to live up to Christ's injunction to love one's neighbour as oneself, now it was a conceptual challenge, too. As Gomes Eanes de Zurara, the Portuguese chronicler, put it, how could those naked "savages", of whom navigators were now bringing home reports, really

Below Columbus' discoveries opened up a New World – and its peoples – to the Europeans, such as these Native Americans from Virginia, in this late 16th-century engraving by Theodore de Bry.

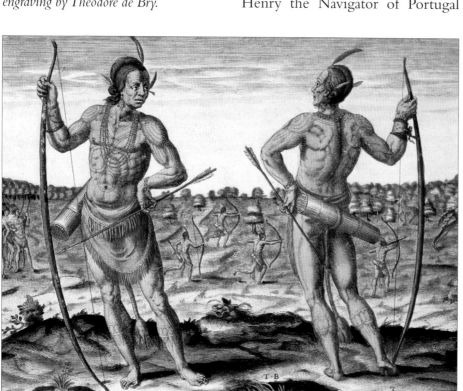

Above Christopher Columbus prepares to set out from the port of Palos, Spain, in August 1492, in this 19th-century fresco by Antonio Cabral y Aguado Bejarano.

be "of the generation of Adam"? Yet, shaped as they were, how could they not be? Were these strangers to be our neighbours? The European idea of the world was being challenged.

REVOLUTIONS

Things got worse. In 1543, Nicolaus Copernicus died. Only then was his great work *De revolutionibus orbium coelestium* (On the Revolution of the Heavenly Spheres) published. Copernicus, a priest himself and one of a family of priests and nuns, had received encouragement in his astronomical researches from fellow churchmen. However, he had been nervous about releasing his conclusions and no wonder: the Church had always followed the view of Aristotle and Ptolemy that the Sun and planets revolved around a stationary Earth. Copernicus believed the Earth and planets went around the Sun in what is called a heliocentric system.

The Church has since accepted this view, but at the time there were fears that it overturned scriptural accounts of the Creation and the cosmos – or that, if it did not, it would appear to do so. When, later in the century, another priest showed support for the Copernican theory, he was tried by the Roman Inquisition. Giordano Bruno faced a range of charges, from blasphemy to heresy: he was burnt at the stake in 1600.

Below Copernicus revealed that the true "harmony of the spheres" was produced by planets' concentric orbit around the Sun, shown in an illustration from Andreas Cellarius' Scenographia, c. 1660.

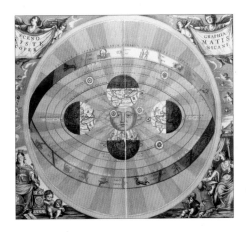

GALILEO'S HERESY

In the early 17th century, another Catholic astronomer, Galileo Galilei, found his own observations lending fresh support to the Copernican case. For this backing he was tried by the Church for heresy in 1633 and was forced to recant his claims. In fairness, Galileo had found discreet support among leading clergy. Several members of the Church hierarchy had acknowledged their support for both the strength of Galileo's observational evidence and the force of his argument that Old Testament cosmology should be regarded more as poetry than as science. Cardinal Caesar Baronius spoke up for Galileo's ideas, joking that "The Bible teaches the way to go to heaven, not the way the heavens go." Officially, though, the Catholic Church had condemned such views.

Above Galileo, shown in a 17th-century painting by the Flemish Justus Sustermans, fell foul of the Roman Inquisition with his public espousal of Copernican astronomy.

THE REFORMATION

IN THE EARLY 16TH CENTURY, MANY BELIEVERS TOOK THEIR STAND WITH THE REFORMER MARTIN LUTHER. IN ENGLAND, KING HENRY VIII PROCLAIMED HIMSELF HEAD OF THE CHURCH OF ENGLAND.

The great indulgence sale in which Pope Julius II set out to fund the rebuilding of St Peter's Basilica in 1505 caused outrage among many people across Europe. Indulgences had been around for centuries, of course, and, so too, had abuses of the system, which was widely satirized throughout the Middle Ages. It would be hard to claim that Julius' behaviour was much worse than anything that had occurred beforehand, yet it came after centuries of supposed reform – and at a time when the Church's overall authority

Below Martin Luther's famous protest is seen as the start of Protestantism. Ferdinand Pauwels' 19th-century painting shows the reformer nailing his "95 Theses" to the cathedral door.

was being questioned. In this climate, cleaning up such abuses within the Church's hierarchy was not going to be enough for the dissenters.

AUTHORITY IN QUESTION

In 1517, Martin Luther, priest and university professor, nailed his "95 Theses" to the door of the cathedral in Wittenberg, Germany, as a protest against the sale of indulgences. His arguments addressed the theology that allowed such indulgences to be awarded. The Church soon found itself under sustained attack from several sides. The scientific and intellectual tumults of the age had not left the Church unscathed. Moreover, the advent of the printing press had for the first time created what might be described as a reading

Above The pope acts as a moneychanger in the sale of indulgences and religious dispensations, as shown in this 1521 German woodcut by Lucas Cranach.

public – before the press, few books were available, and they could often be read only by the clerical elite, educated in Latin.

There was a growing sense that men and women might want to judge things for themselves. So Luther found a receptive ear when, questioning whether or not the Church hierarchy should even exist, he argued that every Christian believer should be his or her own priest. To further that end, he took an interest in making the Scriptures more accessible to the common people. The Church released a bull in 1520, proclaiming Luther's teachings as heretical, and only a few months later he was ex-communicated by the Church.

In 1522, Luther published his German translation of the New Testament, and William Tyndale's English Bible came out in 1525. The Church condemned both of these works: its fear was that the uneducated would be led astray without the interpretative assistance of their priests. However, to an increasing number of the educated middle class now emerging, especially in northern Europe, such thinking simply reeked of condescension.

KING HENRY VIII BREAKS AWAY

British coins still carry the abbreviation "F.D." after the name of the monarch: it means *Fidei Defensor*, or "Defender of the Faith". Ironically, this title was awarded by Pope Leo X to England's King Henry VIII in gratitude for his pamphlet, "A Defence of the Seven Sacraments" (1521), an eloquent response to Luther's criticisms. However, the failure of Henry's queen, Catherine of Aragon, to bear him a male heir led to a conflict between the king and Rome. Henry requested the annulment of their marriage, so he could wed Anne Boleyn, but it was rejected by Pope Clement VII. The king responded in 1532 by announcing that the monarch of England would also be head of the Church of England. He also confiscated the wealth in England's Catholic churches.

Right King Henry VIII puts Pope Clement VII in his place in an approving English satirical engraving of the 16th century.

A SPLIT FROM THE CHURCH
These Christians became known as "Protestants", which is from the Latin word *protestari*, or "to protest". Another meaning for *protestari* is "to affirm" or "to avow", which can also be seen as appropriate for a group whose members sought to seek guidance from the Scriptures, not from the Church's teachings. They believed that the individual person should have his or her own relationship with God. Catholicism never had the right to claim proprietorship over the "keys of heaven". What mattered was the divine Word, as revealed in the Scriptures, which it was the duty of every man and woman to read.

It could be argued that they took more moral responsibility for themselves, and there was no prospect of buying indulgences, or of pattering mechanically through a set of prayers. However, there was a tendency for a self-selecting community to feel that simply by proclaiming their belief they showed themselves to be "saved" and that there could be justification by faith instead of by works.

CALVINISM
In Geneva, John Calvin drew a distinction between the "Elect", marked out for salvation, and the rest, "pre-destined" for damnation by God himself even before they were created. That Calvin rejected Rome and all its works was just the start of his offence, as far as the Catholic hierarchy was concerned. His doctrines affronted their sense of Christian mercy and forgiveness. The way in which Calvin and his followers accepted the consignment of so many to eternal suffering seemed not just ungodly to them but inhuman.

Catholics believed that God, though indeed all-knowing, did not actually pre-ordain the sins of the souls he created, compromising their free will. This meant that the door to salvation would always be left open.

Below The Calvinist chapel contrasted starkly with the ornate Catholic churches of old. Such a chapel is shown in this c. 1565 painting by Jean Perrissin.

THE COUNTER-REFORMATION

IF THE REFORMATION THREW DOWN A CHALLENGE TO CATHOLICISM, IT WAS ONE TO WHICH THE CHURCH WAS ABLE TO RESPOND. AN URGENT EXAMINATION OF CONSCIENCE RESULTED IN FAR-REACHING CHANGES.

While the leaders of the Church were debating its institutional reform at the Council of Trent, a book was causing a stir in Italy. The story of *The Miraculous Life and Doctrine of St Catherine of Genoa* seemed somehow to speak to Catholicism in its crisis. It was hard to see why this should be so. Catherine had died half a century before, and she had barely registered on the consciousness of the Church in her own lifetime. Although nobly born, she had lost any status she had once enjoyed in a loveless, violent marriage; she had never taken orders as a nun. However, she had given her life to God, tending the sick and helping the poor. She had bravely faced the agonies of her last illness.

While Catherine's biography was being read in many hundreds of European homes, a very different life

Above Convened in 1545, the Council of Trent instituted wide-ranging reforms within the Church. The members of the council are depicted in this 18th-century copy of a contemporary painting.

was unfolding far away in a Spanish convent. There, Teresa of Ávila was experiencing visions of Christ that seemed to take possession of her whole being, body and soul. She described these visions in an auto-biography in the 1560s.

PIETY AND PASSION

The experiences of Catherine and Teresa were their own, but they can still be seen as the products of their time. The Church had been ready for two such figures. Both were comparative outsiders and women, and were remarkable not for their services to the Church establishment but for the intensity – the drama, even – of their spiritual lives. Although Catherine's path to God had been arduous and difficult, it was one that many ordinary Catholics could imagine themselves following. Moreover, the passion shown in Teresa's faith proved to be deeply moving to the many people who had been finding themselves increasingly unmoved by a religious life that had become routine.

The Catholics who embraced these women might never have dreamt of turning to Protestantism – any more than Catherine or Teresa would have done – but they were responding to some of the same underlying discontents. Luther's call to Christians was based on rejecting a Catholicism of empty forms for

Left St Teresa of Ávila came to represent a new kind of spirituality – impassioned and intense – as shown in the Ecstasy of St Teresa, *sculpted by Gian Lorenzo Bernini in 1645–52.*

a deep and authentic spirituality, which was founded in the faith of the individual.

THE JESUITS

Among St Teresa's inspirations had been the Spiritual Exercises, written in the 1520s by Ignatius Loyola. This Spanish thinker is now famous as the founder of a great religious order, the Society of Jesus *(see* The Society of Jesus, *opposite page)*, but he always saw faith as being rooted in the individual. His Spiritual Exercises could be seen as a sort of self-help course in Christian devotion, a regime of daily meditations and guided prayer. However, for Loyola, faith had to exist within the framework of the Church: his Exercises had to be followed under the guidance of a spiritual director.

The interconnection between the Church and its followers was perhaps the crucial insight that fuelled the Counter-Reformation. Personal faith, for all its passion, was ultimately

Ignatius Loyola had been born into a noble family in the Basque country and grew up with an exaggerated sense of what that meant. Like the Spanish writer Cervantes' comic hero Don Quixote, he had been addicted to the chivalric romances of the Middle Ages, with their stirring stories of gallantry. On growing up, Loyola enlisted in the army, resolved to win renown in battle, but he found soldiering had changed over the centuries. Instead of exchanging courtesies with fellow aristocrats whom he fought with sword and lance, he lost a leg to a cannonball at the siege of Pamplona. However, even then, Loyola was not disillusioned: recuperating in hospital, he asked for romances to read. Since none were available, he had to make do with reading about the lives of the saints. They inspired him to fight spiritually for Christ instead – but, a true romantic to the last, Loyola conceived of his Society of Jesus, known as the Jesuits, as a chivalric company.

Above Ignatius Loyola thought of himself as a knight in the cause of Christ. This 1556 portrait of him is by Jacopino del Conte.

directionless; at the same time, a large institution could have no soul without developing a fruitful relationship with the individual. What was called for, and what Loyola's Jesuits were able to provide, was a Catholicism in which these two components went together hand in hand.

The same impulse can be seen in the life and work of St Francis of Sales who, in the early 17th century,

Above Pope Urban VIII takes part in celebrations marking the Jesuits' centenary, shown in this c.1640 painting by Andrea Sacchi, Filippo Gagliardi and Jan Miel.

decided to tackle the Reformation head on. As Bishop of Geneva, St Francis had his seat in the very headquarters of Calvinism, but he made it his mission to convert Protestants back to the Catholic Church.

ECSTATIC ART

THE COUNTER-REFORMATION GAVE RISE TO A NEW – AND INTENSELY
EMOTIONAL – AESTHETIC. ARTISTS AND ARCHITECTS LOOKED FOR WAYS
TO DRAMATIZE THE PASSION AND FERVOUR OF RELIGIOUS FAITH.

Art had been one of the issues at the heart of the Reformation controversy. Protestants tended to regard the Church's display of wealth with suspicion. While secular art was one of the vanities that the Christian should be forsaking, "religious art" was really a contradiction in terms. What mattered was the Word of God: sacred pictures and statues were seen as "graven images" that had been prohibited by the Bible, evidence of a heathen adoration of Our Lady and the saints. The Church's collection of artistic treasures was considered one of the trappings of the "Whore of Babylon", their worldly beauties temptations to the struggling soul.

So strongly did Protestants feel about this that some extremists went on sprees of iconoclasm (literally, "breaking images"), smashing statues and stained-glass windows and whitewashing over frescoes. Many English churches still bear the scars – the disfigured statues and blank replacement glass of Ely Cathedral's Lady Chapel are just one example.

Above Flamboyant expressiveness was key to the Counter-Reformation aesthetic, as seen in this 17th-century painting, The Virgin Appearing to St Peter Damian, *attributed to Pietro da Cortona.*

ON THE OFFENSIVE

The Catholic Church responded by redoubling its efforts and launched what amounted to a major artistic offensive. At the same time, religious art took on an altogether different emphasis. Where once the architect had been content to suggest the grandeur of God and the splendour of his Church, the feelings involved in religious faith were now incorporated into the designs. While the artist had previously been content to commemorate worthy piety and honest service, the new spirituality was passionate and intense. Agony, ecstasy, tragedy, triumph: all of these dramatic human sensations were harnessed by artists, designed to both arrest the attention and engage the emotions.

Left Bernini's assistant, Giovanni Battista Gaulli, nicknamed "Baciccia", painted the Il Gesù ceiling, with much of his master's flair, in 1672–85. His work can be seen continuing past the boundaries normally created by barrel vaulting.

The element of surprise was exploited: artists and architects of this period showed an unabashed instinct for showmanship. Rome's Church of the Gesù is a case in point. Its dazzling white façade is elegant in its symmetries, but the overall effect is simple, even chaste. This only heightens the shock (no other word would be appropriate) when the visitor pushes through the doors to be assaulted by the ravishing beauty – and riotous exuberance – that can be found within.

There are frescoes, columns, statues, pilasters and so much ornamentation in marble and gilt that the scene seems to dissolve into a single disorientating vision, with every line and plane being thrown into doubt. The previously used boundaries disappear, with artwork spilling spectacularly across the demarcations made by the barrel vaulting in the ceiling overhead. Christ and his angels appear to waft heavenward through the ceiling itself.

The overall effect is staggering. Whereas the statues and stained glass of the Gothic churches had been visual "books" for instructing the unlettered, this interior was intended to take the senses – and hence the soul – by storm.

HIGH DRAMA
Built toward the end of the 16th century, the Church of the Gesù is the spiritual headquarters of the Society of Jesus, whose founder St Ignatius has his tomb in a side chapel. Beside the altar there is an allegorical sculpture that stands almost 3m (10ft) in height, representing *Religion Overthrowing Heresy and Hatred*. This is the work of Pierre Le Gros the Younger, a French sculptor based in Rome. With the cross of Christianity in one hand and thunderbolts of heavenly anger in the other, Lady Religion stands slightly off balance as she kicks out at Heresy, represented as an ugly old man. Sent

Above What might have been a stagey and schematic scene becomes a powerful human drama in the c.1696 statue Religion Overthrowing Heresy and Hatred *by Pierre Le Gros the Younger.*

sprawling, he appears to be falling over the edge of the sculpture's pedestal: the rules of gravity do not seem to apply. Hatred, a withered old woman, flinches away in fear before Religion's righteous anger. At bottom left, a little angel busily tears up books by the Protestant writers Ulrich Zwingli and Martin Luther.

TOO SENSATIONALIST?
Le Gros' impressive creation is all but overwhelming in its impact. The technical accomplishment involved is also awe-inspiring. It is hard to believe that so obviously schematic a work could be so powerful or that such dynamism could be captured in a lump of cold stone. Yet the miraculous transformation of marble to moving drapery, warm flesh and breathing life seen in this statue was achieved even more astonishingly in Gian Lorenzo Bernini's famous *Ecstasy of St Teresa* (1645–52), another great sculpture of the period.

Inevitably, there have been some criticisms that such sculptures are shallow and sensationalist, being no more than exhibitionistic tours de force by artistic virtuosos. However, these objections miss the real point of the works. They were created by an avowedly evangelizing aesthetic that used sheer emotional force to compel an intensely personal engagement between God and the followers of the faith.

Below Talented Renaissance sculptors could coax strong emotion out of cold stone. The 1674 Beatified Lodovica Albertoni, *by Gian Lorenzo Bernini, is a stunning example of the artist's work.*

TEMPORAL AUTHORITY

ALTHOUGH THE CATHOLIC CHURCH WAS GROWING IN POWER AND MAJESTY AT ITS CENTRE IN ITALY, ELSEWHERE IN EUROPE ANARCHY AND WAR MADE IT HARDER FOR THE CHURCH TO GAIN PRIMACY.

Above Posing with a miniature Aachen Cathedral in an 1825 painting by J.P. Scheuren, Emperor Charlemagne did much to build the bond between sacred and secular power in Europe.

The Church was a powerful force in Rome partly due to two donations. Although it was exposed as a forgery in the 15th century, for several centuries it was thought that the Donation of Constantine had given temporal authority over Rome and its possessions to the papacy. This misconception enabled the Catholic Church to wield an impressive political authority in Rome.

A different donation, made by the Merovingian king Pepin I, was genuine. He reigned over most of France and also over the western part of Germany and northern Italy. In 754, he had given the Church

Below Fought in 1634, the Second Battle of Nördlingen was one of many such encounters in the Thirty Years' War. The battle is depicted in a mid-17th-century painting by Pieter Meulener.

temporal authority over the Duchy of Rome and adjacent regions. Under the Holy Roman Empire, which was established by Pepin's son Charlemagne, these privileges had been upheld and even increased. By the time of Pope Innocent III in the 13th century, the Papal States embraced the whole of central Italy and much of the north-east.

These possessions brought the papacy not just great wealth but also considerable political power: great Renaissance popes such as Alexander VI and Julius II stood on an equal diplomatic footing with Europe's greatest monarchs. However, this was not always such a comfortable place to be, as Clement VII was to discover in 1527, when he was imprisoned during the sacking of Rome. Any idea that the Church was somehow spiritually removed, above politics

and the grubby machinations of international diplomacy, could not credibly be maintained when the pope was practically a king.

CONFLICTS OF INTEREST

Tensions between these secular and religious roles were inevitable. In the early 17th century, for instance, the papacy found itself in dispute with Venice. The city-state had remained Catholic in its allegiances; but, because its economy was based on trade, it was important it kept open its commerce with the Protestant states of central Europe. Also, as a republic, it did not see why it had to be in the control of an external authority.

In 1606, Pope Paul V placed the city under an "interdict" – this effectively excommunicated all its people, denying them the sacraments. This inflicting of a spiritual punishment for what amounted to a rejection of temporal authority was extremely unpopular, not just in Venice but elsewhere, too. While the modern opposition of Church and State had

yet to be formulated explicitly, it is clear that, at some level, the pope was seen to be abusing his power.

THE THIRTY YEARS' WAR

Such goings on in southern Europe soon became parochial when the centre of economic power shifed to the north. Since Charlemagne had founded the Holy Roman Empire, Germany and Italy had been associated, but Germany was now emerging as the greater force. However, as far as the Church was concerned, it was a country that could no longer be relied on, because many of its rulers had embraced the Lutheran cause. The Peace of Augsburg in 1555 had only delayed the showdown struggle between the Catholic and Protestant principalities of what had been the Holy Roman Empire. By the time Pope Gregory XV was enthroned in 1621, war was under way in Germany. Emboldened by the spirit of the Counter-Reformation, the Catholic princes, supported by the Church, had seen their chance to sweep away the Protestant presence in their midst. However, power politics is never so simple: individual rulers pursued their own agendas, and peripheral states were drawn into a rapidly escalating conflict.

The war continued for 30 years, turning the heart of Europe into an inferno. Civilians bore the brunt as mercenary armies embarked on sprees of rape and pillage. One-fifth or more of Germany's people were killed, some slaughtered in the carnage, others caught up in the famines and plagues precipitated by the war and the large-scale population movements it brought with it.

A HOLLOW TRIUMPH

The Catholic powers won, having made significant territorial gains, especially in France. Humanity had, of course, been the loser. Paradoxically, so too had the Church. Under the terms of the Treaty of Westphalia (1648), the principle of *cuius regio, eius religio*, or "whose region, his religion", was set in stone. Protestantism became embedded in several states and even Calvinism was protected.

The Catholic rulers, meanwhile, were ceasing to side automatically with Rome. They had their own strategic aims: France, for instance, had seen the war less as a religious crusade than as a way of containing the expansion of (Catholic) Spain. To thwart the Habsburgs, it had chosen to form an alliance with Protestant Sweden, ignoring the outrage of the pope. This, it seemed, was the shape of things to come: Catholic kings would support their Church when it suited them – and only then.

Above Urban VIII was pope through the most difficult period of the Thirty Years' War. A sculpture of the pope by Gian Lorenzo Bernini sits by his tomb in St Peter's Basilica, Rome.

***Below** Signed at Münster on 24 October 1648, the Treaty of Westphalia finally brought the hostilities of the Thirty Years' War to a close.*

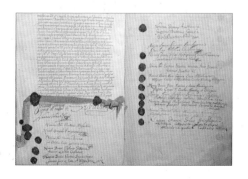

POLITICAL RAMIFICATIONS

THE REFORMATION REPRESENTED A SEISMIC SHOCK FOR THE CATHOLIC CHURCH, BUT ITS REPERCUSSIONS CERTAINLY DID NOT STOP THERE. ITS POLITICAL CONSEQUENCES WERE ALSO PROFOUND.

Above Huguenots are being killed in the St Bartholomew's Day Massacre in this 19th-century painting by François Dubois.

There was no separating the religious sphere from the political world in Renaissance Europe. The stability of the social order rested on the unquestioning respect for authority that the Catholic Church had previously enshrined. With division between the European states, the Church was losing ground.

SECULAR REACTION
Such a blow to the Church's standing compromised the security of the state as far as the Spanish establishment saw it. The Crown in Spain linked its authority explicitly with that of the Church: to be a Protestant was not just to be ungodly but also to be un-Spanish. Given the extent of the country's empire in the Americas and the Pacific, the sponsorship of Spain was not to be dismissed lightly. Meanwhile, demands from French Protestants, known as Huguenots, for religious toleration were met with blunt refusal. In 1572, with an explosion of ferocity, thousands were murdered in the St Bartholomew's Day Massacre. While Henri IV had allowed the Protestants to practise their faith in peace, announcing the Edict of Nantes in 1598, that measure was rescinded by Louis XIV in 1685. The Huguenots saw their property confiscated and their churches closed down; more than 200,000 left the country to live in exile.

Northern Europe, which was the Reformation's heartland, was also a place of political division. In the Netherlands, which was a Spanish territory at the time, the people embraced Protestantism partly in a spirit of nationalist resistance.

REACHING A COMPROMISE
Germany, Luther's homeland, was in theory a single entity under the Holy Roman Empire, but it was actually a patchwork of smaller states. Protestantism had been embraced with genuine enthusiasm in many of these areas. Several local rulers aligned themselves with the new religion to build up their own political power. A compromise was reached in 1555, when the Peace of Augsburg originally agreed the principle *cuius regio, eius religio* ("whose region, his religion"). Where a ruler was Catholic, in other words, Catholicism should hold sway; but where the king was a Lutheran, that religion would prevail in his country.

Instead of a recipe for tolerance it was one for systematic persecution, as rulers cleansed their countries along sectarian lines. Catholic kings were by no means innocent, but in the Protestant states of Germany and in Switzerland, home of Calvinism, priests were burnt at the stake and Catholicism was suppressed.

DISSOLVED IN ENGLAND
The English Reformation had been opportunistic in its origins. King Henry VIII had not disagreed doctrinally with the Church; his conflict was based on his marriage status. Yet Catholicism quickly became identified as a threat to the country and its Crown, and its adherents punished its followers without mercy. Under the Act of Supremacy (1534), Henry became official head of the Church of England, and this allowed him to close Catholic foundations and confiscate their wealth. The Dissolution of the Monasteries shattered an ecclesiastical infrastructure that had been built up over centuries.

The Dissolution had opposition: 1536 saw the Pilgrimage of Grace – an uprising in Yorkshire (where there

Below Half a millennium's Catholic culture came to an end with the Dissolution of the Monasteries. These ruins are all that is left of Fountains Abbey in Yorkshire, England.

was to be a second rebellion, the Rising in the North, in 1569). Catholicism was reprieved in 1553, when Henry's daughter, Mary I, succeeded him and sought to turn the clock back. In the event, the wave of counter-repression she ordered against Protestantism succeeded only in seeing her branded with the nickname "Bloody Mary".

In 1593, Queen Elizabeth I, a non-Catholic, introduced legislation against "recusants" who refused to accept the authority of the Church of England. Those who remained Catholic included many of the country's leading families, especially in the north and the West Country. The father of William Shakespeare is believed to have been a recusant, and there has been speculation that England's greatest playwright was one as well.

King Philip II of Spain, Mary's widower, had supported his wife's mission to re-convert England. It was

Above Protestant Elizabeth I sits in splendour before her Parliament. To her left stands Sir Francis Walsingham, a ruthless hunter of "recusants".

with the intention of restoring Catholicism to England that, in 1588, he dispatched the Spanish Armada, hoping to invade the country. In the event, the *Armada Invencible* ("Invincible Fleet") was stopped by the English navy and dispersed by a "Protestant wind".

UNDERCOVER CLERICS

English priests were trained in continental seminaries and then smuggled back into the country. They slipped in disguise from one private house to another around the country to give Mass. It had to be held in secret because participants never knew when they might be denounced by a suspicious neighbour or a servant with a grudge.

Although a number of these houses had hiding holes for visiting priests, many were caught and executed. Typically, they were hanged, drawn and quartered. Ordinary Catholics were killed, too, but they were often tortured first in hopes that they would give up the whereabouts of other Catholics, particularly their priests. The missionaries were feared by the authorities, not just as religious dissidents but as enemy agents. It hardly helped that the headquarters of English Catholicism were abroad, at Douai in France, and Valladolid in Spain.

Below The Michelade was a massacre of Catholics in Nîmes, after St Michel's Fair in September 1567. Franz Hogenberg captured it in this 16th-century painting.

Above A number of English houses had hiding holes, so priests could quickly be concealed from the authorities. This hiding hole is in the King's Room in Moseley Old Hall, Staffordshire.

S.Catherina
Iris

A WORLD RELIGION

The Catholic religion underwent a major cultural and geographical shift when a Middle Eastern sect became the European Church of Rome. As horizons widened, missionaries ventured out into the farthest reaches of Asia, the Americas and Africa, bringing the Word of God to some of the millions who had not yet heard it.

For a long time in Europe the idea of a godless universe had been – quite literally – unthinkable. In the 17th, 18th and 19th centuries, intellectuals, scientists and politicians began to place their faith in "reason". Christianity was so much superstition, said the rationalists, an instrument of oppression; the Church was a reactionary force. When two secularist ideologies – fascism and communism – plunged the world into chaos in the 20th century, the Church was caught up in the accompanying conflicts. Peace did return, at least for Western Europe and North America, where a new generation grew up in affluent societies. In the consumerist society, everything was a matter of choice – including religious belief and personal morality. Yet most of the world still lived in poverty and the Church had a duty to those people, too.

In the new millennium, Catholicism finds itself facing huge challenges, as it has throughout its history. Time and again, it has shown its capacity to recover from its setbacks and learn from its mistakes while holding firmly to its founding principles to be a guiding light of faith for a struggling world.

Above When the Europeans became established in the Americas, Catholicism quickly spread throughout Latin America. Sister Juana Inés de la Cruz, a Mexican poet, scholar and nun, was painted in the 17th century by an unknown Mexican artist.

Left European explorers introduce the Cross – and Christianity – as they come into contact with previously unknown civilizations in the New World. Théodor de Bry illustrated scenes of these meetings in his 1592 Americae Tertia Pars....

MISSIONS TO THE EAST

THE APOSTLES WERE THE FIRST CHRISTIANS TO SPREAD THE GOSPELS. FROM THE 15TH TO 17TH CENTURY, EUROPEANS BEGAN TO TRAVEL FARTHER EAST, WHERE THEY SPREAD THE MESSAGE OF THE CHURCH.

"Go therefore and make disciples of all nations…" was Christ's command (Matthew 28:19). To the apostles the missionary impulse was part of Christianity. They spread Christ's message through Syria and Asia Minor, and westward to Rome, the centre of an extensive empire. There was even a tradition that St Thomas carried the gospels to India. Christian communities thrived in Iraq and Iran, too, but in the 5th century their Church no longer recognized the authority of Rome when it embraced Nestorianism, a heresy that believes Christ is divided into two: the divine and the human. It was now time for missionaries to carry the gospels to the farthest corners of Asia.

Below China's Mongol emperor Kublai Khan greets the Polo brothers on their visit to China. In this c.1412 illustration from the Book of the World's Marvels, *they receive a letter to deliver to the newly elected Pope Gregory X.*

CENTRAL ASIA

The willingness of the Mongols to adopt Nestorianism may have contributed to the rise of the legend of Prester John *(see right)*. In 1289, Pope Nicholas IV dispatched John of Montecorvino to take messages to Kublai Khan of China and other Mongol leaders. He was the first Roman Catholic missionary in China and translated the New Testament and Psalms into the Mongol language. Missionary work appealed to the enterprising spirit of the new Franciscan and Dominican orders, who sent missions to western and central Asia from the 13th century.

Above St Francis Xavier (1506–52) did more than anyone else to carry the Christian message to the East. This 17th-century portrait is by an unknown painter.

PRESTER JOHN

By the 12th century, the failure of the Crusades and the growing strength of the Islamic world had left western Christendom in a state of demoralization. People were prepared to clutch at straws – even the legend that, somewhere in the East, there was a powerful empire ruled by a Christian king. Prester John had even written a letter, it was said, promising to come to Europe's rescue, attacking the Muslim enemy from the rear. So vague were the stories, and so inexact the geographical knowledge of Europe at this time, that Prester John's realms were variously reported as lying in Ethiopia and Central Asia. In 1177, Pope Alexander III went as far as writing a letter to Prester John seeking his assistance, but his messenger appears to have been lost somewhere in the vastness of Asia.

SPREADING OUT

The missions into Asia were bold but small-scale ventures. Anything more was unrealistic, given Christendom's political and geographical situation. Europe was effectively "boxed in": by Islam on its eastern frontier, by Africa's Sahara to the south and by an apparently infinite Atlantic Ocean to the west. However, the Age of Discovery changed all that, opening a door upon a much wider world. This was a period between the early 15th century and the 17th century in which Europeans explored the oceans, seeking new trading routes. As these great voyages broadened horizons, they brought Christians into contact with nations which had never heard the Gospel Word.

The evangelizing impulse was never lost and found fresh impetus in the 16th century. The Counter-Reformation brought a new spiritual energy, with the Jesuits leading the way. St Francis Xavier founded a mission in Goa, on the coast of India, in 1542. The "Apostle of the Indies" went on to preach Christianity in Indonesia and, from 1549, Japan. The other orders were not idle: the Franciscans were by now well-established in Malacca and Malaysia, and Augustinian friars had a mission in the Philippines from 1565.

THE CHINESE ENDEAVOUR

The greatest challenge for the missionaries at the time was China, a vast and complex country that had an ancient history and strong religious traditions of its own. In 1552, St Francis Xavier was preparing to embark on another mission, this time to China, when he died on an island off Guangdong, on its southern coast. However, 30 years later, his fellow-Jesuits, Michele Ruggieri and Matteo Ricci, established their own mission in Beijing.

The Jesuits were under no illusions about the huge scale of the task that awaited them, and not merely

Above Many missionaries paid the ultimate price for their devotion to their religion. An unknown 17th-century Japanese artist illustrated Jesuits being martyred in Japan in 1622.

Below Jesuit missionary Matteo Ricci and scholar Li Paul Xu Guangqi became friends, shown together in this 17th-century engraving. They translated key works of Western science into Chinese.

because of the enormous population of the country. Chinese society was sophisticated and its sense of cultural identity secure. There could be no pretence that these were "savages" in need of civilization.

A CULTURAL EXCHANGE

The Westerners sought out the Chinese scholarly elite and, addressing them as equals, opened up a dialogue on just about every aspect of life and thought. In the process, they introduced the Chinese to the whole range of Western culture, from art and literature to mathematics and science. They earned the respect and trust of China's rulers – and several Jesuits were even given posts in the imperial administration. Many Chinese intellectuals willingly converted to Christianity.

Sadly, as time went on, dissension between the Jesuits and Franciscans ended up hampering the effectiveness of both. In 1644, moreover, Manchu invaders swept away the old Qing dynasty in China and inaugurated a new order that was far less tolerant toward foreign faiths.

Missions in the Americas

The discovery and exploration of the New World during the 16th to 18th centuries brought with it the discovery of new nations and cultures – and another wave of missions.

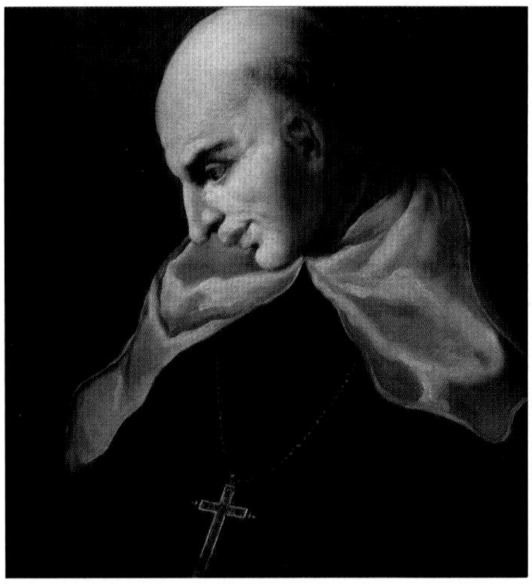

Above *Fray Bartolomé de Las Casas (1484–1566) became Catholicism's conscience in the Americas, with his impassioned pleas for humanity toward the native peoples (artist unknown).*

The newly discovered peoples of the Americas were the subject of an important debate held in Valladolid, at that time the capital of Spain, in 1550–1. Two Dominicans, Juan Ginés de Sepúlveda and Bartolomé de Las Casas, argued the burning question of the day. Were the native peoples of "New Spain" really men and women, like Europeans? They looked like humans, but they apparently went unclothed, like animals, and their customs were alien to Europeans. Should they be treated as equals, or put under subjection?

There were good grounds for taking the latter view, Sepúlveda said. Had not Aristotle himself written that some peoples were by their very nature slaves, and needed to be subjected for their own good? On the contrary, Las Casas maintained. He believed that the "Indians" were entitled to exactly the same treatment as Europeans, but these rights were being scandalously ignored. Both in his Valladolid address and in a series of polemical writings on the subject, Las Casas catalogued every kind of exploitation and abuse that the native peoples were being subjected to. From Columbus' voyages to the Caribbean islands to the conquests of Mexico and Peru, by Cortès and Pizarro respectively, the native peoples, including the Taino, Aztec, Maya and Inca, were harshly treated by the Spaniards.

NEW WORLD, NEW WAYS

Both sides of the debate claimed victory, but the controversy went on for years. The Church was divided:

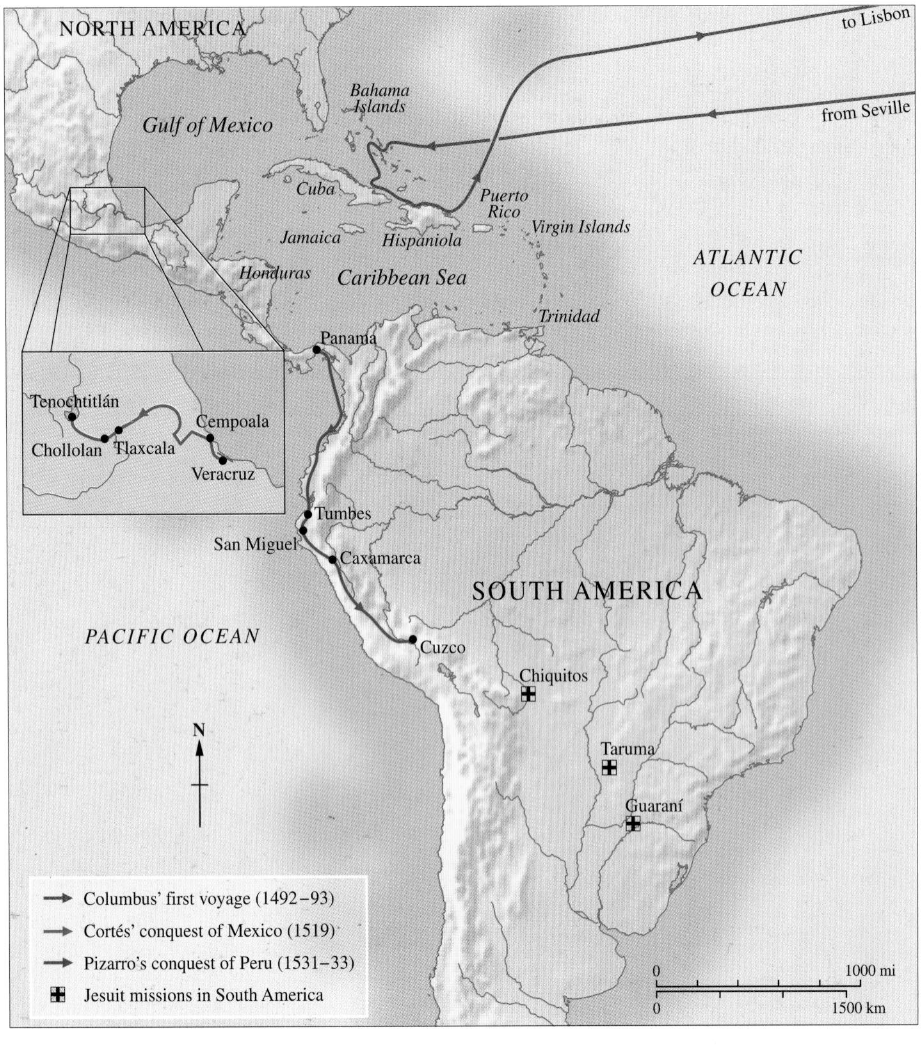

NORTH AMERICA
to Lisbon
from Seville
Bahama Islands
Gulf of Mexico
Cuba
Puerto Rico
Virgin Islands
Jamaica
Hispaniola
Honduras
Caribbean Sea
ATLANTIC OCEAN
Trinidad
Panama
Tenochtitlán
Cempoala
Chollolan
Tlaxcala
Veracruz
Tumbes
San Miguel
Caxamarca
SOUTH AMERICA
PACIFIC OCEAN
Cuzco
Chiquitos
N
Taruma
Guaraní
Columbus' first voyage (1492–93)
Cortés' conquest of Mexico (1519)
Pizarro's conquest of Peru (1531–33)
Jesuit missions in South America
0
1000 mi
0
1500 km

Below *After Columbus' first landfall in the Caribbean, Christianity soon spread down through South America.*

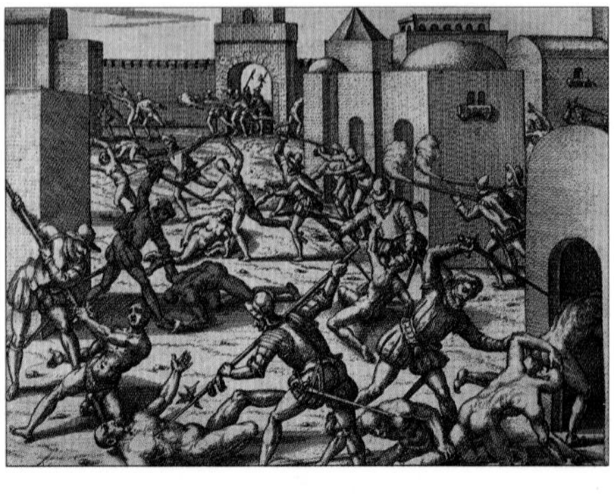

Below *Spanish conquistadors massacre the Inca after capturing their capital, Cuzco, in 1532. The event is captured in this 1602 engraving by Théodor de Bry from the* Historia Americae.

in some places it had become an arm of oppression, while elsewhere it had become a fighter for the indigenous peoples and their rights. An encomienda system was established, in which Europeans took land for themselves, in effect enslaving its indigenous occupiers.

In theory expropriation came with a duty of guardianship. Some took this obligation seriously: the Society of Jesus led the way in trying to make the New World a better one. The Jesuits reigned over *reducciones* ("reductions") that covered most of what is now Paraguay, along with vast tracts in Uruguay, Brazil, Bolivia and Argentina. There they had the rights of the representatives of the colonial power. However, instead of enslaving the indigenous peoples, they settled them around their mission stations, giving them schools and establishing farms to teach skills in agriculture.

The Jesuits' approach could be accused of high-handedness, but their paternalism was preferable to the outrageous exploitation going on elsewhere. The indigenous peoples made it clear where their preferences lay, flocking to the *reducciones* in large numbers. Neighbouring colonists had no alternative but to improve conditions radically if they were to have any hope of hanging on to their subject Indians. As Bishop

Above Made for Aztec offerings, this casket cover found a new role in the Christian liturgy. It is now kept in the Templo Mayor Museum, Mexico City.

of Michoacán, Mexico, from 1537, Bishop Vasco de Quiroga introduced a system of his own. Along with a foundation in Christian education, he had "his" indigenous people taught craft skills, each village being given a different speciality, from weaving and metalwork to pottery. His subjects even had a degree of political autonomy.

Not surprisingly, such utopias sparked controversy and other Europeans lobbied against them. There, lobbying was so successful that in the middle of the 18th century the Jesuits were formally expelled from Spanish and Portuguese America.

NORTHERN MISSIONS

Along North America's eastern sea coast, the main colonial power was Protestant England – with the exception of the colony of Maryland, which was founded by Catholic refugees from the same country in 1633. Farther north, in Canada, the French were in charge. Their intrepid priests played a major part in exploring the interior, venturing up the St Lawrence River to the Great Lakes.

The west coast, though nominally Spanish-ruled, saw little sign of European settlement at first. It was not until the 18th century that encroachments were made down the coast by Russian traders, which created nervousness at home.

In 1769, Father Junípero Serra set out from San Diego with the Spanish soldier and official Gaspar de Portola to build a chain of missions. They founded 21 missions in total, up and down what became known as the *Camino Real*, or "Royal Road". Junípero Serra set up nine of them personally, travelling an estimated 38,000 km (23,600 miles) in the 15 years before he died.

Below A figure of founder Junípero Serra stands before the Mission Church of San Diego de Alcalá, San Diego – California's first church, established in 1769.

THE HURON CAROL

In 1643, the Jesuit priest and explorer Jean de Brébeuf wrote his "Huron Carol", referring to God as Gitchi Manitou – the great deity of the Algonquin people – and giving the Christmas story a new setting in Canada.

*Twas in the moon of wintertime when all the birds had fled
That mighty Gitchi Manitou sent angel choirs instead;
Before their light the stars grew dim, and wondering hunters heard the hymn:
Jesus your King is born, Jesus is born, in excelsis gloria…*

*Within a lodge of broken bark the tender babe was found;
A ragged robe of rabbit skin enwrapped his beauty round
But as the hunter braves drew nigh, the angel song rang loud and high:
Jesus your King is born, Jesus is born, in excelsis gloria.*

THE GOSPEL IN AFRICA

THE STORY OF CATHOLICISM IN AFRICA IS TIED UP INEXTRICABLY WITH THAT OF COLONIALISM IN THE 16TH TO 19TH CENTURIES. TODAY'S CHURCH MUST LOOK BACK ON A RECORD THAT IS DECIDEDLY MIXED.

Exploration of sub-Saharan Africa by Europeans came late. Prior to the 19th century, Africa was for the most part considered only as a place for buying slaves. Sea captains of different nations sailed down the hazardous coast, but generally stopped for only as long as it took to load up with their helpless human cargo. Then the ships set off again – some sailing to the plantations of British North America, but many to the New World colonies founded by Catholic Portugal, Spain and France.

Although this slave trade was a monstrous business, at the same time it was immensely profitable, and the American venture was central to the strategic aims of these great powers. So closely were the clergies

Above To many Africans, such as these slaves photographed in Zanzibar in the 1880s, the Christian message could give meaning to a downtrodden life.

of these conquering countries involved in this project that few seem to have questioned its moral implications for Christians. Although a succession of popes did condemn the trade – such as Gregory XIV in 1591, Urban VIII in 1639 and Benedict XIV in 1741 – with so much at stake they failed to make their message heard.

AFRICAN CATHOLICISM?

Some efforts were made to preach the gospel: indeed, Portuguese priests made great strides in the Kingdom of Kongo (which included much of what is now Angola, as well as parts of the modern Republic of the Congo and Democratic Republic of the Congo). However, in a spirit of tolerance, the Church allowed the incorporation of elements of African religion, and soon Kongolese Catholicism was barely recognizable as Catholicism at all. At the start of the 18th century, for example, a woman named Kimpa Vita mobilized the masses, claiming to be the reincarnation of St Anthony of Padua. She insisted that Christ had been Kongolese, and that St Anthony was a deity alongside him.

Left A contemporary cartoonist addressed the imperial ambitions of the wealthy businessman Cecil Rhodes: Europeans were tripping over one another in their "Scramble for Africa".

A SPIRITUAL SCRAMBLE

The exploration of Africa's vast interior began in real earnest in the 19th century, when it was still seen as a "dark continent" by many Catholics. Nevertheless, the Church was equipped: a wealth of missionary experience had been acquired in the Americas and Asia, and in 1622 a co-ordinating Congregation for Propagation of the Faith had been founded. (In the 20th century this was renamed the Congregation for the Evangelization of Peoples.)

The Catholic Church had competition. The most famous British traveller in Africa, David Livingstone, though today generally thought of simply as an explorer, was just one of many highly motivated Protestant missionaries. Livingstone's explorations, moreover, are difficult to disentangle from the wider British effort to colonize the African interior. Cecil Rhodes' boastful ambition to build a railway "from the Cape to Cairo" typified the colonialists' view of Africa as a blank canvas on which to capture their grand designs. Catholic and Protestant missionaries had brought with them, along with the gospels, an unmistakable message of European supremacy.

ABUSIVE RULERS

The presence of the French Archbishop Charles Lavigerie in Tunisia, a French statesman once remarked, "is worth an army to France". Lavigerie had once said, "as missionaries we also work for France". Where Catholic powers prevailed, the Church often acted as an arm of the colonial administration. Terrible atrocities were committed when the French ruled in what is now the Republic of the Congo.

Still worse was the holocaust committed by Belgium's King Leopold II in the south in his so-called Congo Free State, now the Democratic Republic of the Congo. Mass rape and mutilations were carried out by troops to discourage dissent and boost productivity on the plantations and in the mines. By 1908, up to ten million citizens had been killed by the troops.

These missionaries were fighting a (sometimes unseemly) turf war, analogous to the great colonial "Scramble for Africa" itself, where Europeans competed to claim African territories as their own in the late 19th century until World War I. In some places this had tragic consequences. In Buganda, the main kingdom of what is now Uganda, the local king – a despot of hideous cruelty – kept himself in power by playing Protestant and Catholic missionaries off against one another.

The Catholic missionaries at work in Africa belonged to the Society of the Missionaries of Africa, which was better known as the "White Fathers". The society was founded in 1868 by the Archbishop of Algeria, Charles Lavigerie, who was originally sent to work in French North Africa. The distinctive white garb for which its members were named was modelled on the robes of the desert nomads. Also in the vanguard were the priests of the Society of African Missions, which was founded in 1850 by Bishop Melchior de Marion-Brésillac.

Below French White Fathers pose amid a congregation of local converts outside their traditionally built mission in Urundi (now Burundi) in the years before World War I.

Above A French missionary bulletin of 1878 sends an uplifting message to encourage generosity from back home.

THE ENLIGHTENMENT ASSAULT

FROM THE SCIENTIFIC, INTELLECTUAL AND POLITICAL COMMUNITIES CAME TRENCHANT CRITICISMS OF CATHOLICISM: SOON THE CHURCH WAS STRUGGLING TO HOLD ITS OWN.

The Copernican revolution, in which the 16th-century astronomer claimed that the Earth revolved around the Sun – which meant that the Earth was not, as the Church believed, the centre of the universe – had been only a foretaste of the formidable challenges to come. In 1687, the English scientist Sir Isaac Newton published his *Philosophiae Naturalis Principia Mathematica* ("Mathematical Principles of Natural Philosophy"). While Newton was not an atheist, it was hard to resist a feeling that his far-reaching theories could be suggesting a universe that was governed not by God but instead by mathematics and science.

Below Sir Isaac Newton's theories transformed perceptions of the universe – and, inevitably, of God. This 1687 frontispiece is from the Philosophiae Naturalis Principia Mathematica.

The English poet Alexander Pope, a Catholic, had no difficulty in reconciling his fellow countryman's new science with his deeply felt religious views on the Creation:

*Nature and Nature's laws lay hid
 in night,
God said "Let Newton Be!" and
 all was light.*

In a perverse sort of way, it probably helped that the poet was living in a Protestant country in which anti-Catholic feeling was rife. Catholics had even been blamed for the Great Fire of London of 1666. Under the Penal Laws then prevailing, the poet was not allowed to live in London, but had been forced to take a house outside the city, at Twickenham. Pope's faith was almost certainly steeled by the humiliations he had to undergo.

Above Brilliant in his thinking, vicious in his satire, Voltaire became the scourge of the Catholic Church. This 1811 portrait is by Jacques Augustin Pajou.

THE FRENCH "INFAMY"

In Catholic France, the situation was different: there the Church was closely identified with a monarchical establishment that oppressed the poor and repressed all freedoms. In such circumstances, young intellectuals were more predisposed to regard religion as superstition and to dismiss the liturgy and sacraments as mumbo-jumbo. These intellectuals, and soon the general French public, were quick to adopt anything that seemed to offer a rational explanation for the wonders of creation. *Écrasez l'Infâme* ("Crush the Infamy") became the war cry of François-Marie Arouet, who is much better known today by his pseudonym Voltaire. The infamy he was referring to was the alliance of the Church and Crown against freedom, justice and the rule of reason.

Voltaire was the most famous of the 18th-century *philosophes*, whose work extended far beyond the realm of philosophy as normally understood into just about every area of

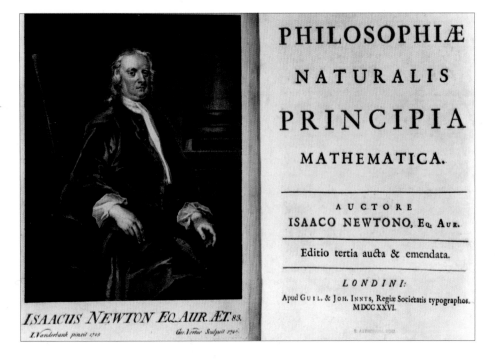

PHILOSOPHIÆ

NATURALIS

PRINCIPIA

MATHEMATICA.

AUCTORE
ISAACO NEWTONO, Eᴏ. Aᴜʀ.

Editio tertia aucta & emendata.

LONDINI:
Apud GUIL. & JOH. INNYS, Regiæ Societatis typographos.
MDCCXXVI.

ISAACUS NEWTON EQ.AUR. ÆT.83.

life and politics. Other prominent *philosophes* included Jean Jacques Rousseau, who said "Man was born free, but he is everywhere in chains". These metaphorical chains were not just those of tyranny but of public institutions, even of morality: children were born innocent, he said, then corrupted by their education. He also claimed that no institution did more to blight the pure soul than the Catholic Church, which was steward of a morality that destroyed the very virtue it claimed to save.

COMPREHENSIVE CRITIQUE

By 1750, under the leadership of Denis Diderot, a group of scholars worked on a great, multi-volume *Encyclopédie*. This was to be a "systematic dictionary of the sciences, arts and crafts", and it was to be drawn up, said Diderot, "without regard to anybody's feelings". They wanted to include every branch of human knowledge.

The Encyclopedists questioned Christianity's most fundamental tenets, arguing that theology was just another branch of philosophical investigation, and that religious doctrine should be submitted to the same sort of scientific testing as anything else.

Above An intimidating late 18th-century French illustration shows an army sapper and a revolutionary exhorting "Liberty, Equality and Fraternity…Or Death".

REVOLUTION

The *Ancien Régime* was finally swept away in 1789. Although the French Revolution did bring a sort of freedom, it also brought its own infamy, too, in the Reign of Terror. The new Republic was defiantly secular in its approach. The idea of *laïcité* was established: France was to be run by and for lay people, not the clergy. Christian values were to be replaced by those of *Liberté*, *Egalité* and *Fraternité* ("Liberty", "Equality" and "Fraternity").

Religion was not actually outlawed (as it would be later in some communist countries), but it was restrained and no longer enjoyed special favours from the state, and it was certainly not allowed to set the tone for ruling the country. Catholicism was given the same slightly grudging tolerance as the Protestants: gone were the days when its cardinals and bishops were active participants in the government of the state.

In the absence of any real understanding developing between the state authorities and the Church hierarchy, the concept of "Ultramontanism" soon grew among the Catholics in opposition to *laïcité*. *Ultramontane* literally means "beyond the mountains": the range in question was the Alps, on the other side of which lay Italy and Rome. French Catholics were told by their clergy that, whatever their state might try to tell them, its authority was trumped by that of their Church.

THE IMPERIAL CATECHISM

In 1804, Napoleon Bonaparte overthrew the revolutionary state, installing himself as Emperor Napoleon I. However, any hopes that the Church might find its old authority restored were cruelly dashed. On the contrary, the ultimate ignominy came in 1806 with the "Imperial Catechism", rewritten by the emperor himself and imposed on France's Catholic educators:

What are the duties of Christians toward those who govern them, and in particular toward Napoleon I, our emperor?

Christians owe the princes who govern them – and we in particular owe Napoleon I, our emperor – love, respect, obedience, fidelity, military service, and the taxes levied for the preservation and defence of the empire and of his throne…

Right *Pope Pius VII and his legates suffered the indignity of being obliged to be present during Napoleon's Coronation in 1804. The pope is the subject of this 1807 painting by Jacques Louis David.*

HOLDING BACK THE TIDE

THE 19TH AND 20TH CENTURIES SAW THE CHURCH ENGAGED IN AN INCREASINGLY FRANTIC REARGUARD ACTION TO DEFEND ITSELF AGAINST FREE-THINKING LIBERALISM AND REFORM.

The Church's identification with its conservative causes was to leave a lasting legacy that would be difficult for Catholicism to live down. It has always insisted that it was no enemy of science or reason – only to the "rationalism" that makes an idol out of human thought. Although Catholicism would come to terms with the discoveries of Newton and his successors, during the 19th and early 20th centuries the clergy often found itself acting as apologists for scientific backwardness, which only seemed to confirm the charge that the Church stood for superstition.

CONSERVATIVE VIEWS

It hardly helped that the most obvious product of the "Enlightenment" had been bloody revolution in Catholic France. The ferment there

Above *Giuseppe Garibaldi led the Italians in their 19th-century struggle for nationhood. Most could not understand why the Church opposed this movement.*

was viewed with consternation in other countries, whose rulers saw their own authority under threat. Rome's unease at the rise of *laïcité* may have been understandable, but it also placed the Church firmly in the camp of the conservatives.

Under the guise of resisting revolution, the Habsburg rulers of Austria, for instance, set themselves against every kind of social change. Backed by the state chancellor and Emperors Francis I and Ferdinand I, they refused the ambitions expressed by subject populations for national sovereignty – not just in Hungary and the Balkans but also in Italy.

THE *RISORGIMENTO*

In 19th-century Italy, a resurgence of national feeling, known as the *Risorgimento*, arose among a people who had for too long lived under Austrian domination. The movement received no encouragement from the Church, which saw any attack on authority as corrosive of its own. Conservatives in Italy shared

Left *By the 1860s, Pope Pius IX was completely dependent on French backing. He blesses Bourbon troops outside the Royal Palace in Naples in this 19th-century painting by Achille Vespa.*

this view, but as time went on and the ferment rose, theirs became an increasingly unpopular position. Because the Vatican identified itself more closely with despotic rulers in Vienna than with the overwhelming will of the Italian people, it severely damaged the Church's reputation.

Pope Pius IX still insisted that, as pope, he was temporal ruler of the Papal States, the central Italian territories traditionally under the rule of the Vatican. Increasingly, the Italians disagreed and, in 1849, Pius IX needed military intervention by France's Emperor Napoleon III to secure his position. Repeatedly, he had to rely on the support of foreign imperialists – sometimes the French, sometimes the Austrians – against the Italian freedom fighter Giuseppe Garibaldi and his patriotic Red Shirt army. Finally, in 1871, papal rule in the city of Rome came to an end. The tiny enclave of the Vatican apart, the former territories were annexed by the state. Rome was now the capital of a unified Italy.

SET AGAINST CHANGE

The episode left a bad feeling behind. Liberals saw the Catholic Church not as a champion but as the foe of freedom; workers saw it as the enemy of change. The Church itself

had been wounded and it lashed out, responding to threats to its authority with a flurry of authoritarian pronouncements. Already, in 1864, Pius IX had issued his Syllabus of Errors, a catalogue of new liberal ideas that he felt were damaging. He summed up by rejecting any notion that the Church should take steps to accommodate "progress…liberalism, or recent civilization". (Called in 1869 to ratify the Syllabus, the First Vatican Council sprang another surprise when, in a statement of 1870, Pius IX proclaimed the dogma of papal infallibility, claiming that popes are divinely guided, so infallible.)

In Protestant-dominated countries, the Church's political position might be more subtly nuanced. For the most part, though, it was identified with conservatism. In Spain, the poor knew better than to look to the Church for support in bettering their situation. They had learned to see the black-garbed priests as scavenging, flesh-eating *corvos* ("crows"). When Civil War broke out in the country in 1936, priests and nuns were massacred in their hundreds.

Below General Franco greets some of his clerical supporters with studied courtesy: relations were not quite so warm between Spain's working people and the Church.

THE WORKERS' POPE

Despite the conservative stand taken by the Church, there was one pope who held a different view. Pope Leo XIII's proclamations on behalf of the world's workers would put many a socialist to shame. He himself was anything but a democrat, putting down one dissenting adviser with an unceremonious *Ego sum Petrus* ("I am Peter") but he saw the need for radical change, if only to rescue the status quo.

In his 1891 encyclical *Rerum Novarum* ("Of New Things"), he addressed the condition of the working classes as one of the great issues of the age. Reasoning that failure to reform would lead to revolution, he called for far-reaching changes in the way modern economies were organized. Denouncing the glaring gulf between rich and poor, he spoke out in support of workers' rights and trade unions, expressing his sympathy for those who went on strike to ensure the welfare of their families.

Above Addressing the Church – and looking to the future – Pope Leo XIII is shown recording his blessing by phonograph in this 1903 print by Achille Beltrame.

DARK TIMES

WITH FASCISTS MARCHING ON ROME ITSELF, NAZISM ON THE RISE IN GERMANY AND COMMUNISTS IN EASTERN EUROPE, THE FIRST HALF OF THE 20TH CENTURY WAS A TUMULTUOUS TIME FOR THE CHURCH.

In 1922, cheering crowds turned out to welcome Benito Mussolini and his "Blackshirts" – the nickname given to members of his Fascist paramilitary – as they made their triumphal entrance into Rome. However, Italy's senior churchmen were rather more muted in their welcome: they had little in common with the young thugs who were following *Il Duce* ("The Leader").

Even so, there was something in Fascism to which these churchmen found themselves able to respond: its reverence for authority, its avowed respect for established tradition. Years of liberalism, with its vaunted freedoms, had brought the country only incessant labour unrest and public immorality – and a press that held the Church and all its values in clear contempt. Worse still, there was evidence everywhere in Europe of the

Below Cardinal Pacelli, the future Pope Pius XII, signs the infamous Concordat with Germany in 1933 on behalf of Pope Pius XI.

advances made by the Communists, who had already established an atheistic state in the Soviet Union.

SENT BY PROVIDENCE

The Holy See had refused to acknowledge Italy's annexation of Rome in 1871, spending the next six decades in denial – and in endless wrangling with successive governments. Under the terms of the Lateran Treaty of 1929, Mussolini agreed compensation for the loss of the old Papal States. Mussolini had discarded the Catholicism of his upbringing, and privately despised it, but he also recognized its importance to the conservative Italians he wanted on his side. He made Catholicism the state religion, made criticism of the Church a crime, outlawed divorce and made religious education mandatory in all schools. All state legislation would be reviewed to ensure that it conformed with canon law. Pope Pius XI declared that *Il Duce* was "a man sent by providence": there were some

Above At the height of his power, Benito Mussolini visits the Vatican in 1932 to meet Pope Pius XI and his officials.

who did not question the moral price the Church would have to pay for this arrangement.

Both Mussolini and Hitler were lapsed Catholics. Like Mussolini, Hitler saw Christianity as a weaklings' creed, but he recognized the value of good relations with the Church. Pius XI signed a Concordat – an agreement between pope and secular ruler on religious matters – with Hitler's government in 1933, eager to have another ally in resisting the Communist advance.

However, the Nazis made more uncomfortable bedfellows than the Italian Fascists, especially when the ugliness of their anti-semitism became evident to all. In 1937, the pope sent out a letter to be read in German churches. *Mit Brennender Sorge* ("With Burning Sorrow") contained a forthright condemnation of the Nazis' attacks on the Jewish population as well as their attempts to establish control over the Catholic Church within Germany.

STANDING BY?

The ensuing Holocaust was one of the darkest episodes of modern history, and the Church is one of many institutions that emerged with its reputation tarnished. Pope Pius XII, who succeeded Pius XI in 1939, has rightly been condemned. Broadly speaking, any good he did

was done by stealth; he was guarded in his public denunciations. He had a love for Germany and its culture (earlier in his career he had been Papal Nuncio – akin to a Vatican ambassador – in the country) and held Hitler's populism in deep disdain. Yet the uncomfortable fact remains that what really excited his moral ardour was the threat represented by Communism in the East. Nazism appeared to him to be the lesser of two evils.

While acknowledging Pius XII's attempts to relieve the plight of World War II's victims, including Jews, some critics charge him and the Catholic Church with a failure of moral leadership. Although there were heroic efforts made by individual priests and nuns, these critics saw the institution as being weak during the war. There was general approval within the Church when, on a visit to Jerusalem in 2000, Pope John Paul II made a heartfelt apology to the Jewish community.

AFTER THE WAR

Fascism had been all but vanquished by the end of World War II, though authoritarian governments endured for a few decades in Spain and Portugal. The Communists gained a strong hold in Eastern Europe, putting the Church there in a weak position. After the lessons of the Nazi era, the Church became outspoken critics of Communist oppression. Yet the Church's earlier links with Fascism meant some Western liberals remained sceptical that the Church's opposition to Communism was truly rooted in principle.

CATHOLICS UNDER COMMUNISM

The Soviet Union had been among the victors of World War II in 1945. With Communism's avowedly materialist principles, there was no place in the Communist scheme for the religious institution. In Russia itself, the established Church had been Orthodox, and its more independent-minded clergy was quickly hounded out by the Soviet authorities. A collaborationist congregation was created in its place. In the Ukraine, Romania and Czechoslovakia, Catholics were forced to join this officially sanctioned pseudo-Church in the tens of thousands, though many of the faithful continued their accustomed worship underground. In Poland, too, a "silent Church" clung on precariously in a mutually uncomfortable co-existence with the Communist state.

Above *Pope John Paul II visited the "Hill of Crosses" in 1993. On several previous occasions the Soviet authorities had attempted to remove this massive memorial to the Lithuanians' faith.*

Above *Pius XI and Mussolini agree upon the Lateran Treaty, as illustrated on the cover of the March 1929 edition of* Simplicissimus, *a liberal satirical magazine published in Germany.*

THE MODERNIZERS

THE 20TH-CENTURY POPES BROUGHT ABOUT RELIGIOUS CHANGES, AND THEIR REFORMS TRANSFORMED BOTH THE PROFILE OF THE CHURCH AND THE EXPERIENCE OF BEING CATHOLIC.

Though Pope Pius XII's pontificate is considered controversial now, in the 1950s his authority seemed impregnable. The pope who had brought the Church through World War II was naturally regarded with gratitude – his own personal role, and that of his Church, were as yet unexamined. In the Cold War climate, moreover, his uncompromising stand against Communism had won him respect well beyond the boundaries of his Church. As the first "media Pope", he became known to the world through newspaper pictures, television appearances and radio broadcasts. Within the Church,

his power was immense, even by papal standards, because he had surrounded himself with elderly and like-minded cardinals.

A CONVENTIONAL CHOICE

Pius XII's unabashedly conservative Church was a frustrating place for the young and the radical. When he died in 1958, some saw a chance to advance reforms. However the cardinals elected Angelo Roncalli, Patriarch of Venice, to serve as Pope John XXIII. The new pontiff was already 77 years of age, and in a long career he had shown himself a meek and unquestioning servant of his

Above Pope John XXIII blesses the crowd as he is carried in to officiate at the opening of the Second Vatican Council in 1962.

superiors. He was not the breath of fresh air the progressives had been wanting. All the evidence indicated that this was what had recommended him as Pius' replacement: he could be relied upon not to rock the boat.

The only issue that appeared to stir up any passion in the new pope was that of Christian unity. John mourned the gradual disintegration of Jesus' Church down the centuries and longed to build bridges with Catholicism's "separated brethren". Hence, he arranged meetings with England's Archbishop of Canterbury and had talks with representatives of other churches. This, though clearly a worthy cause, was hardly an exciting one. There was no immediate prospect of real change.

SECOND VATICAN COUNCIL

John XXIII's dream of Christian unity has remained elusive to this day. However, it was to have one very real and immediate consequence.

Left The scene inside St Peter's Basilica at one of the climactic moments of the Vatican Council. Pope John is enthroned beneath the baldacchino in the distance.

In 1962, the pope called together the Second Vatican Council, and from then onward the Catholic Church would never be the same.

Although some critics might see the changes as superficial, the Council re-emphasized (in some ways reinforced) the hierarchical nature of the Church. At the same time, it acknowledged the need for "top-down" directives to be supplemented by "bottom-up" reform. There was a new tone of openness, and a genuine receptiveness to criticism – lay observers, including women, were encouraged to be involved. Ordinary Catholics were to play a fuller part in the conduct of their faith, and there was to be a drive to make the Scriptures more widely available in the vernacular (people's own languages).

Measures were also taken to give lay Catholics a greater role in the Mass, and in the liturgy, too, there was to be a vernacular component. This process was completed under Pope Paul VI in 1969 when, along with a full transition to the vernacular, the practice of having the priest face the congregation when saying Mass was introduced. Previously, he had faced the altar, which was typically at the eastern end of the church, in the direction of Jerusalem (just as Muslims orientate themselves

Above In 1976 the reactionary Archbishop Marcel Lefebvre defiantly celebrated the traditional Tridentine Mass. This celebration has been encouraged by recent popes.

toward Mecca for daily prayers). Worshippers might feel a sense of wonder at being present for such a sacred ritual, but the new Catholicism wanted to draw parishoners in to make them feel involved.

THE BACKLASH

The Second Vatican Council was in many ways less far-reaching than has since been assumed. Issues that were already becoming controversial, such as contraception and divorce, were mostly unaddressed. Yet Catholicism now had a completely different feel, and Pope John XXIII's critics were in no doubt that there was substance in the changes.

The French Archbishop Marcel Lefebvre led a movement within the Church to return to the old ways and the Tridentine Mass, the Latin liturgy approved by the Council of Trent in the 16th century. Ultimately, he had to lead it from outside the Church. In 1988, he was excommunicated by Pope John Paul II (himself a conservative) after the archbishop consecrated four new bishops without official sanction.

POP RELIGION

The new-look Catholicism was taken up with great enthusiasm, its advent corresponding with that of the 1960s' pop culture. Guitars strummed, children acted out scriptural scenes and kisses of peace were freely exchanged at self-consciously informal "folk masses". This occurred nowhere more so than in Liverpool, England, home of the Beatles and, from 1967, of a thoroughly modern "Metropolitan Cathedral of Christ the King". Although shaped like a stylized crown with a spectacular stained-glass lantern, its circular ground plan was inclusive and democratic. Poet Roger McGough caught the mood with his poem of dedication: "O Lord on Thy New Liverpool Address". The poem has a reference to a priest wearing the cassock, concluding that if it is worn, "Then let's glimpse the jeans beneath".

Above In the modern design of the Liverpool Metropolitan Cathedral, stained-glass windows in the roof complement the colourful lighting that highlights the altar.

THE CHURCH MILITANT

THE CHRISTIAN'S DUTY TO HELP THE POOR IS CLEAR, BUT JUST HOW FAR THE CATHOLIC CHURCH SHOULD BE PREPARED TO GO WAS A QUESTION RAISED BY LIBERATION THEOLOGY.

In the 20th century, many South Americans lived in deprivation and from this arose Liberation Theology. It challenged the Church to make the spirit of the Beatitudes prevail by helping to overthrow established political and economic systems.

> *He has put down the mighty from*
> *their thrones and exalted those of*
> *low degree;*
> *He has filled the hungry with good*
> *things, and the rich he has sent*
> *empty away.*

This is one of the most remarkable passages in the gospels, from Mary's "Magnificat" (Luke 1:46–55).

Below Óscar Romero, Archbishop of San Salvador, was an advocate for the poor and victims of the country's civil war. He was killed in 1980 while celebrating Mass.

Our Lady's words celebrate the Christ who, for all his divine greatness, would keep company with prostitutes and lepers. He is the Christ who, for all his gentleness and his injunction to "turn the other cheek", was moved to violence by the sight of the moneychangers in the Temple. Further, he is the same Christ who, while summoning all to salvation, warned the rich young man that it is easier for a camel to pass through the eye of a needle than for a rich man to enter the kingdom of heaven.

MARX'S "GOSPEL"

Was Jesus not just a saviour but also a revolutionary? It is easy to see why many should have thought so, although it is harder to see what form a real-world Christian revolution would actually take. Especially given that, from the 18th century onward, the revolutionary orthodoxy has seen religion not as an aid to humanity but as a great part of the problem. Karl Marx, the renowned founder of Communism, notoriously saw religion as "the opium of the people" – though to put this into context, it should be noted that he was writing at a time that was lenient toward taking recreational drugs. His suggestion that religion was "the sigh of the oppressed creature", "the heart of a heartless world" showed at least a degree of sympathy for those who sought religious comfort. However, he saw that comfort as illusory.

Marx's later followers took a less nuanced view and settled into the conviction that religion was a cruel hoax designed to reconcile the people to their oppression. In the false hope of salvation hereafter, they

Above Russia's Bolsheviks expressed their antagonism to religion in no uncertain terms, shown in this 1930 print by Achille Beltrame, from the Italian newspaper La Domenica del Corriere.

would accept their lot on the earth: a dismal status quo was thus perpetuated. It was not difficult to find supporting evidence, not just in the sufferings of the world's poor but in the cosy relations between religious leaders and those who held great political power.

20TH-CENTURY RADICALS

That the Church might be letting down the poor had, of course, occurred to many in its history. Even in the 19th century, Pope Leo XIII had met the labour movement halfway with his *Rerum Novarum*, a letter that addressed the condition of the working classes. However, in the 1960s, radicalism was present around the world: this was a time of student sit-ins and anti-war demonstrations. African Americans (as well as Catholics in Protestant-dominated Northern Ireland) marched in the thousands to demand their civil rights; there were general strikes and student riots in France. The aims of the activists might have been vague, but the mood of rebellion was infectious, and many Catholics – the young in particular – felt they should be making their own contribution to the "struggle".

SOUTH AMERICAN LIBERALS

In Latin America, many millions were living in abject poverty while a helpless Church hierarchy looked on. By contrast, the leftists were able to report real achievements. In 1959, Fidel Castro, Che Guevara and their guerrilla army overthrew a repressive regime in Cuba. As proclaimed by Gustavo Gutiérrez, a priest from Peru, Liberation Theology called for a Catholicism that, not content with promising salvation in the next life, would do whatever it took to bring about revolutionary change in this one on earth.

There is no doubting the movement's sincerity in trying to improve the living conditions of the South

Below Pope John Paul II listened to a speech made by Daniel Ortega, leader of the Sandinistas, when the pontiff visited Nicaragua in 1983.

Above Many Catholics reasoned that Christ would have approved of the Nicaraguan Literacy Campaign run by the Sandinistas, but the Church took issue with the Sandinistas' wider aims.

American people – or, for a time, its real significance. Thousands of priests, nuns and lay Catholics were inspired by the Liberationist message, and several important

Catholic figures died for their beliefs. Archbishop Óscar Romero, who had led the popular opposition to El Salvador's oppressive military regime, was gunned down at the altar as he was saying Mass on 24 March 1980. Catholic clerics were well represented among the Sandinistas, who came to power in Nicaragua in the 1980s, including the famous poet-priest Ernesto Cardenal.

However, it was inevitable that the hierarchy of the Church would look askance at such developments, and not only through ingrained conservatism. Liberation Theology failed, as the Marxists would say, because of its contradictions. Despite certain common aims, the marriage of Communism and Christianity was always going to be problematic given the former's refusal to acknowledge the existence of a spiritual dimension. No one could see this more clearly than Pope John Paul II, who had experienced the tyranny that resulted when Communism set out to establish heaven on earth.

CAMILO TORRES

"If Christ were alive today, he would be a guerrilla," claimed Camilo Torres. Born in 1929, and a priest since the early 1950s, he had become disillusioned with the Church's failure to relieve the sufferings of the poor. Deciding that radical action was needed – even violent action if need be – he went as far as enlisting with his country's Marxist guerrillas. The ELN (*Ejército de Liberación Nacional*, or National Liberation Army) was engaged in open war with the Colombian government. However, Torres was killed in 1966 during his first operation with the ELN, becoming the Liberation Army's most famous martyr.

THE PEOPLE'S POPE

TODAY'S PAPACY HAS BEEN INFLUENCED LARGELY BY ONE PARTICULAR POPE, JOHN PAUL II – THE CHARISMATIC HOLY FATHER WHO BECAME A FATHER FIGURE FOR THE WORLD.

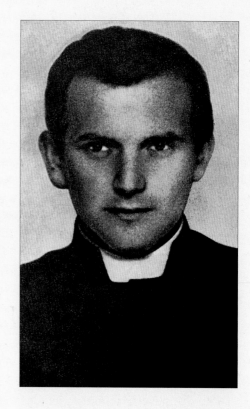

Although the final decades of the 20th century posed new challenges for the papacy, the development of modern technology had presented unprecedented opportunities as well. Pope Pius XII was recognized around the world thanks to television and press images. Pope Paul VI, the first pope of the jet age, was able to embark upon important foreign tours. However, where these previous popes had more or less uncomfortably gone through the motions as media performers, Pope John Paul II took to stardom with the utmost ease.

AN UNEXPECTED STAR

This was in some ways surprising. John Paul II was the first non-Italian pope in half a millennium and he was an intensely serious, scholarly man whose faith had a strongly private, even mystical aspect. The youngest of three children, he was born in Poland in 1920 and named Karol Wojtyla. He had been afflicted in childhood by the loss first of his mother and then of a much-loved elder brother. He'd lost all his family members before he became a priest. In youth, Wojtyla had been a brilliant student

Below A "rock-star" reputation was in many ways ill-suited to a deeply serious, spiritual man, but there was no denying John Paul II's popular appeal. Here he blesses the crowd at St Peter's in 1982.

Above At the time when Karol Wojtyla was a young seminarian in 1942, in Kraków, Poland, the city was under German occupation.

and, more broadly, an intellectual. He was fluent in a number of languages, was widely read, and wrote both poems and plays himself. Wojtyla loved sport, too (playing as a goalkeeper for a soccer team), and had a sociable side that he was able to draw on when making his public appearances as pope.

FREEDOM AND OBLIGATION

His early bereavements apart, the great formative experiences in Wojtyla's life were those of totalitarianism in two different forms. As a young seminarian he lived underground for months at the time of the Warsaw Uprising against the Nazis. He pursued his vocation under Communism and rose to the position of Archbishop of Kraków in a Church that had to keep silent if it was to continue to exist. Wojtyla emerged as an individualist – not an egotist, but a firm believer in the importance of the private voice of conscience. He could never accept that this should be subordinated either to the "collective will" of the Fascists or to the "dictatorship of the proletariat" of the Communists.

It might be expected that John Paul II had little time for Latin America's Liberation Theology. However, those who dismissed him as an old-fashioned reactionary were wide of the mark. He was generally more than ready to condemn the Western powers when the occasion demanded. He was forthright in denouncing the invasion of Iraq in 2003. He was also withering in his assessment of the capitalist system, which he considered was responsible for intolerable economic inequalities and which encouraged a consumer culture that exercised a tyranny all its own.

However, this prophet of freedom had managed to disappoint Western liberals by his refusal to give ground on such issues as contraception, divorce and same-sex marriage. He could never accept that human sexuality could diverge from Church norms. Likewise he resisted calls for married clergy and women priests, reforms that might seem commonsensical to others. He argued that the Church was not just an institution to be brought up to date like any other, but one that was bound by laws lain down by Christ himself.

WIDESPREAD POPULARITY

It was gall to his more progressive critics that John Paul II was so unrestrainedly loved, not just among Catholics but beyond the Church. This was attributable not only to his immense charisma but also to his instinctive gifts as a communicator. He visited 129 different countries, taking his papacy to ordinary people around the world. Wherever he went, he kissed airport runways, cuddled babies, showed himself to vast crowds in his "popemobile" and said Mass to millions at a time. Conservative as his attitudes may have been, his belief that ordinary Catholics should have access to his papacy was entirely in the spirit of the Second Vatican Council.

THE SAINT MAKER

John Paul II's enthusiasm for canonizing saints has been derided (it was said that he beatified more men and women than all his predecessors put together, but incomplete records make this hard to establish). This may speak of an old-fashioned view of Christian heroism, but at the same time it also suggests John Paul II had an utterly modern understanding of media culture. Not since the early Middle Ages had there been such an interest in icons – even if the new ones were singers, models and sports stars. In giving the peoples of the world new saints, the pope was giving them exemplars from their own cultures whose courage and commitment they could aspire to and emulate.

Most of all, his supporters looked up to John Paul II himself, beyond any doubt one of the most popular popes in modern history. This was the man who, as Ireland's young people chorused in their hundreds of thousands at the open-air Mass in Dublin's Phoenix Park in 1979, appeared to have "the whole world in his hands".

Above Pope John Paul II was identified with Solidarnosc ("Solidarity"), the free trade union that helped bring down Communism in Poland and beyond.

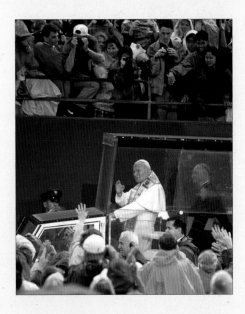

Above John Paul II rides in his popemobile during a tour of the United States in 1995. Everywhere he went he drew enormous and ecstatic crowds.

REACHING OUT TO OTHER FAITHS

IN THE 20TH AND 21ST CENTURIES, THE CATHOLIC CHURCH HAS BEEN EXCHANGING VIEWS WITH OTHER CHRISTIAN COMMUNITIES – AS WELL AS WITH LEADERS OF THE DIFFERENT GREAT WORLD FAITHS.

With the exception of Poland, the Christians of Eastern Europe have historically looked to the Orthodox Church rather than to Rome. The Polish people have always defined themselves against their Russian neighbours (who were often also their oppressors). Their Catholicism was a matter not just of religious faith but of patriotic pride. Yet the Poles were Slavs as well, and Pope John Paul II, who always remembered his Polish origins, was mindful of that ethnic inheritance. The desire for reconciliation with the Eastern Church ran as deep in his heart as, so many years before, it had run in that of Pope John XXIII.

Above An ecumenical service at Paris' Notre-Dame Cathedral is celebrated by leading Catholic prelates alongside an Orthodox metropolitan bishop (centre) and a Protestant minister (right).

A DIVISIVE DIPLOMAT?

In more than a quarter of a century as pope, John Paul II accomplished much for the Catholic Church, but his particular dream of reconciliation had to be deferred. It has been suggested by his critics that the pope himself had created part of the problem: his own instinctive authoritarianism rendered impossible the soft approach that would have been required. It was the same, some critics believe, with his approach to the Church of England, whose doctrine was not so far removed from that of Rome's. Although the decision of the Anglican Church to ordain women priests caused dissension between the two communities, liberal critics have claimed it was a matter in which a less stubborn pope would have found some type of accordance.

On the other hand, John Paul II's charisma propelled Christianity back on to the front page of many of the big newspapers, reminding jaded Westerners that religion could still hold relevance in a modern society. Elsewhere, adherents of the other world religions could find evidence

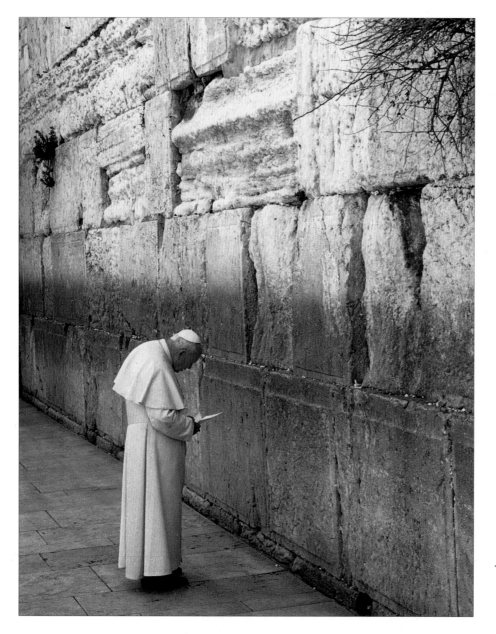

Left In 2000, Pope John Paul II visited Jerusalem and the Western ("Wailing") Wall, where he begged forgiveness on behalf of the Catholic Church for centuries of anti-semitic persecution.

in his energy and enthusiasm that the Christian West was not entirely sunk in cynicism and apathy.

Ultimately, his love of humanity – and the love that humanity felt for John Paul II – made him a more effective bridge-builder than anyone might have expected. His impetuous style certainly helped his cause. A more cautious man might never have dreamt of making his historic (and, at the time, controversial) visit to the Auschwitz concentration camp in 1979. The first-ever papal visit to Israel followed in 2000, where John Paul II's heartfelt apology for centuries of Christian persecution of Jews opened the way to a new era of discussion and co-operation.

COMMON CAUSE

There are, of course, limits to how much progress can be made between different communities. The Catholic creed professes that it is the "one" true Church. John Paul II's successor, Pope Benedict XVI, maintains that, while other Christian Churches and non-Christian religions may offer aspects of the truth and may thereby be instruments of salvation, the

Above In 2006, Pope Benedict XVI met the Orthodox Patriarch in Istanbul, Turkey. It was his first official visit to a Muslim country.

whole truth is to be found only in Catholicism. Although working hard to find points of contact, he has left no doubt that he sees the world's other faiths as fundamentally misdirected, for all their undoubted honesty and zeal.

If anything unifies the world's religions, as far as Benedict XVI is concerned, it is their rejection of modern secularism and the culture it has fostered. The consumerist irreligion, he argues, says that everyone should live as he or she chooses, without reference to any higher laws. Believers of every faith have not just the right but also a duty to make a common cause against this "dictatorship of relativism".

THE POPES AND THE IMAMS

When the Ayatollah Khomeini died in 1989, Pope John Paul II called for his achievements to be reflected upon "with great respect and deep thought". There have been more effusive eulogies, perhaps, but the pope's was still strikingly cordial in the circumstances. John Paul II had refused to lend his authority to other Christian leaders who earlier that year had expressed sympathy with the leader of Islam in Iran. The Ayatollah had issued a *fatwa* – a religious decree – calling for the killing of author Salman Rushdie for writing his novel, *The Satanic Verses*, which was said to be blasphemous. The years that followed would find John Paul II continuing his dialogue with Islam's leaders, and in 2000 he became the first pope to pray in a Muslim mosque.

Contact with the Muslim world has continued during the papacy of Benedict XVI, despite the offence caused by his quotation from an anti-Islamic text by a medieval writer in a talk at the University of Regensburg, Germany, in 2006. Relations soon recovered, and in 2008 Muslim scholars were invited to a joint seminar with Catholic thinkers held in Rome.

Right Pope Benedict XVI clasps hands with the head of Turkey's Religious Affairs Directorate after talks about Catholic–Islamic relations and terrorism.

NEW CHALLENGES

THE NUMBER OF CATHOLICS DECREASED IN MANY WESTERN SOCIETIES DURING THE LAST CENTURY. THE INFLUENCES OF CAPITALISM AND CONSUMERISM ARE PERHAPS PARTLY TO BLAME.

In recent years, the Church has seen its support ebb away in the advanced industrialized societies. In the mostly Protestant and Anglo-Saxon countries of Europe, Catholicism was long regarded as a peasant creed that was associated with "backward" regions: southern Italy, Spain, remote parts of France – and pre-eminently with Ireland. Yet Christ had always loved the poor, and the poor had always reciprocated, offering their sons and daughters into his service.

CHANGING SOCIETIES

When a previously poor region begins to thrive, no one mourns the passing of mass poverty – however, economic development often brings

Below Sardinians process through their village as they have done for so many centuries, but can Catholicism offer more than history and local colour?

problems as well as benefits. In some places, historical tendencies can be traced. For example, that most Spaniards say they no longer bother to go to Church may reflect resentments dating back to the Franco era and beyond. Italy is another country in which the Church's most visible adherents recall an authoritarian past. Although comparatively few Italians have rejected the Church outright, it is for many now no more than a part of their cultural rituals – baptisms, marriages and funerals – and is otherwise ignored.

Increased wealth has resulted in population shifts, which have created their own impact. The old overcrowded communities of the cities have been dispersed to suburbs, where more secular attitudes have prevailed. One example can be seen in St Anthony's parish in Jersey City in New Jersey, USA. In the 1950s, a

Above Falling levels of attendance and reduced collections have sent parochial incomes tumbling, a formidable challenge for the Church in the new century.

typical Sunday Mass was attended by around 10,000 Christians; today, less than 300 people turn out.

The problem has partly been that there is so much more to do at weekends for families with cars and money to spend – but who have precious little quality time together. Although Christ was clear in his insistence that material wealth was not spiritually enriching, Catholics are not immune to the attractions of material consumerism. Nor are they immune to the consumeristic attitude that encourages people toward the various spiritual options available these days, from yoga and meditation to New Age practices.

A DECLINE IN CLERGY

Something is clearly wrong with the Church when Ireland is running out of priests. In 2007, 166 priests died, while only 9 new ordinations were made. The priests constitute an ageing population: in the next generation, their numbers are bound to fall further. This is because as

societies prosper, life expectancy increases and families feel more secure. With this security, families tend to have fewer children. This has happened in many industrialized countries, regardless of religious culture. It has certainly occurred in Ireland, which has enjoyed great economic success in recent decades. The youths who would once have gone into the Church no longer exist in such abundance, and they have other life choices and distractions. Ireland faces the kind of administrative adjustments with which Catholics in the United States and Great Britain have become familiar, with small groups of priests and lay helpers taking charge of sprawling parish clusters.

NEW OPPORTUNITIES

The difficulties can hardly be denied, yet given the age of the institution, talk of doom and gloom is misplaced. In 2,000 years, Catholicism has come through many more challenging times. Despite all its claims for apostolic continuity, the Church has shown the capacity to reinvent itself again and again down the centuries.

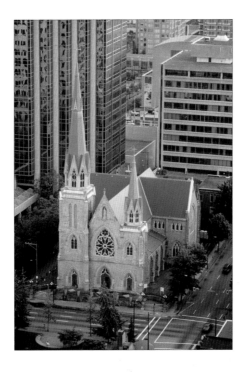

Above Once Vancouver's Holy Rosary Cathedral dominated the skyline. Today the Christian message risks being lost amid the pressures and distractions of modern life.

Below A businessman finds comfort confiding with his priest in the confessional, something that many middle-class Westerners have decided is not for them.

That it will have to do so again has become clear, with its great structures perhaps learning to accommodate a more administratively flexible, "small is beautiful" community-based system. There could be scope for lay Catholics to play a far greater role in their local communities, which has been an official goal ever since the time of the Second Vatican Council.

THE SINS OF THE FATHERS

The Church has admitted it has not always been worthy of its members' trust. Catholics have been rocked in recent years by a series of allegations of sexual impropriety on the part of members of its clergy. From the mid-1980s onward, a series of scandals in the United States, Ireland, Australia and other countries focused attention on alleged sexual abuse of young people by diocesan priests and members of the religious orders. In some cases the Church hierarchy was accused of attempting to cover up accusations, and even of moving sexual abusers away from one scandal and into a position where he or she could offend again.

In the United States, the Church made financial settlements of $2 billion to victims of sex abuse in the past 60 years. In the largest settlement, in 2007, the Archdiocese of Los Angeles paid $660 million (£324 million) to settle 508 cases of alleged sexual abuse.

Pope Benedict XVI has departed from this shameful stance. He has gone out of his way to meet members of victims' groups and to express his shame and sorrow on behalf of the Catholic Church.

FACING COMPETITION

IN TODAY'S SOUTH AMERICA AND AFRICA, THE CATHOLIC CHURCH IS BEING CHALLENGED BY OTHER CREEDS THAT MAY APPEAR MORE ENERGETIC, AND MORE IMMEDIATELY RELEVANT TO PEOPLE'S LIVES.

As recently as a generation or so ago, South America was one of the bastions of world Catholicism, a region consecrated to Christ and the Virgin Mary, utterly loyal to the pope. The idea of a Protestant Brazil or Chile was practically unthinkable. Catholicism was in the culture, in the air the people breathed.

Nevertheless, Pentecostalism has spread like wildfire throughout the region in recent decades. This new form of Christianity first appeared in the United States at the beginning of the 20th century. Rooted in a range of different Protestant churches, Pentecostalism is a faith of enthusiastic evangelism that demands that the believer be born again in the Holy Spirit – just like the disciples at the first Pentecost.

AN ALTERNATIVE CREED

The explanations given for such a quick expansion in South America vary. Pentecostalism is strongly emotional in its emphasis, which offers the individual Christian a spiritual (or, perhaps, merely psychological) high. Catholicism has always tended to distrust this type of extravagant emotionalism. Yet the importance of the ecstatic sense of self-worth it brings to the Pentecostalist convert can hardly be exaggerated. However, in some ways, it is the logical outcome of the attentions given by dedicated missionaries, hard at work for decades among poor people who may well feel that their traditional religious leaders have often taken them for granted.

Some South Americans have pointed to the remoteness of a conservative clergy, reluctant to involve itself with the problems of the masses. Others have seen the failure of ideologically driven Liberation Theology to see the poor as real people. Either way, the Protestant missionaries have made huge strides.

By 2005, an estimated 13 per cent of Latin America's huge population had embraced Pentecostalism; that is, 75 million out of 560 million people. This overall figure conceals the fact that there are areas in which Catholicism has been in headlong retreat. In some of Rio de Janeiro's poorest districts, Protestant chapels now outnumber Catholic churches in a ratio of seven to one.

Above A worshipper is energetically welcomed to a Pentecostal congregation in Rio de Janeiro. Latin Americans have been flocking to the new chapels in their thousands.

A PLACE OF SAFETY

In some areas, politics have certainly played a part. For example, through the many long years of vicious state repression in Guatemala, courageous priests and nuns made a stand against the military, which also made them targets. The conspicuously apolitical stand of (overwhelmingly American) Pentecostalist missionaries made their church a refuge from the violence and turmoil of the time. Middle-class Guatemalans, who were instinctively uneasy at the thought of any association with the leftists, have turned to Pentecostalism in large numbers. Today about 20 per cent of the population now considers itself Protestant; that figure rises to almost one-third among the urban middle class.

COMPETITION FROM ISLAM

In West and Central Africa, the main competition is not from Pentecostalism but from Islam. This is not surprising since Islam's history in the region is at least as long as Catholicism's. Muhammad's faith was first brought south across the Sahara by

Left Pentecostalism is not just for the poor. These bourgeois Brazilians have crossed the ocean to be baptized in the sacred waters of the River Jordan.

desert traders; nomadic tribes thereafter carried it farther to the south. A kind of frontier has long existed across this part of the continent, with – broadly speaking – Islam to the north, Christianity to the south. In reality, this border has been highly porous, with any number of communities to be found on the "wrong" side, and with close contacts, even family relations, between the two.

MODERN RADICALS

Peaceful co-existence has until recent history been maintained, but the emergence of Islamic fundamentalism has altered the dynamics. With its agenda being as much political as religious, radical Islamic groups have engaged in direct competition for converts with Catholicism, and their evangelization has to some extent paid off.

Conflict has flared as well, most famously in the Sudan, whose Islamic Khartoum government has for years been at war with the Catholic communities of the south. Elsewhere, too, there has been trouble, most notably perhaps, in parts of Nigeria, where attempts have been made to introduce the full rigour of Sharia law.

RESPONDING TO CHANGE

Ultimately, the only way for the Catholic Church to respond to such changes will be to change itself, while staying true to the central principals of so many centuries. Rome may remain its centre, but a Eurocentric Church will hardly be able to provide Catholicism with the worldwide guidance and support it needs. The ethnic mixture of the hierarchy has already been transformed by the addition of new African, Asian and

South American faces, and more changes may occur in the years to come. It would seem strange indeed if the first great world religion were unable to meet the challenge of globalization. Despite its past difficulties, the Catholic Church appears well placed to face the future.

Right Théodore-Adrien Sarr celebrates Mass after being made a cardinal by Pope Benedict XVI in 2007. Senegalese Muslims also joined in acclaiming the new Cardinal.

Right Followers of Islam gather to pray outside the main mosque in Asmara, Eritrea. Islam is on the rise across much of North and Central Africa.

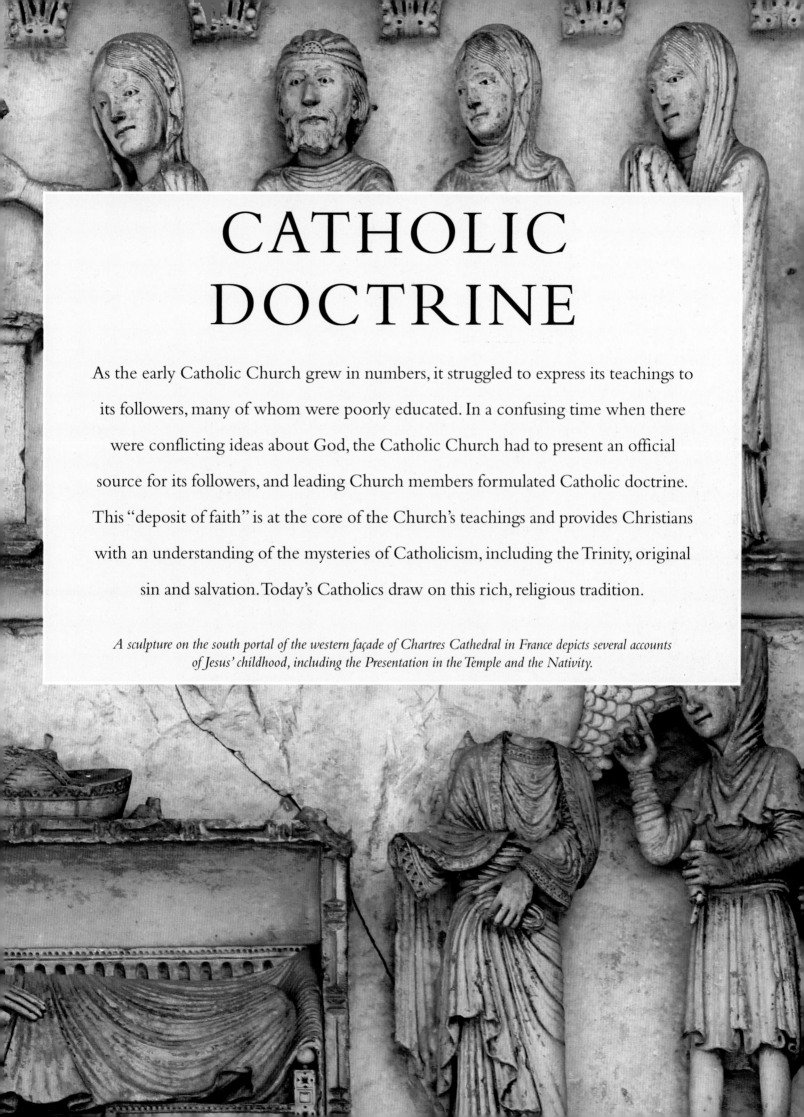

CATHOLIC DOCTRINE

As the early Catholic Church grew in numbers, it struggled to express its teachings to its followers, many of whom were poorly educated. In a confusing time when there were conflicting ideas about God, the Catholic Church had to present an official source for its followers, and leading Church members formulated Catholic doctrine. This "deposit of faith" is at the core of the Church's teachings and provides Christians with an understanding of the mysteries of Catholicism, including the Trinity, original sin and salvation. Today's Catholics draw on this rich, religious tradition.

A sculpture on the south portal of the western façade of Chartres Cathedral in France depicts several accounts of Jesus' childhood, including the Presentation in the Temple and the Nativity.

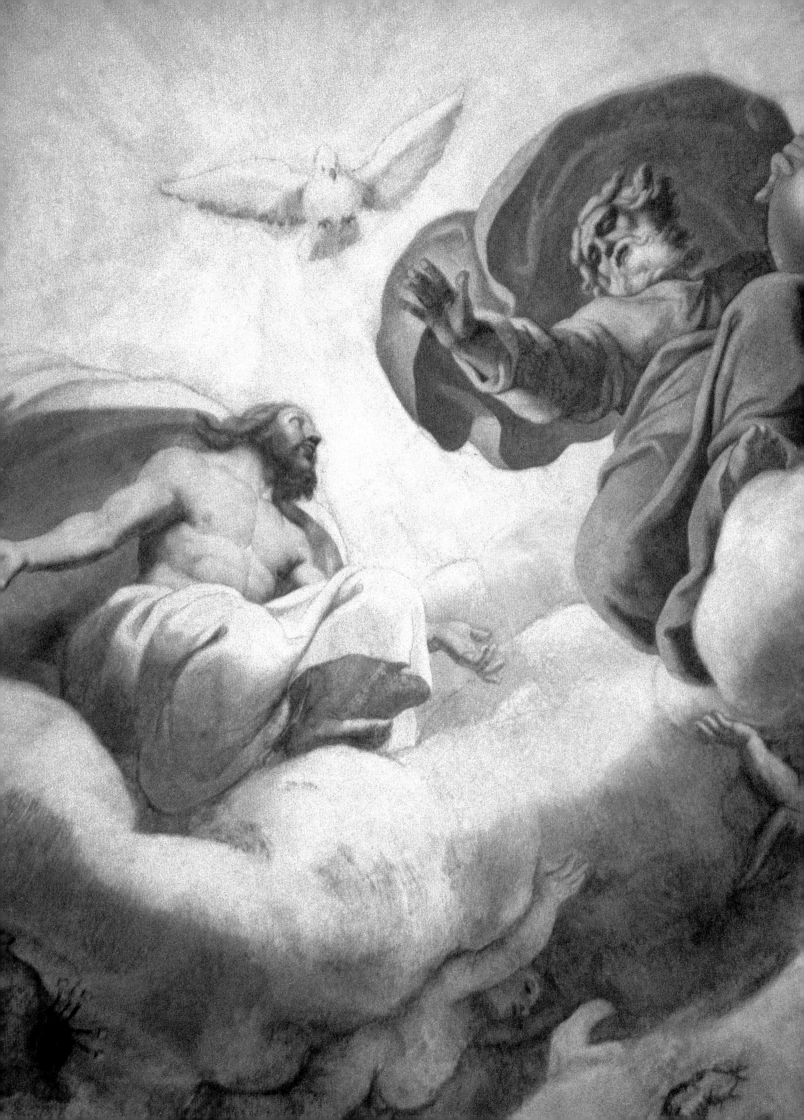

THE MYSTERY OF FAITH

As the nascent Catholic Church began to develop its doctrines in the first centuries after Christ's death, it was faced with many challenges, including persecution, the difficulty of communicating abstruse concepts, such as the Trinity, to an uneducated and superstitious populace, and the constant threat of heretical beliefs and teachings. Such challenges forced early ecclesiastics and Catholic theologians to be vigilant and proactive as they formulated and disseminated Church doctrine.

The early Church councils acted as both the universities and the senates of the Church to standardize beliefs and promulgate them as law. The early Church was blessed with a number of brilliant early thinkers such as Sts Augustine, Athanasius, Jerome and Thomas Aquinas, whose devotion to understanding Christ and his teachings, as well as to the development of the Church, was absolute. As Catholic beliefs developed into officially disseminated teachings and practice, they became part of the "deposit of faith", the vast bulwark of accepted Church tradition that had its genesis in the earliest oral apostolic teachings, the canons of the New Testament and in the decisions and decrees of the Church councils.

At the core of Church doctrine are the Trinitarian nature of God, the Incarnation of Christ as God-Man, his real presence in the Eucharist, his suffering and death, and his resurrection for our salvation. All other Catholic beliefs and teaching are nourished from the deep wellspring of these particular articles of faith.

Above The Eastern European influence on the early Roman Church is evident in this Byzantine-style, mid-8th-century Russian illustration of the First Ecumenical Council of Nicaea, which convened in Turkey in AD 325.

Left The three persons of the Trinity – Christ, the Holy Spirit (in the form of a dove) and God – are the focus of this 17th-century painting by Pierre Mignard. Christ's bare chest alludes to his crucifixion, when he was stripped of his garments.

GOD IN THREE PERSONS

CATHOLICS BELIEVE IN THE TRINITY OF GOD, OFTEN TRADITIONALLY PORTRAYED WITH THE FATHER AS A REGAL OLDER MAN, THE SON AS A YOUNG, SORROWFUL MAN AND THE HOLY SPIRIT AS A DOVE OR FLAME.

Belief in the Trinity is an absolutely central tenet of the Roman Catholic faith, but it is also an item of doctrine that has a controversial past among Christians. It is a paradox that is difficult to understand rationally. The doctrine states that there is only one eternal, almighty God, who exists without beginning or end, and who is the creator of all that exists. However, there are three "persons" – the Father, the Son and the Holy Spirit – existing "one in being" as that God. The three are equal and eternal, each existing without beginning or end.

THE SAME BUT DIFFERENT

As stated in the Nicene Creed, which deals specifically with the nature of Christ, the Son is said to be "eternally begotten" of the Father, but "not made", emphasizing that there was never a time when he did not exist and that he partakes of the substance of the Father even while he is another person. The Holy Spirit "proceeds" from the Father and the Son – this is an active verb that emphasizes a continuous being, a kind of eternally advancing horizon of existence. The Greek word for

Above In this 13th-century French image, the "Creator of heaven and earth" takes the measure of his raw materials with a compass. This image may have influenced William Blake's 1794 Ancient of Days.

proceed emphasizes "movement out of". The Greek word *perichoresis*, meaning "permeation without confusion", is also used by theologians to express how the persons of the Trinity interpenetrate each other, yet remain distinct.

DIVINE BEINGS

The three persons of the Trinity are perceived by most Catholics as having particular, appropriate divine aspects. The Father is the Creator, the maker of all and the interlocutor with Adam and Eve. The Son's defining attribute is that he was made man. He demonstrated the infinite depth of divine love by becoming human, walking among us and acceding to an agonizing sacrifice of his simultaneously human and divine self as an

Left The Catholic mystery of the Trinity is shown in this 15th-century European painting. They are intimately connected yet distinct, with God the Father holding his crucified Son, while the Holy Spirit as a dove rests on Christ's halo.

offering to re-open the possibility of man's freedom from Adam and Eve's original sin.

The Holy Spirit, as implied by his name, is the only divine persona without a human form in traditional Catholic iconography. He is usually artistically represented as either a dove or a tongue of flame, the form in which, ten days after Christ's ascension to heaven, he descended to inspire the apostles as teachers of the Word of God (the day now known as Whitsunday, or more commonly in Catholic theology, Pentecost). Metaphorically, in his role as bringer of grace and an inspirer of wisdom, he is spoken of as a mighty wind or as the inspiration or breath of God. He is also known as the "Paraclete", or advocate, which refers to his role as a spiritual teacher or guide.

A CONTROVERSIAL TIME

The doctrine of the Trinity was fiercely debated by the bishops and Church fathers in the early days of Christianity. The 4th-century controversy surrounding Arianism — a heresy that claimed the Son of God

Above The Holy Spirit is the only person of the Trinity who never speaks, but we can almost hear the whirr of his wings in this graceful French c. 1490 illumination by Jean Colombe.

Above At Jesus' baptism, the heavens opened, the Holy Spirit descended and the Father spoke, "This is my beloved son…" Giovanni Guercino's 17th-century painting shows a powerful God the Father.

was not truly God but was created by God — in particular, served as a spur to bishops to set and define the immanent divinity of the three persons of the one God as a crucial and defining Catholic doctrine.

Arianism argued that Christ was inferior to the Father in that "there was a then when he was not" — in other words, there was a time when Christ did not exist. Christ was described as the first of the Father's created beings, not "eternally begotten", but simply "begotten", thus denigrating his divine nature as a being without beginning or end.

The Council of Nicaea was convened in AD 325 by Constantine, Emperor of Rome, in large part to counteract Arianism. The Nicene Creed that was formulated at the council, then finalized at the Council of Constantinople in AD 381, is still the familiar creed recited in Roman Catholic churches today.

Even more contentious was the relationship of the Holy Spirit to the Father and the Son. The Nicene Creed of AD 325 merely stated "we believe in the Holy Spirit". In AD 381, the "filioque" ("and the son") clause was added, stating that the Holy Spirit "proceeds from the Father and the Son". It was disagreement about this "dual procession" doctrine that caused the Eastern Christian Church to split from the Roman Church in the Great Schism of 1054.

THE TRINITY

The term "Trinity", from the Latin noun *trinitas*, meaning "three at once", does not occur in the Bible, but the gospels do contain references to the divinity of the Father, Son and Holy Spirit. For example, after Christ rose from the dead, he bid the apostles to "go forth and teach all nations, baptizing them in the name of the Father, and of the Son and of the Holy Spirit" (Matthew 28:20). The term Trinity in relation to the Godhead was first used by Tertullian, the 3rd-century son of a Roman centurion and an early convert to Christianity, who was a prolific writer and contributor to evolving Christian theology in the early centuries after Christ's death.

CHRIST THE REDEEMER

IN CATHOLIC THEOLOGY, ORIGINAL SIN IS THE METAPHORICAL "STAIN"
ALL HUMAN BEINGS ARE BORN WITH — AND IT IS THE REASON WHY
CHRIST SACRIFICED HIMSELF TO REDEEM THE HUMAN RACE.

Original sin is inherited, like a genetic disease, from the first man – our ancestor Adam – and all humans have inherited it. The Catholic catechism says, "The whole human race is in Adam". This does not mean that original sin is a sinful action of Adam that we imitate or recreate. It is, rather, our tragic patrimony, meaning that we have been born deprived of the original grace that was God's initial endowment to our ancestral parents, Adam and Eve. The poet John Milton (although not a Catholic himself) expressed it well:

> Of man's first disobedience,
>   and the Fruit
> Of that Forbidden Tree,
>   whose mortal taste
> Brought Death into the World,
>   and all our woe…

FORBIDDEN FRUIT

The actual sin, described in Genesis, was eating the fruit of the Tree of Knowledge of Good and Evil, the only tree in paradise prohibited by God to Adam and Eve. Eve was tempted by Satan in the guise of a serpent, who told her she would be like a god and understand good and evil. Adam then took the fruit from Eve and ate as well.

As a result of Adam and Eve's wilfully disobedient act, Catholicism teaches that we are born fallen, with our souls deprived of sanctifying grace, not fully and freely open and receptive to God's love. The fall of the first man infused not just humanity but the entire world – the originally harmonious world made by God became discordant. Instead of every type of fruit tree, God prophesied that the earth would bring forth thorns and thistles. Instead of being blissfully unaware of their nakedness, Adam and Eve perceived it as shameful and hid. Original sin set man against himself and the earth – first intended to be our garden of delight – against man.

Catholics believe that death became part of life with original sin. As a direct response to Adam and Eve's disobedience, God pronounced, "In the sweat of thy face shalt thou eat bread till thou return to the earth out of which thou wast taken: for dust thou art, and into dust thou shalt return" (Genesis 3:19).

Left Eve, having already eaten from the forbidden fruit, colludes with the serpent, who places the apple in her waiting hand as she draws Adam close. This detail is from a 16th-century German triptych.

Above Because of original sin, death gained power over us and took us from the garden of paradise. In Evelyn de Morgan's 1890 The Angel of Death, *death has wings.*

BODY AND SOUL

Although the concept of original sin already existed, it was first defined as a doctrine in the 5th century AD by St Augustine of Hippo. Augustine had lived a dissolute life before his conversion from Manichaeism (a type of gnostic religion) to Catholicism, so he was particularly alert to man's sinful nature. The Second Council of Orange in AD 529 specified that while death of the body was the punishment for original sin, death of the soul was the sin itself.

Death of the soul is emphasized because original sin is responsible for destroying our first intimate union with God. Adam and Eve's action deprived them of the original grace that was their birthright, and this loss introduced the tendency toward corruption into the world, as though the previously perfect fabric of Creation was rent with a fatal flaw, weakening it so that it easily became tattered. Original sin is also responsible for allowing our

CHRIST'S CRUCIAL SACRIFICE

At both the Council of Orange in AD 529 and the Council of Trent in 1546, the Church fathers defined the doctrine of justification. This emphasized that our redemption was not possible without Christ's mediation, or the merit that he obtained for us by his obedient death, to make restitution for our disobedience. Redemption is not possible by human good works and good behaviour alone. The Church fathers pronounced anathema (a kind of doctrinal condemnation) on anyone who believed humans could save themselves without Christ – specifically, Pelagius, an Irish monk whose heretical beliefs triggered the Council of Orange's pronouncements.

Pelagius believed we could save ourselves by our good works and he de-emphasized the role of God's Grace. The Catholic Church teaches that we need the grace that Christ first obtained for us by his sacrifice. Additionally, we also require the sanctifying grace that fills our soul in baptism, the educating aid of the Holy Spirit that comes to us through participation in the sacraments, and continuous obedience to God's commandments in order to avoid damnation and find eternal life with God.

Above Pelagius (AD 355–425) *believed that original sin was not every man's inheritance, and that man could save himself without Christ's sacrifice.*

inferior worldly and carnal desires, known as "concupiscence", to prevail over our reason.

SEEKING REDEMPTION

The counterpoint to this tragic fall from grace is our ability to essentially re-enact our first parents' temptation and choice – but this time, individually, because we still retain the free will with which they were endowed by God, to choose to turn toward God, or *conversio ad deum*. The possible redemption of each individual is a direct result of the offering Christ made of himself to the Father: as man out of his own free will chose to turn away and reject God's love (*adversio ad deum*) and instead act to satisfy his own egotistical desire, Christ out of his own free will did not resist actual torture on the Cross to pay the price to redeem man. The Latin word *redemptio* is related to Hebrew and Greek words meaning "a ransom price".

Right Our first defence against original sin comes through the grace of baptism. In this late 16th-century painted stone, St Augustine, once a libertine, and his illegitimate son Adeodatus are baptized by St Ambrose.

THE EUCHARIST

LIKE THE HOLY TRINITY, THE DOCTRINE OF THE EUCHARIST, WHICH
CELEBRATES JESUS' LAST SUPPER WITH HIS APOSTLES, IS ONE OF THE
MOST IMPORTANT, CENTRAL BELIEFS OF THE CATHOLIC CHURCH.

The Roman Catholic catechism calls the Eucharist "the source and summit of the Christian life". Most Catholics would probably agree that the Eucharist is a particularly special doctrine. It is one that each practising Catholic is introduced to at an early age, and it continues through the years, becoming a customary thread of the faith drawing together generations of families.

Almost any person brought up in the Catholic faith will have specific memories of their first Holy Communion, because it is a joyful day that has delightful worldly celebrations

Above The most sacred moment of the Mass is the consecration, when the bread and wine are transubstantiated into the body and blood of Christ, as seen in this 15th/16th-century image by Giovanni di Giuliano Boccardi.

surrounding it. It is also the first time that a child is called to participate in one of the central mysteries of the faith, the Eucharist. This is a particularly special occasion, when the child is first asked to try to extend his or her perception to encompass a numinous dimension of the infinite by participation in a very specific individual act.

THE LORD'S SUPPER
The word "Eucharist" comes from the Greek *eucharistein*, or "grateful, thankful". It is the name given to the communion that has been repeated through the centuries at every Catholic Mass. Its origin lies in the Last Supper, the story of which is engraved on the consciousness of every Catholic. The Last Supper is described in almost the same words in Matthew 26:26–28, Mark 14:22–24 and Luke 22:17–20. Celebrating the paschal meal with his apostles, and well aware that he was about to be betrayed and put to death, Christ took bread, broke it and offered it to his apostles, saying, "Take

THE LAST SUPPER
Leonardo da Vinci's renowned mural painting, *The Last Supper* (1495–8), depicts the paschal supper at which Christ broke bread and offered wine. The painting dramatizes the moment described in the gospels when Jesus, "troubled in spirit", announces "Amen, amen, I say to you, one of you shall betray me." The disciples therefore looked upon one another, doubting of whom he spoke.

Despite the press of the apostles around the table and the apparent furor caused by Christ's words, there are two figures who remain alone with their thoughts. Judas' hand hovers slightly above a dish, illustrating Christ's words, "he that dippeth his hands with me in the dish, he shall betray me". All the other apostles lean toward Christ or toward each other, exchanging glances. Judas leans away from Christ without touching anyone else, and while the others look at Christ beseechingly, Judas simply stares. Christ's arms extend down with his palms turned upwards in a gesture that is one of submission, yet he also seems to be gathering power from the heavens toward which his hands open. Although Christ's gaze is directed away from Judas, the entire side of his face is angled toward him, almost as if he were offering a cheek to be kissed – and, of course, it is with a kiss on Jesus' cheek that Judas will betray him to his captors on the following day.

Above Da Vinci's late 15th-century painting The Last Supper *not ony recalls the last meal between Jesus and his apostles but is also full of symbolism, referring to the momentous event that will occur when Judas betrays Christ.*

ye, and eat. This is my body." Taking the chalice, he gave thanks, and gave it to them, saying, "Drink ye all of this. For this is my blood of the new testament, which shall be shed for many unto remission of sins." During this supper, Christ spoke the simple words, "Do this in memory of me." This quiet command is the genesis of the Eucharistic sacrifice around which a great world religion has been formed. In allusion to the Last Supper, communion is sometimes called the Lord's Supper.

Christ prefigured these actions before his death when he fed a crowd of people that had come to hear him preach and who were hungry, yet with little food. In the hands of Jesus, on that day the five loaves and two fishes available miraculously became enough to feed the multitude. When preaching in the synagogue at Capharnaum soon after performing this miracle, Jesus said, "I am the bread of Life…. He that eateth my flesh and drinketh my blood have everlasting life: and I will raise him up in the last day."

BREAD AND WINE

Through the centuries, the central act of Mass has been the priest's consecration of wheaten bread and grape wine into Christ. The Council of Trent in 1546 defined the Eucharist as "the Body and Blood, together with the Soul and Divinity of our Lord Jesus Christ, and therefore the whole Christ, is truly, really and substantially contained in the sacrament of the Holy Eucharist."

Various theologians over the years have attempted to define the Holy Eucharist as a symbol of the body and blood of Christ (16th-century Zwinglians), or as a dynamic trans-

Right A literal interpretation of the doctrine that the host is transubstantiated into the entirety of the body and blood of Christ can be seen in this 14th-century painting by Ugolino di Prete Ilario.

ferral of the efficacy of Christ's body and blood to the souls of the elect at the moment of reception of the host (Calvinists), but the Church declared all such limitations on the definition of the Eucharist to be heresies.

THE CONSECRATION

Catholic doctrine is specific regarding the holiest moment of Mass. This is known as the consecration, when the priest repeats the words of Christ at the Last Supper. "This is my body" is spoken when the priest raises the

Left The first Holy Communion is an inspiring milestone in the lives of Catholic children. In this late 19th-century painting by Carl Frithjof Smith, a young girl proudly wears her new crucifix.

bread and "This is my blood" is uttered with the wine, and at each and every Mass a miracle occurs and the bread and wine are changed, or "transubstantiated", into the body and blood of Christ. How the change occurs when the priest speaks the words is a mystery known only to God. What is changed is the entire substance – the being – of the bread and wine into the entirety of the substance, or being, of Christ, with only the "species", or appearance, of bread and wine remaining.

The Church holds that, in essence and in actuality (not symbolically), Christ is present in the Eucharist. In order to skirt an association with cannibalism, the Church does not usually emphasize (but it would not deny) that Christ is physically present (like the person sitting next to you in Church, for example), but that he is substantially present, which is known as the "Real Presence".

THE CLASSIC CREEDS

THERE ARE THREE CLASSIC CREEDS OF THE CATHOLIC CHURCH: THE APOSTLES', NICENE AND ATHANASIAN CREEDS. EACH WAS DEVELOPED TO SHIELD THE CHURCH FROM A SPECIFIC HERESY.

Many modern Catholics can usually repeat by rote the Nicene Creed, imprinted on their memory since childhood. However, they may not realize that in the early centuries after Christ's death, when Christianity was still seeking to define and establish itself in the face of uncertainty, danger and opposition, creeds were developed and perceived as true badges of faith. They were developed to fight heresies, to establish, teach and promote right doctrine, and, in the words of the Catholic catechism, to be "the spiritual seal, our heart's meditation."

THE FIRST SYSTEM OF BELIEF
The Apostles' Creed is the oldest. It originated in the first century after Christ's death and sets forth the teachings of the Church under the leadership of St Peter, the first pope.

During the Middle Ages it was believed that the first 12 apostles had composed the Creed on Pentecost, the day that the Holy Spirit descended to inspire them; however, this is probably a legend.

About two-thirds of the Apostles' Creed sets forth in straightforward language beliefs about the identity of Jesus Christ. This is because, during the first five centuries of the Church's existence, when the Apostles' Creed was formulated, Gnosticism was an influential heresy. Followers of this faith believed that the material world was completely corrupt (beyond the "tendency to sin" of the doctrine of original sin) and, therefore, although they were willing to believe that Jesus was God, the Gnostics denied that he had ever been a true man, a flesh and blood corporeal man who had died, as well as being divine.

Above St Athanasius, shown in this 18th-century Greek icon, was an Egyptian theologian known as the Father of Orthodoxy. His fight against Arianism was influential in the development of the doctrine of the Trinity.

Below The ravaged body of Christ, showing he was flesh and mortal, stands out in a contemporary landscape, an attempt by a 16th-century French artist to help refute the Gnostic doctrine that Christ had never been truly mortal.

By denying Jesus' humanity, the followers of Gnosticism were also denying that he died for us, which was a blatant contradiction of a bedrock Catholic doctrine. The Apostles' Creed refutes this Gnostic heresy by dwelling on the corporeal history of Christ on earth, stating that he "suffered, died and was buried". This creed may have been used as a profession of faith for early Christians about to be baptized, and even today the Apostle's Creed is part of the baptismal rite.

ONE IN BEING

The second of the classic creeds, the Nicene Creed, which is also known as the Niceno-Constantinopolitan Creed, clarified Jesus' standing. It was developed in the 4th century and endures today in both the Roman and Eastern Catholic Churches. During the 4th century, Arianism – essentially the belief that Jesus, while divine, was an inferior divinity to the Father – became such a widespread and contentious issue that it threatened the stability of the Roman Empire itself. In the Edict of Milan (AD 313), Constantine declared that Christians were free to practise their religion, so the disputes over Catholic doctrine, freed from the earlier need for secrecy, became even more acrimonious than before.

Constantine ordered a council of bishops to be convened in Nicaea (in present-day Turkey) to make a ruling on the heated issue. The Nicene Creed, which was developed at that conference, declared in its

Above Simon Magus, shown in this 14th-century French manuscript, was a Gnostic teacher and magician known as the "first heretic". Legend says he fell to his death from the Roman Forum while trying to prove to St Peter that he could fly.

most significant line that Jesus was "one in being with the father". The most significant Greek term used in this phrase was *homoousios*, or "consubstantial", meaning of the same substance, not *homoiousios*, which means "similar" (but not the same) substance.

In AD 381, the creed was revised to expand its definition of the Holy Spirit. The earlier AD 325 version had only noted "We believe in the Holy Spirit", somewhat short-changing the third person.

THE STERNEST CREED

The newest of the three classic creeds, the Athanasian Creed, is a resolute profession of doctrines on the nature of the Trinity and of the Incarnation (particularly with regard to the divinity and humanity of Jesus). It also declares the absolute necessity of belief in these doctrines in order to achieve one's salvation.

The creed was written in a series of declarations that were clearly and inclusively formulated in an obvious attempt to stifle all the various heresies on the Trinity and the nature of Christ that plagued the Catholic Church, among them being Arianism, Modalism, Sabellianism, Apollinarianism and Eutychianism. To emphasize that this was a serious matter, the creed contains a series of clauses that outline two stark choices: belief, or the road to damnation. It concludes: "This is the Catholic faith, which except a man believe faithfully and firmly, he cannot be saved."

Below The large hands of the Madonna protectively enfold the Christ child in this 15th/16th-century painting by Giovanni Bellini. He grasps his mother's thumb, even as he asserts his divinity by offering a blessing.

OF UNKNOWN ORIGIN

The Athanasian Creed is also known as the Symbol Quicunque for its first Latin words, "*Quicunque vult salvus esse…*" ("Whosoever wishes to be saved…"). Tradition has ascribed the Athanasian Creed to Athanasius, the 4th-century Bishop of Alexandria, but this has been proved untrue. Although many plausible theories have been put forward as to its origin, none have been conclusive. However, scholars tend to agree that it was written in France *c.* mid-5th century.

THE CATECHISM

TO HELP THE FAITHFUL LEARN THE BELIEFS OF THE CATHOLIC CHURCH, ALL ITS GREAT THEOLOGICAL TEACHINGS HAVE BEEN SUMMARIZED IN WHAT IS POPULARLY KNOWN AS THE CATECHISM.

"Catechetics" comes from the Greek *katechesis*, meaning instruction by word of mouth. A "catechumen" is the person being instructed in religious doctrine. The New Testament portrays the 12-year-old Jesus as an exceptional catechumen:

And it came to pass, that, after three days, they found him in the temple, sitting in the midst of the doctors, hearing them and asking them questions. And all that heard him were astonished at his wisdom and his answers. (Luke 2:46)

THE WORDS IN WRITING

A catechism is doctrinal instruction provided in written form. It is in a question and answer format because the Church considers it the best method for ensuring that the doctrine being taught is correct and uniform – which is important in a religion where shades of meaning are crucial and confusion can unwittingly lead to heresy.

In Catholicism's early history, written doctrinal instruction was generally sparse, a deficiency that contributed to the Church's

Above A youthful Jesus turned the usual catechetical order inside out by teaching the rabbis. In this 15th/16th-century painting by Albrecht Dürer, Jesus amazed them with his preternatural wisdom.

vulnerability to the Reformation. Fifteenth-century parish priests, who were often poorly educated in abstruse Church doctrines themselves, were usually unable to help their confused parishioners. Poor instruction and misunderstanding of the complexities of the doctrines, including the plenary indulgence, enabled corrupt practices, such as selling indulgences for money. Martin Luther was one of the reformers who pounced on these practices, and many left the Church to join the reformers as a result.

The first-ever Catholic catechism was published in Vienna in 1555 by Peter Canisius, a Dutch Jesuit. Canisius compiled a single volume

Left Peter Canisius (1521–97), shown in this 17th-century Flemish painting, wrote three Latin and German catechisms and helped to found the University of Fribourg, Switzerland, still an influential school of Catholic theology.

that contained 222 questions and 2,000 scriptural quotations. This catechism is still a favourite of theologians and historians centuries later; however, at the time it was first published, it was too sophisticated to be of much help to the ordinary priest and parishioner.

EDUCATING THE CLERGY

The Church recognized the need for, in the words of the 16th-century Council of Trent, "...a formulary and method for teaching the rudiments of the faith, to be used by all legitimate pastors and teachers". This was to take the shape of a simpler catechism that would be helpful for ordinary priests as they cared for the souls of their flocks. The resulting Roman catechism was published in 1566 and translated into the vernacular languages used by all Catholic countries.

The Roman catechism was intended to educate the clergy, and parish priests were ordered by their bishops to memorize it and to pass on that rote knowledge to their parishioners. It was the work of a number of distinguished theologians and cardinals of the day, and the authority of the Roman catechism was considered unimpeachable.

THE DISCIPLINE OF THE SECRET

In the early centuries of the Church, during and just after the Roman persecutions, admission to the mysterious doctrines and rites of the new religion called Christianity was treated with great reserve. Scriptural support for a gradual revelation of the mysteries was provided by Matthew 7:6: "Give not that which is holy to dogs; neither cast ye your pearls before swine, lest they trample them under their feet, and turning upon you, they tear you."

The gradual revelation of the doctrines and rituals of the Church was known as the Discipline of the Secret. In particular, early Christians considered that the teachings of the Trinity and the Eucharist should be revealed to postulants only after careful preparation, because the doctrines imparted to the poorly prepared could easily be misconstrued as tritheism (the Trinity) or cannibalism (the Eucharist). As Christianity became more established, the practice of the Discipline of the Secret began to diminish and it was for the most part finished by the 5th century AD.

MODERN VERSIONS

New catechisms continue to be developed. The catechism familiar to Americans is the Baltimore Catechism. In 1829, American bishops asked for a catechism adapted to the needs of the diverse American Catholic audience. *A Catechism of Christian Doctrine, Prepared and Enjoined by Order of the Third Council of Baltimore*, was issued in 1855 and became the standard United States catechism. A modernized edition of the Baltimore Catechism is still available today.

Another new catechism, entitled *Compendium of the Catechism of the Catholic Church,* was started on the 20th anniversary of the Second Vatican Council, brought to completion by Pope John Paul II and published by Pope Benedict in 2005.

Below Founded in 1253 by the Chaplain of Louis V, the Sorbonne was an institution of education, famed for its influential, but conservative, school of theology.

Below A nun from the Missionaries of Charity, the order founded by Mother Teresa, is engaged in the traditional catechetical method of oral instruction.

IN ACCORDANCE WITH THE SCRIPTURES

CATHOLICISM VIEWS THE SCRIPTURES AS THE WORD OF GOD, PASSED ON BY WRITERS INSPIRED BY THE HOLY SPIRIT. THEY ARE CONSIDERED DIVINE REVELATION IN WRITTEN FORM.

The Scriptures that form the sacred canon are the biblical books accepted by the Church as genuine. Catholicism sees the Old Testament, which existed years before the birth of Christ, as part of a divine plan, calling the Old Testament an "active and steady preparation" for the revelations of Christ in the New and credited with tilling the ground for the coming of the Messiah. According to the Catholic catechism, this is a covenant that is "strikingly fulfilled" in the New Testament. It says the Old Testament books:

> …*give expression to a lively sense of God, contain a store of sublime teachings about God, sound wisdom about human life, and a wonderful treasury of prayers, and in them the mystery of our salvation is present in a hidden way.*

"Typology" is the term that describes seeing the revelations of the New Testament prefigured in the books and stories of the Old.

THE DEPOSIT OF FAITH

Unlike Protestant Christianity, the Catholic Church does not view Scripture as the sole source of divine revelation. This was a major issue during the Reformation, with the Protestant reformers claiming that all belief required specific evidence or *sola scriptura* ("scriptural proof"). The Catholic Church, in contrast, argued that scripture should be read from the perspective of a sacred tradition, and that it should include the non-scriptural compendium of teachings and traditional beliefs – referred to by the Church as the "deposit of faith". These teachings and beliefs were revealed by Jesus

Above Moses keeps a protective arm around the second tablets of law written by the hand of God in this 17th-century painting by Laurent de la Hyre. Moses had smashed the first tablets when he saw his people worshipping a golden calf.

to the apostles and passed down through the apostles and early Church fathers to become Catholic customary belief and practice through the centuries.

At the same time, the Church does not encourage individualistic interpretations of Scripture, especially when they are not supported by valid study and scholarship. Instead, the ultimate authority for scriptural interpretation is the magisterium, or the teaching authority of the Church comprised of the pope and the bishops of the Church. The magisterium's scriptural interpretations, according to Church doctrine, are infallible because they are inspired by the Holy Spirit. That said, the Catholic Church does encourage serious biblical study, so that readers will not react to the Bible only according to their own subjective emotional responses.

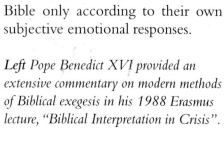

Left Pope Benedict XVI provided an extensive commentary on modern methods of Biblical exegesis in his 1988 Erasmus lecture, "Biblical Interpretation in Crisis".

THE BACKGROUND

In "The Interpretation of the Bible in the Church", a 1993 document written by Cardinal Joseph Ratzinger (who became Pope Benedict XVI in 2005), the cardinal freely asserted that the Bible would be more fully appreciated if its readers had a working knowledge of the society, history, languages and geography that influenced its writers. Of this "historical-critical" approach, Cardinal Ratzinger pointed out that the "eternal word" of God, the Bible, was brought into being during specific historical periods, and that readers of the Bible must necessarily be grounded in the cultural and social details of those eras for proper and accurate comprehension of the text.

However, an overemphasis on these methods could obscure what the Church refers to as the "spiritual sense", a dimension of the Scriptures that extends far beyond the reality of other human texts. Benedict warned that modern historical-grammatical methods of interpretation can lead to the distancing of God's original words if too much emphasis is put on the human dimension of the words.

Benedict went on to assert that while approaching biblical exegesis (or interpretation) with the proper respect for the texts, as God's Word requires, all the possible methods of interpretation – historical, philological, sociological – should also be given their due. It is essential for Catholics to keep in mind that the principal aim of their studies should be the deepening of their faith.

DIFFERENT TESTAMENTS

The Protestant and Catholic Bibles differ in the number of canonical books contained in their respective Old Testaments. Catholic Bibles have 46 books, Protestant Bibles, 39. The reasons for the discrepancy go back to ancient political and religious history. Early Christians accepted as divinely inspired the *Septuagint* (Greek for 70, referring to the 70 translators from Hebrew into Greek) version of the Jewish Old Testament. When the *Septuagint* was translated from Hebrew into Greek, it contained seven newer Greek books that had never been in the Hebrew language, but they were still considered part of the divinely inspired canon by Jews at the time of Jesus.

In AD 100, Jews purged their canon of these non-Hebrew books, known as the Deuterocanonical (for second canon, because they were newer) books. Christians chose to keep the seven, because at the time of Christ, they had been considered inspired texts. However, in 1517 during the Reformation, Martin Luther advocated the old Hebrew canon, partly because he objected to references to Purgatory in some of the Deuterocanonical Books. Even today, many Protestant Bibles include the seven disputed books only at the back of the volume and refer to them as the Apocrypha (hidden) books. The Seven Books of the Apocrypha are Baruch, Maccabees I and II, Tobit, Judith, Ecclesiasticus (or Sirach) and Wisdom.

Below The English translation of the New Testament by William Tyndale (1494–1536) was the first based on Hebrew and Greek texts.

Above Biblical exegesis – the critical explanation of the text – takes many forms. This medieval French Bible Moralisée *from c. 1230 features brief biblical passages interspersed with moral or allegorical lessons.*

THE EVANGELISTS

THE "FOUR EVANGELISTS" – MARK, MATTHEW, LUKE AND JOHN – ARE
CREDITED IN THE TRADITION OF THE CATHOLIC CHURCH AS THE
AUTHORS OF THE GOSPELS IN THE NEW TESTAMENT.

"Evangelist" is from the Greek for "one who proclaims good news", so the title when referring to the gospel writers emphasizes they are spreading the word of Jesus' life to inspire others to believe in Jesus as God. The earliest Gospel, Mark, was written about 40 years after Jesus' Resurrection. In that intervening time, accounts of Jesus were passed on orally, and all the Evangelists used this oral tradition for the content of their gospels. The four gospels were composed from about AD 65 to 100.

AUTHOR UNKNOWN

Secular biblical scholars generally agree that the actual authorship of the gospels is anonymous; the titles "according to…" (not "by") Matthew, Mark, Luke or John, were added in the late 2nd century. Secular scholars also believe that the gospels were written according to the oral traditions of, rather than written by, the particular Evangelists. Yet the Church, while acknowledging the likely accuracy of the historians' position, has essentially declared that scholarly

Above A portrayal of the four Evangelists eschews symbology and shows the four as reverent scholars, each cradling his precious gospel (Greek school, 18th century).

debate over the specific human authorship of the gospels is beside the point. In *Dei Verbum* (or "Word of God"), a "dogmatic constitution on divine revelation" issued by Pope Paul VI in 1965, the Church stated that as whoever "wrote" the gospels was inspired by the Holy Spirit, the real author of the gospels is God – and as such, the Church accepts them in their entirety as sacred and canonical. In other words, the authors, no matter who, were divinely inspired.

THE ORATORS

Tradition describes the Evangelists as four distinct people: Mark was a missionary with Paul, and Peter's follower. Matthew, one of the apostles, was a tax collector from Galilee. Luke, another missionary with Paul, was a Greek doctor, and is also believed to be the first Christian

Left Tradition says that St Luke painted some of the earliest icons of the Virgin Mary. This has become a popular subject in art, as in this 16th-century painting by Maerten van Heemskerck.

FOUR CREATURES BOUND TOGETHER IN SPIRIT

For centuries, the four Evangelists have been magnificently illustrated in Christian iconography and art as the "four living creatures" that flank God's throne in Revelation and Ezekiel. Described as six-winged and "full of eyes", the living creatures are fierce testaments to God's majesty and power. Traditionally, the first living creature, a lion, symbolizes Mark; the second, an ox, Luke; the third, a man, Matthew; and the fourth, an eagle, John. Each creature encompasses certain virtues: Mark's lion is royal and courageous; Luke's ox represents endurance and sacrifice; Matthew's man suggests the primacy of human intellect; and John's eagle, spirit and aspiration.

The Book of Kells, the superb 9th-century illuminated manuscript produced by Irish monks on the island of Iona, devotes a full page to the four living creatures. They frequently guard the portals of medieval cathedrals and glow in the light of ancient stained-glass windows. The symbols of the Evangelists are most often seen together, reflecting the beautiful words of St Irenaeus of Lyons (AD 120–202), "He who was manifested to men, has given us the gospel under four aspects, but bound together by one Spirit."

Right The symbols of each of the four Evangelists are shown in this introductory page to the Gospel of St Matthew, from The Book of Kells.

painter (he is often portrayed holding a brush and is said to have painted the Black Madonna of Czestochowa, now the centrepiece of a Polish shrine). John was the beloved youngest apostle of Jesus.

THE "SYNOPTIC GOSPELS"

The first three gospels, Mark, Matthew and Luke, which are similar in content, are known as the "Synoptic Gospels", meaning they "see with the same eyes". Scholars believe the Synoptics have a common, lost source document, which is referred to as "Q" (from the German *Quelle*, or "source"). The Gospel of John, which is notably different, is known as the "maverick" gospel.

Each gospel was developed with unique characteristics. Mark is referred to as the "action" gospel,

because it contains the most miracles and has a quick narrative pace – in fact, the word "immediately" appears 39 times. Luke contains more parables, and, as befitting a doctor, has a somewhat scientific tone. Its opening words state that it is intended as an orderly account for attaining knowledge. Matthew opens with a genealogy of Jesus, with frequent references to the Old Testament, and it emphasizes that Jesus is the prophesied Messiah. His work appears to have been written for a Jewish audience.

John opens with the famous passage, "In the beginning was the Word: and the Word was with God: and the Word was God." John is the most spiritual of the four gospels and the only one to state an evangelical purpose, "that ye might believe that Jesus is the Christ, the son of God; and that believing ye might have life through his name". John is also the only Gospel not to describe Jesus offering bread and wine at the Last Supper (the acts that instituted the Eucharist). In its place is the account of Jesus washing the apostles' feet.

Right Christ walking on water, as depicted in this 20th-century painting by Frederic Montenard, is described in the gospels of Matthew, Mark and John. The miracle is prefigured in the Old Testament when the River Jordan parts for Joshua. "Jesus" is Latin for the Hebrew name Joshua.

OUR LADY

MANY OF TODAY'S CATHOLICS GROW UP SURROUNDED BY IMAGES OF THE VIRGIN MARY, BUT IT WAS NOT UNTIL THE 5TH CENTURY AD THAT MARY'S UNIQUE STATUS AS GOD-BEARER WAS EVEN RECOGNIZED.

Mary's eminent position in the Catholic pantheon was slow to develop. St Paul does not mention Mary, mother of Jesus, in any of his epistles. The Bible does not mention Mary's ultimate fate after Christ's death on the Cross. The last mention of Mary is in Acts 1:14, when she was present with the apostles as they persevered in prayer after Jesus' Ascension and just before Pentecost. We do not know where, how or even if Mary actually died. The Scriptures are silent on all of these things.

THE GOD-BEARER

Mary's status in the Church began to develop after she was declared *Theotokos* (Greek for "God-bearer") by the Council of Ephesus in AD 431. As was their wont, the early Church

Below Mary spreads her cloak in a gesture of protection in this detail from a c.1422 painting by Jean Miralhet. The Sub Tuum Presidium, *a hymn dating from the 3rd century, begins, "Beneath thy compassion, we take refuge, O Theotokos".*

fathers debated for a long time before endowing Mary with this title. Its ultimate conferral was yet another means for the Church fathers to promulgate the concept of Christ as God-man, indivisibly true man and true God. By officially proclaiming Mary "God-bearer", it meant that she did not give birth to just the "man" aspect of God, as believed by Nestorius, the 3rd-century Bishop of Constantinople. Calling Mary *Theotokos* was just one more way to affirm the indivisible divine-human nature of Christ.

A PRAYER FOR MARY

It was only after the Council of Ephesus that liturgical feasts were held in Mary's honour, though the earliest known prayer to Mary, the *Sub Tuum Praesidium* ("Beneath Thy Compassion"), dates from *c.* AD 250. The prayer is a plea to Mary in her role as an intercessor for humanity with God. Pope John Paul II mentions this important mediatory role of Mary in *Redemptoris Mater*, his 1987 encyclical letter concerning Mary, noting that she intercedes "…not as an outsider, but in her position as mother". Mary, as both mortal woman and mother of the God-man, has a special attentiveness to the needs of mankind as well as a unique intimacy with her son. As a suffering mother, she has earned the right to be an adviser – even to God.

CONCEIVED WITHOUT SIN

There are three Catholic doctrines regarding Mary. The Immaculate Conception claims that alone among human beings, Mary was conceived without the inherited stain of original sin. It states "…the most

Above As he hung on the Cross, Christ placed Mary under the protection of the apostle John, shown in this painting by Rogier van der Weyden. Christ spoke words to each in turn, "Woman behold thy son…Behold thy mother."

Blessed Virgin Mary, from the first moment of her conception, by a singular grace and privilege from Almighty God and in view of the merits of Jesus Christ, was kept free of every stain of original sin."

This dogma sets forth the utter singularity of Mary. No other human being received this privilege from God. Besides the logic that the woman who was to bear and raise God would be free of a fallen nature, this doctrine also endows Mary with a special role, if not of our Redeemer, as is Christ, then as the one who made redemption possible through her obedience.

PERPETUAL VIRGINITY

Mary was a virgin at Christ's conception and remained so despite his gestation and birth and indeed for the rest of her life. Known as Perpetual Virginity, in the words of the Lateran Council (AD 649), Mary conceived "without any detriment to her virginity, which remained inviolate even after his birth". Mary's lasting virginity was accepted by most of the early Church fathers, although Tertullian disagreed with it.

The doctrine provided a prototype for the monastic movement as it gained strength in the Church, starting *c.* the 4th century with St Anthony. Mary's celibacy is also representative of the metaphor of being "wedded to Christ", or so devoted to Christ that this relationship subsumes all others. The Church is known as the Bride or Spouse of the Lamb, nuns are brides of Christ and the Church continues to insist on the celibacy of priests, so that their devotion to God remains completely unchallenged by earthly vows.

THE ASSUMPTION

Celebrated by Catholics each year on 15 August, the Assumption is the doctrine that "…at the end of her

Below The Eastern Catholic tradition of the Dormition (falling asleep) of Mary teaches that she died a natural death, surrounded by all of the apostles except Thomas, who was late. The scene is shown in this 14th-century Byzantine mosaic.

earthly course, Mary was assumed into heavenly glory, body and soul". This is the 1950 definition given by Pope Pius XII, in a decree (*Munificentissimus Deus*) whose solemnity is apparent from the fact that it is the only ex-cathedra invocation by a pope since the doctrine of papal infallibility was established in 1870.

Pius XII's decree leaves vague the question of whether or not Mary actually died before she was raised by God into heaven. A variety of early non-scriptural accounts of the Assumption exist, some written by early saints, such as Gregory of Tours and John of Damascus.

Eastern Orthodox Catholics tend to favour more explicit stories concerning Mary's actual death, stating that she was surrounded by 11 of the apostles at the moment of her death. They refer to this death as Mary's Dormition, but believe along with Western Catholics that she was bodily assumed into heaven after her burial; the Dormition is also celebrated on 15 August. In any case, the Assumption is viewed by most Catholics as prefiguring the final redemption of all observant Catholics on the Last Day.

MOTHERLY LOVE

Despite all the unusual doctrines that surround Mary, the Catholic fascination with this figure seems to be related to something intimate and simple: her motherhood. The familiar enveloping motherly relationship and the idea that Jesus had a special fondness for Mary were illustrated when he did favours for her (turning water into wine at the wedding at Cana). Some of his last words as a living man were spoken to her as he hung from the Cross, where he appointed his apostle John to care for his mother. These actions seem to simplify Jesus' humanity into something that we can understand, even while he maintains his godliness. A simple emotion in powerful people is always resonant, and through Mary we can find this in Christ.

Above Mary rests her cheek on the head of her thriving son, whom she closely resembles. This early 16th-century Madonna and Child *by Raphael emphasizes the natural maternal bond.*

MARIAN APPARITIONS

APPARITIONS OF THE BLESSED VIRGIN MARY HAVE BEEN REPORTED
FOR MANY CENTURIES. THE CATHOLIC CHURCH REFERS TO SUCH
VISIONS AS "PRIVATE REVELATIONS".

Probably the earliest of the Marian revelations dates back to AD 40. It occurred before Mary's Assumption into heaven, when the apostle James, who was in Spain trying to spread the gospel, had a vision of the Virgin atop a marble pillar. She instructed him to build a church on the site, and that church today is said to be the first of the thousands of churches that have been dedicated to and named for the Blessed Virgin.

GUADALUPE

The three most influential Marian apparitions occurred at Guadalupe in Mexico, Lourdes in France and Fatima in Portugal. Guadalupe is notable because the visionary, Juan Diego, was an Aztec and a recent convert to Christianity. Mary appeared to him in 1531 at the site of a former temple to the Aztec gods,

and as a proof of her appearance she left her image mysteriously imprinted on Juan Diego's tilma, a type of cactus-fibre cloak. The image and the cloak have never decomposed and even today, more than four centuries later, the cloak (protected by bullet-proof glass) can still be seen at the basilica that was built in Guadalupe. Juan Diego's vision was influential in converting many indigenous Mexicans to Christianity, although these people were initially disinclined to do so because of their subjugation by the Spanish.

LOURDES AND FATIMA

Probably the best-known Marian vision occurred at Lourdes in 1858. The lady who appeared to a poverty-stricken and sickly shepherd girl said very little, mainly directing her supplicant to pray the rosary and to do penance. Yet the simple, intense, committed (and lifelong) piety and certainty of Bernadette Soubirous so impressed the clergy who examined her that Bernadette remains today the exemplary believable visionary in the eyes of the Church. Lourdes is also known for Massabielle, the spring blessed by the Virgin that has been responsible for dozens of otherwise inexplicable cures.

Fatima is remarkable for both the number of the visions and the loquacity of the Virgin Mary. Appearing six times in 1917 to three young children, Mary foretold the end of World War I but warned of a

Above Our Lady, atop a pillar carried by angels, is illustrated in a c.1629 painting by Nicolas Poussin. She appeared to the apostle James as he prayed by the banks of the Ebro River in Zaragoza, Spain.

worse war to come. She provided the children with a brief vision of hell and requested that Russia (this was during the Russian Revolution) be consecrated to her Immaculate Heart. Pope John Paul II, who felt that Our Lady of Fatima was

Left The Basilica of Guadalupe in Mexico is the most visited Catholic shrine in the world; on the feast of Our Lady of Guadalupe, millions make the pilgrimage – some on their knees.

THE PRINCIPAL REVELATIONS

At least 75 visions, or private revelations, have been reported over the centuries, but the Church has deemed "worthy of belief" perhaps 30 of them. Of these, there are nine principal, approved Marian apparitions:

Guadalupe (Mexico, 1531)
Rue du Bac (France, 1830)
La Salette (France, 1846)
Lourdes (France, 1858)
Pontmain (France, 1871)
Knock (Ireland, 1879)
Fatima (Portugal, 1917)
Beauraing (Belgium, 1932)
Banneux (Belgium, 1933)

responsible for his own survival from an assassination attempt that occurred on the feast of the Lady of Fatima, did perform such a consecration in May 1984. As a gesture toward Russia, he mentioned the nations that "particularly needed to be… consecrated" in the consecration.

THE DEPOSIT OF FAITH

The Church teaches that even the private revelations they dub "worthy of belief" do not constitute part of the "deposit of Faith" (the approved doctrines) of the Catholic Church, and that Church members are not bound to believe even the "approved" apparitions. The Church holds that the sum total of crucial Catholic revelations was given in apostolic times and, in particular, is contained in the doctrines of Christ's birth, death and Resurrection. Cardinal Ratzinger (who is now Pope Benedict XVI) commented in 2000 that the "…mystery of Christ as enunciated in the New Testament" was the utter, complete revelation of God to humanity, and that the Church neither needs nor expects anything more. There is no need for further divine manifestations. The Church feels that revelation is complete and that "secrets" revealed by visions cannot add to it.

MODERN REVELATIONS?

The attitude of the Catholic Church to Marian apparitions is cautious. The amount of attention paid to contemporary apparitions (such as the "disapproved" manifestations in Bayside, Queens, New York City) can quickly get out of hand due to the speed and widespread nature of modern publicity and ease of travel for pilgrims. The Church is concerned

Right Our Lady of Fatima asked the three shepherd children to whom she appeared to pray the rosary daily; today there are nightly candlelight processions to the shrine, where the participants pray.

Sainte Bernadette

Ton sourire divin illumine ma vie
Et lorsqu'au dernier jour vers toi prenant l'essor
Mon âme aura quitté l'exil pour la patrie
O Vierge Immaculée viens me sourire encor

that such charismatic phenomena will spread false doctrine and corrupt its magisterial authority. In essence, the devotees of particular Marian visions run the risk of developing into cultists.

Catholic doctrine also teaches that private revelation is not something to aspire to. St Teresa of Ávila

Left A personal supplication to St Bernadette of Lourdes (1844–79) is inscribed on this little holy card, together with an image of Bernadette (shown with a halo) after the pious woman entered the Sisters of Charity.

(though she herself had visions) reflected the sentiments of the Church when she said, "They desire to see; faith holds on without seeing." In other words, you should not need visions to believe. Christ himself said, "More blessed are they who have not seen and have believed."

Modern-day investigations of Marian apparitions are instituted by the bishop of the relevant diocese. If the messages being relayed by the apparition to the visionary are in any way contrary to the accepted doctrine of the Church, that alone is enough to have the apparition declared invalid. Investigations will also probe the mental, physical and spiritual health of the visionary and consider whether the messages being conveyed by the apparition are considered beneficial to the spiritual health of the faithful.

ALL SAINTS

THE MOST FAITHFUL SERVANTS OF GOD WHILE THEY WERE ON EARTH
ARE KNOWN AS SAINTS, AND CATHOLICS BELIEVE THEY ARE REWARDED
WITH A PARTICULAR INTIMACY WITH GOD IN HEAVEN.

The word "saint" comes from the Latin *sanctus*, or "holy, consecrated". In the general sense, the Catholic Church believes that anyone who has died and been accepted into heaven has earned the status of saint. However, there are also people who have been judged worthy of canonization by the Church hierarchy here on earth because of their exemplary behaviour as Christians. These saints are considered to have an especially intense beatific vision of God.

THE FIRST SAINTS

In the early centuries of Christianity, saints came from the ranks of the martyrs, those who in Roman times chose death rather than renounce their faith. After Christianity was legalized by the Edict of Milan in AD 313, the learned of the faith such as bishops or theologians ("doctors") were often considered for sainthood. Anchorites, or hermits, were also likely to achieve the designation by popular reputation. A saint chosen

Above St Matthew was stabbed in the back by a hired assassin while saying Mass in the church he built in Ethiopia. He is a saint by virtue of being an apostle and a martyr. This 14th-century illustration is from an altarpiece of St Matthew showing scenes from his life.

by reputation would be venerated by the people, who might visit the person's tomb or celebrate the day of his or her death.

After many years, the ecclesiastical authorities became involved and eventually created an official process for declaring someone a saint. The first saint for whom official canonization documents exist is St Udalricus, who was canonized in AD 973. In the early days of canonization, it was part of the practice to exhume the presumed saint's body and place it under an altar, apparently to facilitate the practices of veneration and pilgrimage that often resulted. An alternate way to express canonization is "to be

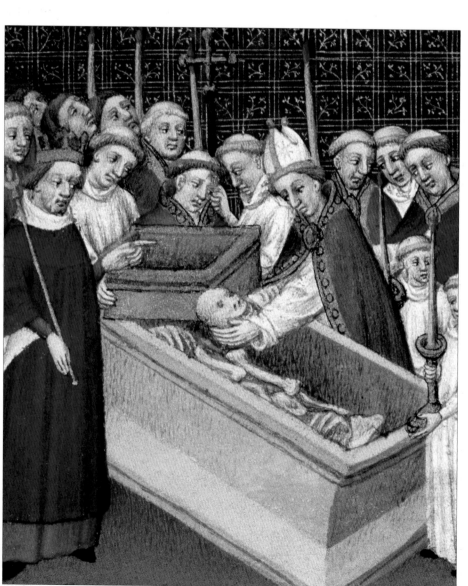

Left In this 15th-century painting, the bones of King Louis IX of France are disinterred (for reburial under an altar) by Pope Boniface VIII, who later canonized Louis.

THE LONG ROAD TO CANONIZATION

There is a set procedure to follow for a person to be made a saint. First there is The "Opening of the Cause", which occurs when the diocesan bishop agrees that there is enough evidence to initiate an investigation into the life of a deceased resident of his diocese, by popular opinion known as outstandingly holy. Usually, there is a five-year waiting period after the candidate's death, but in the case of Pope John Paul II, Pope Benedict XVI waived this waiting period. At this point the candidate can be called "a servant of God". The report that results from the investigation is sent to the Congregation for the Causes of Saints, the Vatican investigative body that vets saintly nominees. If the Vatican agrees the report profiles a saint in waiting, the candidate is called "Venerable".

A posthumous miracle, evidence of the candidate's intercessory influence with God, must be verified. After verification, the candidate is beatified. Mother Teresa was beatified in 2003. After beatification, the candidate is called "Blessed". The Congregation for the Causes of Saints must verify that a second miracle occurred after the beatification before the candidate can be called a "Saint".

Above *The widely held conviction that Pope John Paul II was an exceptionally holy man caused Pope Benedict XVI to open the cause for canonization only weeks after John Paul's death.*

raised to the full honours of the altar". Even today, saintly bodies reside under altars in some of the most surprising places – the body of St Mother Mary Frances Cabrini, for example, is under the altar of the chapel at Mother Cabrini High School in New York City.

VENERATION OR WORSHIP?

The modern Church recognizes saints as people of exemplary holiness who are worthy of veneration, which is not the same as worship. The act of worshipping a saint would violate the first commandment – "thou shalt not have strange gods before me". Catholicism is emphatically a mono-theistic religion. The Church makes a specific distinction between *latria*, or "worship", due only to God, and *dulia*, which is "honour or venera-tion", due to saints. The Blessed Mother has her own intermediate category, known as *hyperdulia* – a very high degree of veneration due only to her.

Right *St Anne's status as grandmother of the Holy Family means that she is asked to intercede on family matters. Shown here in this 17th-century French painting, she is patroness of expectant mothers, women in labour and of the sick.*

Worship and veneration can seem similar, since their practices (prayers to the worshipped or venerated, for example, or kneeling before statues, and feast days) are alike. However, the difference between worship and veneration is found in the believer's heart. When he or she worships, he or she is recognizing that the object of worship is divine. There is an element of awe rather than respect. When you venerate or honour, you are recognizing that the object of

your veneration is due your respect – in the case of the Blessed Mother, the highest respect – but there is no awe and no intent to confer or recognize divinity.

Catholics who pray to saints do so not to obtain grace or favour straight from the saints themselves, but to ask the saint to intercede with God. This is because the saint is so close to God that their intercession is likely to smooth the way of the prayers of the petitioner.

A State of Grace

An individual's state of grace (whether or not he or she will receive sanctifying grace from God) depends on his or her efforts to gain salvation by turning to God through free will. Yet, one has to only briefly consider contemporary scandals that fill the newspapers' headlines to realize that humankind's sinful nature has not changed much over the centuries since early ascetic monks and doctors of the Church, such as Thomas Aquinas, created the Christian vocabulary to talk about sin. The seven "deadly" categories still apply – pride, avarice, greed, lust, gluttony, envy and sloth – leading men and women into both public and private trouble and strife. What has changed over the centuries is the emphasis that the Church places on forgiveness rather than punishment, and most particularly on the manner in which it defines not only punishment, but reward.

Also enduring is the human metaphysical longing for answers to ultimate questions and the craving to put our faith in something that is unified, peaceful and eternal. Catholicism defines this as the Trinity, the ultimate end of our seeking. The emphasis that the modern Church places on our personal relationship with God and on our eventual either beatific union with or desolate divorce from him is evidence that the Church has shifted the promise of heaven's glory and the threat of hell's fires and mutilations from the pointedly physical to the ineffably spiritual. The Church offers the heaven of rest and union with God.

Above The seven deadly sins all imply gross self-absorption. This attribute is evident in the oblivious expression and callous disregard of the child's pleas displayed by the overstuffed man in a scene depicting gluttony from Hieronymous Bosch's late 15th-century Tabletop of the Seven Deadly Sins and the Four Last Things.

Left In contrast to many paintings of the Harrowing of Hell, Giotto di Bondone portrays Christ as a tender and kind, rather than glorious and triumphant, liberator in his c.1320–5 painting, Descent into Limbo.

THE SOUL REDEEMED

CATHOLICS HAVE DISAGREED ON WHAT PEOPLE NEED TO DO TO GAIN
REDEMPTION FROM ORIGINAL SIN. IN ADDITION TO CHRIST'S SACRIFICE,
INDIVIDUALS MUST ALSO CONTRIBUTE TO THEIR OWN SALVATION.

Debates between Christians on what sinful humans need to do to attain salvation involved some of the most divisive issues of the 16th century, leading to the Protestant Reformation. Shuffled around in the debates were issues of grace, faith and the relative significance of human good works, along with the role of Christ's sacrifice on the Cross. The Catholic Magisterium, or teaching authority, and Martin Luther – the Catholic priest responsible for starting the Protestant Reformation by nailing his influential 95 Theses to the door of a church in Wittenberg – agreed on one important issue: that Christ's ultimate sacrifice on the Cross was the absolutely necessary prerequisite for human redemption.

Above Faithful Catholics pray before
The Way of the Cross, *a sculpture that
emphasizes the physical reality of Christ's
sacrifice. The weight of the Cross seems to
drive Christ into the ground, with only
the help of Simon of Cyrene keeping
him from falling.*

GOD'S GIFT

As a result of original sin, humans are viewed as helpless to effect their redemption on their own. (Pelagius, a 5th-century theologian, disagreed and thought that people could handle their redemption without God's intervention; the Catholic Church declared him a heretic.) Both Catholics and Lutherans also agreed that salvation is a gift from God. God has no obligation or need to save sinful humanity.

Fortunately, even the grievous fact of original sin was not enough to destroy God's love for humanity – his Creation – and his infinite goodness is displayed in the mystical balance of Christ's redemptive sacrifice. As the 20th-century theologian Jaroslav Pelikan has noted, Christ's obedient passion and sacrifice on the tree of the Cross undid the damage that humankind had done next to the tree of disobedience.

Left The Catholic Church recognizes
seven sacraments, while the Lutheran
Church practises only two – baptism and
the Eucharist. In this detail from a 1561
altar front from Torslunde, Denmark,
Martin Luther, who was once a Catholic
monk, performs both.

140

HAVING FAITH

Luther believed that *sola fide* (or "faith alone") was the sole active principle in humankind's salvation. People would be saved by their faith in Christ's life, death and Resurrection. Christ basically earned redemption that is "imputed", or credited, to us if we have faith. Although Luther agreed that due to their faith in Christ, people develop a disposition to do good works, known as the process of sanctification, he thought that these human good works would never be enough to have any active effect on our redemption. Christ's sacrifice, and our faith in it, are all that matter. Luther is said to have declared, "Good works are useless."

CATHOLIC BAPTISM

In contrast, Catholicism teaches that not only can we be active contributors to our own salvation, but in fact, we must be so, in order to be saved. Faith alone will not be sufficient. Catholics view salvation as a process, so unlike Protestants they do not say, "I've been saved". Their ultimate salvation will be decided on their particular Judgement Day.

Catholicism teaches that we are redeemed through the progressive and co-operative interactions of first (and most crucially) Christ's initial sacrifice, the prerequisite that has made our personal redemption possible. Next we need to participate in a baptism, which is like our first purifying bath to cleanse us of original sin and infuse us with an initial dose of sanctifying grace. This act of baptism can be seen as an introductory step toward the process necessary for spiritual salvation.

JUSTIFICATION

Catholic theologians call what happens at baptism "initial justification". Justification is defined as making a person righteous in the eyes of God. However, to keep the spiritual introduction received at baptism

Above On the day of the final judgement, Catholic tradition declares that soul and body will be reunited. This 15th-century fresco by Giovanni Canavesio shows bodies rising from their graves on this ultimate day.

vigorous, Catholicism teaches that we need to participate actively in the Church and its sacraments, especially attendance at Mass, reception of the Eucharist and good works. Through these sincere acts of participation in the Catholic community, we become more immune to sin – and we also turn into more vigorous spiritual beings. This level of participation is known as "progressive justification".

Above The scallop shell is the traditional Catholic symbol of baptism. John the Baptist is said to have baptized Christ with water poured from a scallop shell. Here Pope John Paul II baptizes a child in the Sistine Chapel in 2001.

THE NATURE OF SIN

CATHOLICISM RECOGNIZES DIFFERENT TYPES OF SIN, FROM THE ORIGINAL SIN OF ADAM AND EVE TO THE UNFORGIVABLE SIN. IT IS OUR CHOICE TO TURN TO GOD AND NOT SIN OR TO TURN AWAY FROM HIM.

To understand how sin is viewed in Catholic doctrine, one needs to consider the concept of *aversio ad deo*, or "turning away from God". Sin is an insult to God, an almost unimaginable rudeness when considering that, in the Catholic view, God has offered us the most superb gift, his love. Sin is perverse, in that it says "no" to the love of God; the Catholic catechism says that sin contradicts the love of God.

Sin is the refusal to accept this priceless love and to choose instead to turn down the blind alley of self-love or toward a false attraction to worldly objects or persons. It is a disordered perception (as a result of original sin) of the value of attractions of the temporal world that we

Below Man's fallen nature leaves him vulnerable to the attractions of the temporal world, including riches, corporeal delights and secular power, shown in Jean de Gerson's 1462 Mirror of Humility.

mistakenly define as love. The more complete the degree of turning away from God, the more distance we put between ourselves and the grace we receive in his presence, and thus the more likely we are to continue to sin.

PERSONAL SIN
When we resist or turn away from God's love for us, we cannot receive his grace, and without God's grace we lose the most effective means to avoid our tendency toward personal sin. While original sin is inherited from our ancestral parents, personal sin is our own production (though we can blame Adam and Eve for the fact that we were born imperfect). Regardless of excuse, Catholic doctrine teaches that after Adam and Eve's fall from grace, humanity retained, in weakened form, its free will. Since we still have free will, even in a fallen world we can choose to "turn toward God", or *conversio ad deo*, and not sin.

Above A 15th-century Italian illustration shows Jesus uttering the famous words, "He that is without sin among you, let him cast the first stone at her".

VENIAL VERSUS MORTAL
Catholics classify sins as either venial or mortal (theologians break these sins down into smaller categories, but for most of us the mortal/venial distinction is sufficient). To continue the metaphor of turning away from God, a venial (from the Latin word *venia*, or "forgiveness, pardon") sin would be a slight acknowledgement, and a mortal (from Latin *mortalis*, or "death") sin would be turning one's back, which is the rudest of cuts that would sever all social ties (*see Before the Mortal Blow, opposite*). Biblical reference to the venial versus mortal sin distinction can be found in 1 John 5:16–17:

> He that knoweth his brother to sin a sin which is not to death, let him ask, and life shall be given to him, who sinneth not to death. There is a sin unto death: for that I say not that any man ask.

Venial sins (those little rudenesses to God) do not in and of themselves sever all ties and destroy our hope for eternal life with God. However, like any rudeness, they can damage the relationship between us and him and lead in time to the final rift unless

BEFORE THE MORTAL BLOW

Unconfessed and therefore unforgiven mortal sins cause the death of the soul and consign the sinner to hell – eternal punishment. However, God is fair and just, so mortal sins are not easy to commit. You cannot "accidentally" commit a mortal sin. Before you turn away from God and choose the devil, three ominous conditions must be present:

Grave Matter: The act, to any person of normal reason, would be understood as evil.

Full Knowledge: The potential sinner must know that the act is evil. A person with a mental illness, such as schizophrenia, for example, may not have full knowledge that an act he is about to commit is heinous.

Deliberate Consent: It is up to us. The choice is ours, because God endowed us with free will. We can choose to turn toward the Dark or the Light. If you hit someone with your car accidentally and kill him or her, that is not a mortal sin; but if the accident happened because you drank alcohol at a party, knowing that you planned to drive home, then the accident is a mortal sin because you acted irresponsibly.

Right St Augustine thought one of the most terrible results of the fall of man was libido dominandi, *or "the lust for dominance". Cain, son of Adam, enacts a tragic result of that lust – fratricide – in* The Killing of Abel, *a detail from the 1379–83 Grabower Altarpiece by Master Bertram of Minden.*

we mend our ways. As this particular passage makes clear, mortal sin leads to the death of the soul.

THE UNFORGIVABLE SIN

The New Testament refers to an eternal, or unforgivable, sin. In Mark 3:22–30, Christ says, "All sins will be forgiven the sons of men, and whatever blasphemies they may utter; but he who blasphemes against the Holy Spirit never has forgiveness, but is subject to eternal condemnation." Christ also refers to unforgivable sin in Matthew 12:3–32, when Pharisees, who witness Christ cast out demons, claim Christ had the power of Beelzebub (the devil).

The unforgivable sin is connected to a wilful rejection of God in the face of all the manifest good that is clearly vouchsafed to us. This sin consists of seeing good and perversely calling it evil. It blasphemes against the Holy Spirit in his role as a "convincer of sin", which is what Pope John Paul II called the Holy Spirit in the 1986 encyclical, *Dominum et Vivificantem*. John Paul pointed out that the Holy Spirit's role is to purify humankind's consciences, so that they are able to call good and evil by their proper names. When we radically reject the Holy Spirit, we are no longer able to see our good and our salvation even when they stare us in the face. This is the unforgivable sin.

Right A 14th-century biblical illumination shows the fool who said, "There is no God" (Psalm 53). The sin of apostasy, or rejecting God, is called the unforgivable sin.

THE SEVEN DEADLY SINS

SINCE THE 5TH CENTURY, CATHOLIC THEOLOGIANS HAVE DISCUSSED A LIST OF PARTICULAR SINS FOR THE FAITHFUL TO AVOID, BUT IT WAS ONLY IN THE 12TH CENTURY THAT A CREED LISTED THE SEVEN DEADLY SINS.

Although the list of the seven deadly, or cardinal, sins has traditionally been paired with a list of virtues, it is the sins that are remembered. The seven deadly sins (and the corresponding virtues), in the order of descending gravity, are: pride (humility), avarice (generosity), envy (kindness), wrath (patience), lust (chastity), gluttony (temperance) and sloth (diligence).

The Catholic catechism refers to these sins as capital vices, noting that they are capital because they produce other sins. In fact, the seven deadly sins are actually categories of sin, and

Below Hieronymus Bosch's 15th-century Tabletop of the Seven Deadly Sins and the Four Last Things *shows the deadly sins balanced with four medallions of the four last things: death, judgement, heaven and hell.*

sins falling within those categories are not always mortal. For example, eating two desserts when you really needed only one – or none – would be a sin classified as gluttony, but it would not be enough to send you to eternal punishment (unless it was a symptom of a much larger problem).

EARLY MENTIONS

The tradition of the seven deadly sins originated in the writings of John Cassian, a 5th-century monk and ascetic. In his book *Collationes*, he provided a list of eight vices that were particularly tormenting to ascetic monks, as follows: gluttony, impurity, covetousness, anger, dejection, accidia (or boredom), vainglory and pride. Pope Gregory the Great included a similar list in his book *Moralia on Job*. Cassian and Gregory

Above The virtue of flourishing generosity is seen in opposition to the deadly vice of avarice in this 1945 illustration, Allegory of Generosity and Avarice, *by Rémy Hetreau.*

may have been influenced in turn by *Psychomachia*, an allegorical poem by the 4th-century Roman Christian poet Aurelius Prudentius Clemens. His poem featured a battle between personified virtues and vices in the style of the *Aeneid*. Prudentius may have influenced later authors who made specific use of the deadly sins in their writing, in particular, Geoffrey Chaucer and Dante Alighieri. Of the church fathers, Thomas Aquinas in his *Summa Theologiae* (1265–73) paid attention to the seven deadly sins, for example, analysing multiple manifestations of gluttony, such as *studiose*, or "eating too daintily", and *laute*, or "eating too expensively".

BY COUNCIL DECREE

The wide dissemination and subsequent popularity in public discourse of the seven deadly sins can be traced back to the Church's Fourth Lateran Council (1214). One of the decrees of the council was the

In 2005, the Church published a "Compendium of the Social Doctrine of the Church", which reasserted the humanist position of the Catholic Church on all social issues. The widely publicized list of the seven "social sins" derived from this compendium. The social sins of the 21st century are:

1: Bioethical violations, such as birth control
2: Morally dubious experiments, such as stem cell research
3: Drug abuse
4: Polluting the environment
5: Contributing to the widening gap between rich and poor
6: Excessive wealth
7: Creating poverty

The compendium states that social sin falls into two categories: "On the one hand, the all-consuming desire for profit, and on the other, the thirst for power, with the intention of imposing one's will upon others." Bishop Gianfranco Girotti also stated that, "While sin used to mostly concern the individual, today it has mainly a social resonance, thanks to the phenomenon of globalization."

Above The oil industry often displays social sin. It pollutes the Earth in its desire for great wealth.

requirement that Catholics attend yearly confession. In order to make a good confession – or any confession at all – the ordinary communicant needed to be educated in the concept of sin and given a vocabulary to talk about it. Parish priests as well had to learn the language of sin. In the Lambeth Constitutions of 1281, Archbishop of Canterbury John Peckham provided the clergy with a syllabus that included the seven deadly sins (as well as the seven virtues and the seven sacraments).

THE NUMBER SEVEN

Many Christians have asked why there are only seven deadly sins and have noted some considerable

Above St Thomas Aquinas, one of the Church's most erudite theologians, provided an exhaustive analysis of the seven deadly sins in his Summa Theologiae. *This portrait of Aquinas is by Alessandro Botticelli (1445–1510).*

omissions from the list, such as cruelty to others. This is because seven was considered a number of significance in the Old Testament, starting with the creation of the world in seven days, and it has reappeared in many other guises as an important ordering principle in Scripture, in particular, in the "Book of Sevens", Revelation. Seven is generally considered a number of high sacred significance.

JUDGEMENT DAY

ACCORDING TO CATHOLICISM, EACH PERSON IS JUDGED AT DEATH (PARTICULAR JUDGEMENT). CHRIST WILL RETURN ON JUDGEMENT DAY TO JUDGE THE LIVING AND THE DEAD (GENERAL JUDGEMENT).

The Catholic vision of Judgement Day is a particularly specific one. Catholic tradition teaches that there are two separate and specific judgements: the particular and the general. The particular judgement, as the name implies, has more significance for the fate of each person, while the general judgement is the Judgement Day that will see the Second Coming of Christ and the end of the world as we know it.

AT DEATH

Particular judgement happens at the exact moment of individual death, when the soul separates from the body. Catholic sacred tradition teaches that the particular judgement is instantaneous, so that the soul will simply know, immediately, what the verdict is and go on its own in the right direction. The choices are heaven, which is reserved for the perfectly pure; Purgatory, for the vast group of the imperfectly pure

(those with venial sins that are still unconfessed and unforgiven); and hell, for the definitely not pure (those with mortal sins that remain unconfessed and unforgiven).

A PAPAL BULL

This belief in the prompt fulfilment of the sentence was a controversial one within the early Church. Some Church fathers argued that either the bliss of the beatific vision (for example, the intuitive knowledge of God) or the suffering of the tormenting fires of hell would be postponed until the general judgement. Pope Benedict XII convened a commission to decide the question, and after four months of testimony

Below During the Second Coming of Christ, saints will be rewarded with the beatific vision of Christ, implied in this early 15th-century German painting by his larger size in relation to the others and the blissful expression of the saints.

Above Aided by its guardian angel, this soul is slipping away to its judgement (fresco detail from the Last Judgement, *Voronet Monastery, Moldavia, Romania). The soul will be reunited to the body it leaves behind at the general judgement.*

from various theologians, he issued the 1336 papal bull, *Benedictus Deus*. This bull proclaimed, once and for all, that your fate was indeed determined right away.

GENERAL JUDGEMENT

The judgement that has been traditionally depicted in Western art – full of angels, demons, writhing naked bodies and a just Christ sitting on a throne with a group of saints in attendance – is known as the general judgement. It is a popular theme of medieval and Renaissance paintings.

Church tradition teaches that at the general judgement, all bodies, both the saved and the damned, will be rejoined to their immortal souls. The wicked, unfortunately, will not be happy to meet their bodies again, as noted in Revelation 9:6, "The wicked shall seek death, and shall not find it, shall desire to die, and death shall fly from them…"

Scripture specifically assigns the general judgement as a role for Christ. In John 5:28, it states, "…for the hour cometh wherein all that are in the graves shall hear the voice of the Son of God." This is why the general judgement is also referred to as Christ's Second Coming.

It will be during the general judgement that the Godhead's ultimate purpose for mankind will finally be fulfilled.

The general judgement appears to have the same function as a public trial: although a particular judgement has already been pronounced, the general judgement is needed so that all may witness the justice of the final decrees. General judgement features an aspect of public proclamation, as described in the Athanasian Creed, "at whose coming all men must rise with their bodies and are to render an account of their deeds". The general judgement is the day of public accounting and is a final judgement.

THE FINAL JUDGEMENT

Catholicism teaches its followers that when Christ returns, it will be for the final judgement and that the resulting reign will be eternal and in heaven. Over the centuries, however, Christians have held different

Below Weighing souls after death, shown in this 12th-century Catalan fresco, was an ancient belief of Egypt and Greece as well as early Christianity. Traditionally, the archangel Michael escorted souls to God on Judgement Day and weighed them.

views on what will happen during the final judgement (*see* Final Judgement and the Millennium, *below*). Pre-millennialism describes this as an actual return of Christ for a thousand years, before the final judgement. However, post-millennialism prefers to describe an achieved perfection on earth due to the preaching of the gospel, as a result of which the entire earth will be Christianized. After the thousand years of earthly Christian perfection, then Jesus returns to conduct the final judgement. Pre-millennialism posits a return and reign of Christ on earth prior to

Above A phalanx of saints are in attendance above, the mouth of hell gaping is on the right and delight or dismay (as applicable) are shown on earth in The Last Judgement *by Bartholomaeus Spranger (1546–1611).*

the final judgement, whereas post-millennialism believes in a period of achieved perfection on earth prior to the final judgement.

The Catholic Church refutes pre-millennialism and also rejects the post-millennial view that there will ever be a period of perfection on earth prior to the final judgement (this view would contradict the

---

FINAL JUDGEMENT AND THE MILLENNIUM

The Book of Revelation, and Chapter 20 in particular, is problematic for Catholics. This difficult chapter describes a thousand-year period when Satan will be bound with chains in a pit, after which he will be "loosed for a little while" and emerge to deceive again. This thousand-year period when Satan will be bound is known as the millennium. There are many gradations of opinion (much of it Protestant evangelical) on the millennium, but most understand it as a thousand-year "golden age" of the triumph of Christianity, a reign of Christ himself (pre-millennialism) or of the Christian religion (post-millennialism) on earth that will be distinct from the final judgement and distinct from eternity.

VISIONS OF HEAVEN

THE WRITERS OF THE BIBLE REFERRED TO HEAVEN AS A PHYSICAL PLACE, GOD'S FIRMAMENT. HOWEVER, TODAY'S CATHOLIC CHURCH DESCRIBES HEAVEN AS A STATE OF BEING.

The Bible uses several descriptive phrases when referring to heaven, including a kingdom, a crown, the city of God, a reward and even an inheritance. This metaphorical variety on the part of biblical writers shows that the early Christians felt a certain liberty in their attempts to imagine heaven, as long as it provided a good image.

In the popular imagination, both in the past and present, heaven is often seen as being palatial, expressed in the term "pearly gates", which derives from the opulent description of heaven as the "New Jerusalem". In Revelation 21:21, its gates "are twelve pearls, one to each: and every several gate was of one pearl". In paintings and movies, heaven is

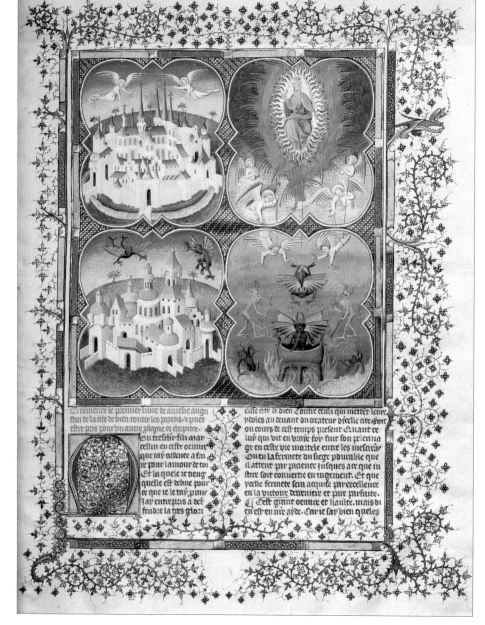

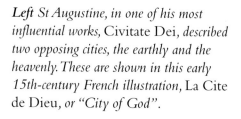

Above Orderly groups of saints approach the fortified portal of paradise in this 1480 detail from the Last Judgement, *Voronet Monastery, Moldavia, Romania.*

dreamy, awash in clouds that are often shot through with pastel rays of effulgent light. In common usage, "heavenly" is the adjective of choice for anything highly pleasurable, from pizza ("a slice of heaven") to relaxing in a hot bubble bath.

GOD'S FIRMAMENT

Despite these images, the etymology of the word "heaven" derives from words referring to "a roof or covering", confirming the majority view that heaven is above us. Genesis 7:10 describes God making the "firmament", which serves as a vast buttress that divides the elemental regions of the earth: "And God made a firmament, and divided the waters that were under the firmament, from those that were above the firmament... And God called the firmament heaven...".

Left St Augustine, in one of his most influential works, Civitate Dei, *described two opposing cities, the earthly and the heavenly. These are shown in this early 15th-century French illustration,* La Cite de Dieu, *or "City of God".*

This soaring support of the world came to be associated with the abode of God, "…a building of God, a house not made with hands, eternal in heaven" (2 Corinthians 5:1). Medieval cathedrals aspired to represent in earthly architecture the inspiring span and lofty height of heaven.

A STATE OF BEING

Catholic doctrine, however, is circumspect in describing heaven as an actual physical place. No doctrine of the Church has ever attempted to establish the latitude and longitude of heaven, and although it is the traditional concept, the modern Church is even cautious in describing heaven as the dwelling place of God. This is because by doing so, it would imply that God can be contained in a particular place.

Instead, the Church describes heaven as a state of being achieved only by those who are pure of all sin. The Catholic catechism says that when we enter into the state of being of heaven, we will have a "beatific vision" of God. Unless God makes himself open to an individual for contemplation, God cannot be seen. If this contemplation takes place, our spiritual and intellectual perceptive capacity will be unbound from its earthly limitations so that we will be able to perceive and receive God – this is a beatific vision. Such an encounter "is what the perfect happiness of heaven will consist of".

In 1336, Pope Benedict XII defined belief in the beatific vision (for those who attain heaven) as a dogma of the faith. Theologians, however, put limits on even the beatific vision. They state that while we will see God (such as in the Trinity) entirely, our vision will not have the absolute and infinite clarity with which God perceives himself. The Church also believes that there are degrees of beatitude granted to the Blessed; saints have a more extensive vision of God.

Above New residents, borne on the backs of obliging angels, are welcomed to heaven with open arms in this 15th-century work from Hastings Book of Hours.

BEING REUNITED

There is also a more homely aspect to heaven. The Church teaches that in heaven we will be reunited with our beloved family and friends who have gone there before us, and the language of some of the prayers for the dead in the Church emphasizes that heaven is the true home of the righteous and that our arrival in heaven will actually be a homecoming. In the service that is given for the dead, the Prayer of Commendation states:

> *May you return to [your Creator] who formed you from the dust of the earth.*
> *May holy Mary, the angels, and all the saints come to meet you as you go forth from this life…*
> *May you see your Redeemer face to face.*

The sense is of a family's loving, eager greeting to one of its members who has been too long away. Heaven is also a homecoming in that we return to our first home, paradise, redeemed from a long sojourn in the fallen world. St Augustine said, "Thou hast made us for Thyself (O God) and our heart is troubled till it rests in Thee."

Below The Madonna and saints contentedly work, read and play in a walled garden in this c.1410 German painting, Paradise Garden. *The garden is the earthly mirror of paradise, which is from the old Persian word for "a walled garden" or "park".*

PURGATORY

CATHOLICS BELIEVE THAT AFTER DEATH THERE ARE MANY SOULS THAT ARE NOT DESTINED FOR HELL BUT THAT ARE NOT READY TO ENTER HEAVEN WITH GOD – THEY GO TO PURGATORY TO BE CLEANSED OF SIN.

The Catholic doctrine regarding the concept of Purgatory has developed from the Catholic belief that God is both merciful and just. Because God is merciful, sinners can atone for their non-mortal sins even after death, but because he is just, this atonement is a requirement that must be met.

Purgatory (from the Latin word *purgare*, "to make clean, to purify") is where that atonement happens. The Church teaches that Purgatory is where those who die without mortal sin on their soul, but also without making full satisfaction to God for their sins, must suffer for a time to purify their souls and to make recompense to God. Purgatory is different from hell because it is temporary. Souls suffering in Purgatory know that eventually they will be with God. In traditional teaching, Purgatory is a place; however, in more contemporary teaching it is a state of being.

A DEVELOPING CONCEPT

The early church Councils of Lyons (1274), Florence (1438–43) and Trent (1545–63) all made statements describing, with varying degrees of

Above Few theologians were as aware of the struggle between good and evil as St Augustine. In this 15th-century French woodblock print, he focuses on his work despite the clamour of demonic distractions around him.

specificity, the Church's developing concept of Purgatory. In *The City of God*, St Augustine expressed his belief that there would be temporal punishment after death, and Pope (later St) Gregory the Great, influenced by Augustine, was principally responsible for refining the idea of *purgatorius ignis*, or the "cleansing fire", into doctrine.

Going to Purgatory is not completely inevitable. The pure do not go to Purgatory, and Catholics also believe that those who, through no fault of their own, have suffered terribly in life (say an unjustly convicted prisoner), essentially pay recompense for their sins by experiencing Purgatory here on earth. However, those who have been less than pure will go to Purgatory.

PURGING OUR SINS

Purgatory is necessary, in most cases, even if you have made an appropriate confession of your sins and have been forgiven. The Catholic concept of penance is that temporal punishment is required to discharge our debt

Above Purgatorial punishments match the earthly sin. In an illustration in Le Trésor de Sapience *by Jean de Gerson (1363–1429), the prideful are pushed into the ground and trodden on, expiating their arrogance by being forced to grovel in flames.*

of sin as a necessary condition of absolution. The Church makes the point that Purgatory is necessary not because God is vengeful but because our sins, like a stain, have worked into our essence. Only the spiritually clean can truly see God, and being spiritually cleansed is difficult work, a sense expressed by the early Church father, Gregory of Nyssa, in his reflections on Purgatory:

> *...we may figure to ourselves the agonized struggle of that soul which has wrapped itself up in earthy material passions, when God is drawing it, his own one, to himself, and the foreign matter, which has somehow grown into its substance, has to be scraped from it by main force, and so occasions it that keen intolerable anguish.*

INTERCEDING SAINTS

Catholicism also teaches that the prayers of the faithful still residing on earth can help the souls in Purgatory. The Communion of Saints refers to the belief that all faithful members of the Church, whether living or dead, are united as members of a single spiritual community and can help one another; therefore, the saints in heaven can intercede with God to help us on earth, and by offering suffrages – our prayers, fasting and works of charity on earth – we can obtain divine mercy for the souls in Purgatory, perhaps even hastening the time that they will be released into heaven.

Above Part of a larger panoramic 15th-century French painting by Enguerrand Quarton, The Coronation of the Virgin, *this detail depicts Purgatory in an unexpected location – just beneath the walled city of Rome. It includes a few fortunate penitents who have completed their time in Purgatory and are rising from the depths, with the aid of angels.*

HEAVEN SHOULD NOT BE FOR SALE

Indulgences, or remission of time spent in Purgatory, became a hot trading commodity during the early 16th century. The trade in indulgences reflected the extreme concern with the afterlife during this era when the Black Death (plague) had decimated Europe's population. Pope Leo X took advantage of this situation to enrich the Church coffers by selling indulgences – though selling them is a mortal sin (Leo, a member of the Medici family, was extremely corrupt). Leo was selling plenary indulgences, a particular type of indulgence that provides total remission of the temporal punishment (time in Purgatory).

Indulgences are legal in the Church, but because of this earlier history they are often misunderstood as being a kind of coupon for time off from Purgatory that the Church offers in exchange for cash. However, what many do not understand is that even forgiven sins may result in some time in Purgatory after death, before an individual is in acceptable spiritual shape for heaven. Plenary indulgences can free you from that prospect, but there are conditions attached. First, they should never be offered solely in exchange for money. Sins must be forgiven by confession; the person receiving the indulgence must go to confession and receive Communion for a week, and the person must perform charitable works prescribed by the Church.

Above Johann Tetzel, a Dominican prior, sells indulgences in Germany in this 18th-century woodblock print.

VISIONS OF HELL

MODERN CHURCH DOCTRINE ON HELL IS RELATIVELY TAME IN COMPARISON TO THE LURID VISION OF ETERNAL DAMNATION THAT HAS GRIPPED THE POPULAR IMAGINATION SINCE THE MIDDLE AGES.

The Scriptures contain a number of references to a hell with a fearsome aspect, describing it as a place of fire and darkness. Among these are: "pool of fire" (Revelation 19:20), "everlasting fire (Matthew 18:8; 25:41; Jude 7), "unquenchable fire" (Matthew 3:12), "furnace of fire where they will weep and gnash their teeth" (Matthew 13:42, 50), "exterior darkness" (Matthew 7:12; 22:13; 25:30) and "mist" or "storm of darkness" (2 Peter 2:17; Jude 13).

ETERNAL DAMNATION

These are all arresting descriptions, particularly when coupled with the concept of being never ending, because hell, of course, is eternal. Contemporary Catholic clergy are

Above The license allowed in portraits of Satan is evident in this 15th-century rendition, which depicts him with belled horns, wings like ribbed leaves and tusks.

unlikely to dwell for long on these descriptions. However, in medieval times and up to the Second Vatican Council (1962–5), priests and nuns often invoked the grim spectre of hell in an effort to scare their congregations into good behaviour. The Church considered meditation on the "Last Things," which are death, judgement, heaven and hell, as salutary to spiritual health.

We are indebted to the medieval period for many of our images of hell as a place of gruesome punishments and apocalyptic landscapes. The vision literature of the Middle Ages featured an entire genre of texts that recounted personal tours of hell, featuring horrible retributions that were tailor-made to suit the sin. This early vision literature influenced the great Florentine poet Dante, who in his *Inferno* described hell as a series of nine concentric circles, with limbo, the least severe, at the outer rim and Satan confined at the centre.

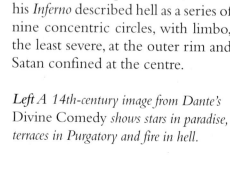

Left A 14th-century image from Dante's Divine Comedy *shows stars in paradise, terraces in Purgatory and fire in hell.*

Right A demon delivers a new soul to
hell to join eternally tormented souls in
this detail from a 15th-century painting
by Enguerrand Quarton.

HELLFIRE

The fires of hell are supernatural:
they do not require fuel and they do
not consume those they burn, but
blaze eternally. Traditional Catholic
theology describes hellfire as *poena
sensus*, meaning the "pain of sense".
Poena sensus is considered a corporeal
pain, because Scripture specifies that
after the last judgement, the damned
will be rejoined to their bodies. Some
have noted that *poena sensus* was an
appropriate pain, because mortal sin
is often allied to excessive desire for
physical and material pleasures.

THE CHURCH'S VIEW

The Second Vatican Council did
not mention hell, but the gentling
of Church rhetoric on hell dates
from then. The current Catholic

Above The damned make their way to
hell and the pure to heaven in Rogier
van der Weyden's 15th-century painting
of the Last Judgement.

definition of hell, as noted by Pope
John Paul II, states that the ultimate
punishment for sin itself is hell, and
that it is "more than a physical place".
Hell represents the state of those who
have chosen freely and completely to
"separate themselves from God".

The Catholic catechism describes
hell as a state of being where the
individual chooses to reject God's
love, thereby dying in mortal sin. By
choosing to exclude him or herself
from God, and by not repenting, he
or she will be separated from God for
eternity – this is hell.

To older Catholics whose lifetime
spans the expositions of both the
older eternal, infernal physical
punishment vision of hell from
before the Second Vatican Council
and today's metaphysical "eternally
separated from God" hell, the
difference can be striking. This is a
situation in which the Catholic
Church has exercised its magisterial
authority to interpret Scripture.
Here we see the evolution of Church
tradition at work.

John Paul II also went on to say
that we need to understand the
meanings presented by the images of
hell in Scripture, which illustrate an
empty and frustated life if living
without accepting God. The Pope
calls the scriptural words on hell

"images" and says, not that they "are"
hell, but that they "show" a state of
being. So, heaven is unity with God
and hell is separation from God.
Although John Paul II did not
repudiate the old concept of hell, he
did go so far as to redefine the terms
of the discussion.

THE PAIN OF LOSS

Poena damni, or the "pain of
loss", refers to psychic pain. The
Church describes *poena damni*
as a real, intense pain, rooted in
the loss of the beatific vision. The
damned still retain the human
need for God, even if they have
rejected this desire, and so are
tormented eternally by the
unquiet described by Augustine
in his *Confessions*, "…You have
formed us for yourself, and our
hearts are unquiet until they find
rest in you." The disquiet of the
damned can never be stilled, so
they burn with eternal despair.
It is the *poena damni* that Pope
John Paul II emphasized in his
definition of hell. "Damnation"
comes from the Latin word
damnum, which means "loss",
emphasizing that the essence of
hell is in the pain of loss.

VISIONS OF DAMNATION

THE ARTISTIC REPUTATION OF PAINTINGS OF HELL HAS ALWAYS ECLIPSED THOSE OF HEAVEN. BLISS SEEMS TO LEAVE ARTISTS AT A LOSS, BUT THEY APPEAR TO HAVE A PASSION FOR PAINTING ETERNAL PUNISHMENT.

Hell was by no means an unusual subject in religious art. Two popular themes are of "The Harrowing of Hell", when Christ descended into hell after his Crucifixion, before his Resurrection, and the Last Judgement. Numerous artists, including Giotto di Bondone (*c.*1267–1337), Fra Angelico (*c.*1387–1455), Hans Memling (*c.*1440–94) and Michelangelo (1475–1564), have depicted hell. Giotto's hell is a fiery nether region dwarfed by a conquering Christ who was enthroned in an orderly heaven with the righteous in attendance.

Memling's triptych *The Last Judgement* depicts hell as a flaming pit into which the undifferentiated bodies of the damned tumble, superintended by colossal and well-armed demons. Jesus holds centre stage as the archangel Michael weighs the souls. The left panel shows the pure being led to heaven, while the right panel shows the damned.

Fra Angelico's hell is honeycombed with flaming caverns where bleeding, naked people are bound, speared and burnt by gleeful demons resembling diabolical monkeys, or the unfortunate occupants are eaten in great gulps by Satan himself, looking like a great ape.

THE MASTER OF HELL

Pre-eminent among all the painters of the horrors of hell is Hieronymus Bosch (*c.*1450–1516). He was an unassuming Dutchman who never travelled far from 's-Hertogenbosch, his village in the duchy of Brabant (modern-day Netherlands). In a small house on the market square, besides making devotional wood-cuts, he painted hell and its countless demons in endlessly inventive, startlingly modern, gruesome detail.

In contrast to many of the other illustrations of hell, Bosch's chaotic, brightly coloured depictions are typically overrun with life, albeit in monstrous forms: strange demons that resemble insects or sea creatures, monstrous birds, odd plants with pod-like excrescences, enormous ears, mussel shells, eggs, unusual ice skaters and odd little bathyspheres with grilles for doors. One representative Bosch monster is a fish swallowing another fish, with lobster legs and a spiny tail.

Bosch's demons tend to have long whip-like tails resembling the stingers on stingrays. The damned are not simply burnt or bound, but are

Above The descent into the mouth of hell was a standard subject of medieval "doom" paintings. In a detail from Hans Memling's 15th-century version, the damned souls tumble with arms and legs extended in almost balletic poses.

tortured in an indescribable variety of obscene manners by a wealth of phantasmagoric creatures. Hellfire burns on the outskirts of Bosch's canvases, in dark regions shot with red light; unlike the typical painting of hell, the flames are not the principle torture of the damned.

THE FIRST SURREALIST

Because he married an heiress, Bosch did not depend on the Church hierarchy for commissions of his work, unlike many other artists. Free from the need to submit his compositions to the censorship of the Church, he was able to produce beautifully painted works featuring imagery not found in any Scripture.

Bosch's technique came to him naturally: several of his relatives were also painters, including his grandfather, father, brother and three uncles. The Flemish style of slender, restrained human bodies and of

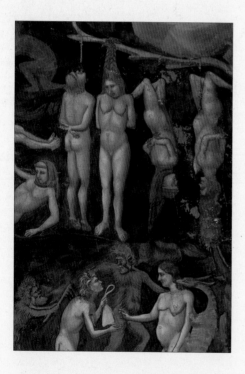

Above The damned are subjected to various forms of torture applied by tiny demons, from being suspended by the hair to the racking of bare skin, in this detail from Giotto di Bondone's *c.*1303 painting, The Last Judgement.

Right *Looking at Hieronymus Bosch's imagery, such as* The Garden of Earthly Delights *(c.1500), it is hard to believe that he lived and painted in the 15th century. His imagery and technique still look startlingly modern today.*

meticulous attention to detail is evident in his work. However, Bosch's iconography is like no other religious painter's and is a precursor in its hallucinatory specificity to the early 20th-century work of the Surrealists, artists that were hailed as "revolutionary" more than five centuries after Bosch.

A DEVOUT BROTHER

Surprisingly, the little-known story of Bosch's life suggests that he participated in the conventional pious observances of society: he was a sworn member of the Society of Our Lady, a devout brotherhood founded in 1318. The society was a powerful but exclusive group, and

Bosch was allowed to become a member upon marriage because his wife was already one. The studies of the brotherhood may have contributed to Bosch's obsession with hell: they were said to conduct daily readings of accounts of hell.

Despite his deeply unconventional work, during his lifetime Bosch became enormously popular among the laity, if not the Church itself. King Philip II (1527–98), the Spanish monarch known for his collection of saintly relics, was a particular admirer of Bosch. He was a keen collector of his works and kept Bosch's painting of a wheel depicting the seven deadly sins in his bedroom at the Escorial Palace.

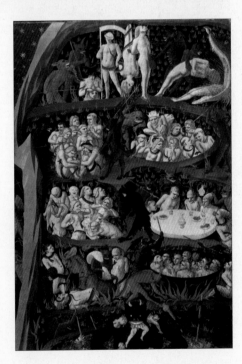

Left *Only in the hell of Bosch would one find what resembles a penguin on ice skates, as seen in this 1503–4 detail from* Die Hölle. *The horror of Bosch's hell is its complete lack of logic and reason — all the universe is askew.*

Above *Fra Angelico's vision of hell exemplifies the "cooking and eating" motif, with a cauldron of unfortunates being boiled, Satan gorging on their flesh and lesser demons contemplating bodies massed for their delectation.*

LIMBO

A REGION ON THE EDGE OF HELL, LIMBO WAS RESERVED FOR THOSE WHO DIED FREE FROM SERIOUS PERSONAL SIN, YET, THROUGH NO FAULT OF THEIR OWN, WERE STILL IN A STATE OF ORIGINAL SIN.

The name "limbo" derives from the Latin *limbus*, meaning "hem", "border" or "edge", reflecting its juxtaposition with hell. The concept of limbo was developed as an extension of the doctrinal importance that the Church ascribes to original sin and baptism, added to its belief that only those who are free of all vestiges of sin will be worthy of the beatific vision of God.

There are two categories of candidate that can go to limbo. These are either virtuous people who died before Jesus redeemed them from original sin, or babies who died before being baptized.

GOD'S GIFT

Original sin is an inescapable fate for all humans, with only the Virgin Mary being conceived without it. Romans 5:18 says, "Therefore, as by the offence of one, unto all men condemnation; so also by the justice of one, unto all men justification of life." This scriptural syllogism makes clear the direction of the Church's thinking: if salvation, that gift of God, is going to apply to all people, then so must the unfortunate predecessor to salvation: the hereditary stain that marks all the unbaptized as exiles from God. In other words, the unbaptized are at risk.

Above The halo over Mary in Pietro Lorenzetti's 14th-century painting, The Birth of the Virgin Mary, *is a clue that she was conceived without original sin.*

THE TWO LIMBOS

Catholic tradition originally taught that there were two limbos: *limbus patrum*, for virtuous but unbaptized adults (*patrum* refers to "fathers"), reflecting the belief that the Old Testament patriarchs – including Abraham – would go there, and *limbus infantium*, for unbaptized infants. The two limbos were required because *limbus patrum* would end with the Second Coming, whereas *limbus infantium* was permanent. The fathers could not be baptized because Jesus Christ had not yet redeemed man. The babies were not baptized because they had died before anyone had baptized them.

In fact, this is why the Church teaches that in an emergency, anyone can baptize a baby by making the sign of the cross over the infant and

Left Abraham holds the souls of the righteous in this 12th-century French manuscript. Because he lived before Jesus was born, Abraham was not redeemed before he died and went to limbo.

speaking the words, "I baptize thee (NAME) in the name of the Father and of the Son and of the Holy Spirit." Many doctors, nurses and midwives have performed such baptisms over newborns they feared would not survive.

INNOCENT BUT IN LIMBO

The ultimate fate of the innocent but unbaptized was controversial, as were so many theological issues before their applicable doctrines were established. St Augustine was the most severe: this 4th-century theologian believed that the innocently unbaptized would be punished, though more mildly than the truly damned. The theologian Peter Abelard (1070–1142) believed that the innocent but unbaptized suffered no physical pain, only the pain of the loss of God, and Pope Innocent III (1160–1216) agreed.

St Thomas Aquinas held an even more soothing concept, stating that limbo was a place of "natural happiness", but with the crucial exception that its residents were deprived of the transcendent joy of true union with God (known as supernatural happiness). However, the Council of Florence (1438–43) seemed to backtrack, stating, "the souls of those dying in actual mortal sin or in original sin alone go down at once into hell, to be punished, however, with widely different penalties". Yet the teaching of Aquinas remained the somewhat equivocal general Church position – crucially, it was never a definitive doctrine – right up until the 21st century and the pontificate of Pope Benedict XVI.

Above The theologian Peter Abelard, shown in this 19th-century engraving, supported the idea of limbus infantium. Pope Innocent III accepted his view.

A 21ST-CENTURY DEBATE

Centuries of debate about limbo continue. In April 2007, the International Theological Commission, an advisory panel to the Vatican (previously headed by Cardinal Ratzinger, now Pope Benedict XVI) published a report endorsing the belief that *limbus infantium* was too limiting when it came to salvation. The report affirmed the superabundance of God's Grace over sin, noting that Christ's relationship with humankind must be stronger than any links with Adam. In a contest between original sin and salvation where no personal guilt is involved, the power of Christ's mercy vanquishes the power of Adam's sinfulness. The report, however, does not repudiate the Church's doctrine of original sin or the need for baptism. Instead, it theorizes that in the case of unbaptized infants, God can give his Grace without the need of the sacrament being given in baptism.

Above In the Harrowing of Hell, between death and Resurrection, Christ went to limbo to free the just who died before him. It is depicted in this 15th-century fresco.

INDEX

Page numbers in bold denote illustrations.

*Above Spaniards and Mexicans celebrate
Mass in this 16th-century painting,*
Lienzo de Tlaxcala, *printed in*
Antigüendas Mexicana.

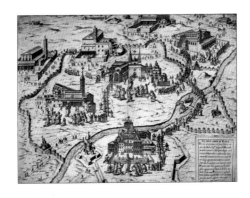

Above The seven pilgrim churches of Rome, seen from above in this 1575 copper engraving by Antonio Lafreri.

PICTURE CREDITS

Abbreviations ADO: Alfredo Dagli Orti; BL: British Library, London; GDO: Gianni Dagli Orti; Priv Coll: Private Collection; V&A: Victoria & Albert Museum, London.
akg-images 1m, 5bml, 9bl, 13t, 19tl, 21br, 25b, 26tr, 33bl, 36tr, 37br, 38b, 39tr, 39bm, 40tr, 42-43, 44tr, 48bl, 49tl, 60bl, 61bl, 62tr, 65tr, 70tr, 71l, 72tr, 75tr, 78b, 80tr, 81l, 81br, 82tr, 83tm, 90tr, 90bl, 91tr, 100tr, 118tr, 119bl, 122tr, 126tr, 126bl, 129bl, 133bl, 138-139, 143br, 146tr, 147bl, 149tm, 150bl, 151br, 154tr, 154bl, 155bl, 156bl, 159t. **Alamy** 82b, 87tm, 103br, 111tm.

Ancient Art & Architecture 15b.
The Art Archive 2, 3t, 3, 4bml, 4bm, 5bm, 5b, 6t, 8tm, 8tl, 9bl, 9b, 10-11, 12-1, 14br, 17b, 18tr, 20tr, 22t, 22m, 22b, 23tr, 23b, 24tr, 24b, 25t, 27t, 28bl, 29, 30tr, 30b, 31t, 31b, 33, 35t, 35b, 35br, 37b, 38tr, 40bl, 42tm, 43tm, 44bl, 45b, 45b, 47bl, 51b, 52try, 55b, 58t, 58bl, 59br, 62b, 63, 64t, 64bl, 65b, 66tr, 66bl, 68tr, 69br, 70bl, 71r, 73br, 74tr, 76tr, 76bl, 77tl, 77br, 78tr, 79tr, 79br, 80bl, 84tr, 85tr, 86tr, 89, 91bm, 92tr, 92br, 93tm, 94bl, 96bl, 97tm, 98bl, 99br, 104tr, 117tm, 118b, 119tr, 120bl, 121br, 123tm, 123bl, 124tr, 124, 125tm, 130bl, 131br, 133b, 136bl, 137br, 139tm, 140bl, 141tr, 142bl, 144tr, 148tr, 149br, 150tr, 152tr, 155br, 156tr, 157b, 157br, 158b, Endpaper. **The Bridgeman Art Library** 4bl, 5bl, 15, 16t, 18, 19b, 20bl, 21, 27b, 29tr, 34tr, 36bl, 46tr, 47tr, 50t, 52b, 53t, 53, 56-5, 57t, 59t,

60t, 63tr, 67b, 67br, 68b, 68br, 69tr, 73tr, 74b, 75br, 77bm, 83br, 84b, 85br, 87bl, 87br, 88-89, 94tr, 95bl, b, 96tr, 97br, 101bl, 116-11, 120tr, 122b, 125b, 127bl, 128t, 129b, 130t, 131tr, 132b, 134tr, 136tr, 142tr, 143t, 144bl, 145t, 146b, 147t, 151t, 152tr, 153t, 153b, 155tr.
Corbis front cover tl, tmr, tr, b, front flap, back flap, back cover tl, tr, bml, spine, 4br, 14tr, 16bl, 17, 32b, 55tr, 72bl, 86b, 99bl, 102t, 103tl, 104b, 105tm, 106b, 107bl, 107br, 108t, 108bl, 110tr, 113br, 114-115, 132tr, 134bl, 135tm, 135br, 137tr, 140tr, 141br, 145br, 148b.
Getty Images 51tl, 98tr, 102bl, 105bl, 106tr, 109tr, 110bl, 111bl, 112tr, 112bl, 113tr, 121tr, 128br.
Heritage-Images 48tr, 50br, 61br. **Photolibrary** 7.
Rex Features 101br, 109br. **Robert Harding** 54tr. **Sonia Halliday Photographs** 26bl, 28tr, 54bl.
TopFoto 34bl, 100tr, 127br.